Kardinal John Bonaventura

Meditations on the Supper of our Lord and the hours of the passion

Kardinal John Bonaventura

Meditations on the Supper of our Lord and the hours of the passion

ISBN/EAN: 9783741163562

Manufactured in Europe, USA, Canada, Australia, Japa

Cover: Foto ©Lupo / pixelio.de

Manufactured and distributed by brebook publishing software (www.brebook.com)

Kardinal John Bonaventura

Meditations on the Supper of our Lord and the hours of the passion

Meditations

on the Supper of our Lord, and the Hours of the Passion,

by
Cardinal John Bonaventura
the Seraphic Doctor.

Drawn into English Verse by Robert Manning of Brunne.

(ABOUT 1315—1330.)

EDITED FROM THE MSS. IN THE BRITISH MUSEUM AND
THE BODLEIAN LIBRARY, OXFORD,

with Introduction and Glossary

BY

J. MEADOWS COWPER, F.R.H.S.,

EDITOR OF 'THE TIMES' WHISTLE,' 'ENGLAND IN HENRY VIII'S TIME,' 'THE SELECT
WORKS OF ARCHDEACON CROWLEY,' ETC. ETC.

LONDON:
PUBLISHED FOR THE EARLY ENGLISH TEXT SOCIETY,
BY N. TRÜBNER & CO., 57 & 59, LUDGATE HILL.

MDCCCLXXV.

INTRODUCTION.

I. DESCRIPTION OF THE MS.

The MS. from which the poem here presented to the reader has been copied is known as Harl. MS. 1701, and marked Plut. LXXII. B. The volume, which is about 12 in. × 9 in., contains three poems:

- a. *Handlyng Synne,*
- b. *The Medytacyuns,*
- c. *Roberd of Cyssille.*

The first two leaves are blank; *a.* occupies 83 leaves and part of the 84th, ending in the second column of the first side of leaf 84. It is immediately followed by our poem, which, it will be seen, commences in the second column of leaf 84. It closes on the second page of leaf 91 (fol. 91, back), of which it occupies somewhat more than half. On leaf 92 commences *Kyng Roberd of Cyssille,* which closes on the first side of leaf 95.

The headings of the divisions of the poem are all written in red ink; a few of the capitals are illuminated, and the lines are all bracketed in pairs with red ink. In " the fourþe poynt of þe soper " five ¶'s have been introduced, but whether by the original scribe or by a later one I am unable to say: they are done in blue. The handwriting is very regular and very clear; a few omissions occur, but nearly all have been supplied by the original scribe with the usual mark (ʌ) underneath. These are all noted, as well as a few which I have thought to be required: one whole line has been supplied from the Bodleian MS.

INTRODUCTION. I. DESCRIPTION OF THE MS.

A few words have their meanings written over them, thus:—

	wraþþe		euer
l. 345	mode	l. 1030	ay
	place		soper
l. 440	ce to ce	l. 1111	cene
	haste		take
l. 821	reke	l. 1114	nome

The punctuation of the MS. is so very slight, that it has been disregarded altogether. I have expanded the contractions where I could see clearly what was intended, and have marked the expansions according to our custom. In a few cases the mark of contraction seemed doubtful, and these I have noted at the foot of the page where they occur. Frequently *gh* has a mark through it, thus, gh̄, and it will be found so printed in the text, even where it perhaps ought to be followed by a *t*: thus tagh̄ in the MS. is not expanded into tagh̄t; and thogh̄ is printed thogh̄ without any expansion. In line 554 the words "crucyfye, crucyfye" have a slight curl, or it may be *g*, over the *ye*; a curl somewhat similar is found over such a word as "our," which I have expanded into oure; but the word "crucyfye" I have left. MS. B. has "crucyfige." The word is in the imperative mood, singular; and "crucyfye" or "crucyfyge" will correspond with the grammar of the poem, as will be seen further on.

The only other known copy of the poem is in the Bodl. MS. 415, which also contains the *Handlyng Synne*. Mr Geo. Parker of Oxford has kindly read my transcript with the Bodleian MS., and noted all the variations between the two. They are but slight, but the Bodl. MS. has supplied one whole line (248) as stated before, and correct readings in ll. 214, 216; while l. 1102 seems to be corrupt in both MSS.

II. GRAMMATICAL NOTES.

The few notes I have made upon the grammatical forms of this poem are such as presented themselves to my mind in reading the MS., aided by a hint from the Rev. W. W. Skeat, which is referred to below. The forms I have tabulated are intended for those readers who are interested in the grammar of our language, and they will, I trust, be of some use to those who are more competent than I am to

INTRODUCTION. II. GRAMMATICAL NOTES. vii

draw correct conclusions as to the date of the poem and the locality in which it was written. My object has been simply to tabulate forms; and if at any time I have ventured to give utterance to an opinion of my own, or to deduce any principle from the facts before me, I have done so with the utmost deference to the opinions of others.

1. VERBS.

(i.) Verbs in the third person singular, indicative mood, present tense, end generally in *eth*, some few in *th*; as:—

wytnesseþ	l. 51	kalleþ	l. 535
putteþ	71	goþ	571
boweþ	148	bereþ	572
wasseþ	151	suffyseþ	693
cleppeþ	152	endyþ	775
kysseþ	152	suffreþ	782
gouerneþ	211	wexyþ	825
foleweþ	295	seeþ	848
preyeþ	310	accepteþ	913
kepeþ	404	answereþ	1004
seyþ	408	shameþ	1081
cumþ	418	ȝyſþ	1106
chargeþ	470.	cryeþ	1106
wadeþ	520	geþ	1122
sheweþ	524		

Once only have I noticed the verb in the *second* person singular, indicative, present tense, to end in *th*:—

"Fy! þat goddes temple *dystroyþ*" (674).

(ii.) Verbs in the third person plural, present indicative, end in *eth* and in *en*. The following end in *eth*:—

bygynneþ[1]	p. 1	scorneþ	l. 429
blyndyþ	l. 427	syngeþ	429
boffeteþ	428	dyspyseþ	673
seyþ	428	seeþ	848

The following end in *n, en*:—

ben	l. 122	pycchen	l. 612
sen	232	cleuyn	616
crepyn	286	beren	667
callen	292	doun	755
deluyn	347, 611	dyen	755
axen	430	lakkyn	884
leyn	521	wounden	911
dryuen	593	wrastyn	911
dyggen	611	shullen	1108

[1] In B. *bygynnen*

(iii.) Imperatives in the singular have two terminations -e (sometimes omitted), and th in the proportion of rather more than two of the former to one of the latter. Bearing in mind Mr Skeat's distinction between "thou and ye" in *William of Palerne* (Intro. xli), I have endeavoured to classify these imperatives to see whether the author followed any definite system in their use.[1] At first all seems confusion—e and þ being apparently used indiscriminately.

Omitting the expletives "þenk"(e), "beþenk"(e), and "beholde," used only by the translator to his reader, which never end in þ, they may be divided thus:—

(a) The translator addressing the reader, *or equal addressing equal*, uses the e termination generally, as:—

say	l. 8		receyue	l. 218
opone	10		here	219
hyde	10		do	298
take	17, 43, 297, 371		loþe	299
loke	167		crucyfye	608
haue	179		se	826

Christ addressing His Father—*Equals*—also uses the e termination:—

kepe	l. 259, 354, 366, 368	ryse	l. 338
bowe	312	forgyue	649, 711
lestene	312	graunte	650
here	313	ssue	651
dyspyse	313	slake	696
see	316	take	746

The Father to the Son—*Equals*:—

Com	l. 750	sytte	l. 754
Come	754		

The Virgin to death:—

Come	l. 791	do	l. 792

The Virgin to her Son:—

haue reuþe on me l. 832

The mob to Christ:—

telle who þe smyt	l. 428	saue þy selfe	l. 675
Come to þy dome	483	come adowne	676

The Virgin to the disciples:—

dysmay ȝow nat l. 1090

St Michael to Christ in His agony:—

cumforte þe weyl l. 398   do manly l. 398

---

[1] I am reminded that *ye* for *thou* is regularly Northern; it is first found in the *Tristrem*, then in the *Havelok*.

The last two ought, perhaps, to be classed with the following three, as exceptions to the rule :—

Be	l. 2	graunte	l. 5
sauc	4		

These occur in the translator's invocation to the Deity. And lastly, *se*, 701, used by the Virgin to God. This may be an error of the scribe, as Mary, we shall see, in every other instance uses the termination *th*.

We may then, I think, conclude that equals address equals without the final *th*.

(*b*) I come now to examine the imperatives which end in *th*. Among these are no expletives to be struck out.

Christ addressing His disciples, Superior addressing inferiors, use *th* :—

makeþ	l. 196	weteþ	l. 254
kepeþ	247	aryseþ	280

The Virgin, apparently assuming superiority, says to the women, seeþ (809) ; to the disciples :—

takeþ	l. 950	lateþ	l. 994
beryeþ	951	douteþ	1105
abydeþ	991, 1047	beþ	1107
goþ	994		

The Virgin to the Jews who came to remove the bodies from the cross :—

pyneþ	l. 847	ȝyueþ	l. 848
brekeþ	847	haueþ	850

In these last instances, although the Virgin appears as a suppliant, yet we cannot doubt but that the poet intended to represent her as the superior of the "houudes" who came to break the legs of those hanging on the cross, and to cast their bodies into the ditch close by. Once, as we have seen (1090), Mary uses "dysmay" when addressing the disciples, and only once. John, too, uses the forms under notice twice ; once, addressing these same Jews at the cross, he says, "goþ hens" (873), and again, in addressing the women, "beþe of gode cumforte" (895). A seeming inconsistency appears in this last, but it must be remembered that to him was given the care of the Virgin ; and with this charge he seems to have had the care and command of all the women.

So far, then, we should be tolerably safe in saying equals addressed equals without the *th*, and superiors inferiors with it; but another class will compel us to modify what would have been a convenient division, and one which could have been accounted for by *number* (as the division, perhaps, will be after all), namely, that imperatives singular end in *e*, while in the plural they end in *th*. The class which remains for examination is that in which inferiors address superiors.

The Virgin in her prayer to God uses

kepeþ	l. 458	ȝeldeþ	l. 468
beþ	459	helpeþ	471
doþ	465	bryngeþ	472
lateþ	467		

Broadly stated, then, we may say, equals address equals in *e*, and unequals address unequals in *th*.

We may also say that all imperatives in *e* (except dysmay followed by the pronoun) are in the singular number, and that all in *th*—*nine* exceptions—are in the plural number.[1]

(iv.) A few verbs occur in the second person indicative, terminating in *est*, as: þenkest (21), takest (202), seest (205), forsakest (727), betakest (728), suffrest (868), and sentest (317). We have also byt for bade (305), and byst for biddest (1015); fynst for findest (557), shust for shouldest (714), and bynte for bind (427).

(v.) The present participle ends in *ing* (yng) throughout; to this I find no exceptions; unless memorand, ll. 32 and 195, are taken as participles.

II. NOUNS.

Of Nouns not much need be said. Generally the plural ends in *s*, *es*, or *ys*, as opyuyons, wurdes, hertys; but a few end in *en*, as:—

teren, tears	l. 634	sostryn, sisters	l. 647
yen, eyes	357	shamen, shames	672
breþren	647	honden, hands	912

The possessive (several exceptions) ends in *s*, *es*, *ys*, as:—

Martyals legende	l. 51	goddes grace	l. 9
Sones passyun	3	crystys passyun	14

---

[1] See *Morris's Specimens of Early English*, Introduction, xxxiii.

III. PRONOUNS.

The Personal Pronouns are, Singular—

1.	2.	3.
y	þou	he, she (also *se*), hyt
my, myn	þy, þyn	hys, here
me	þe	hym, here, hyt

Plural—

1.	2.	3.
we	ʒe	þey
oure	ʒoure	here
vs	ʒow	hem

The interrogatives *who* (106, 551) and *ho* (526, 790) occur; also the relatives *whiche* (812) and *þat* (215). *He* occurs once as a neuter unless we say 'world' is masculine:—

    And ʒyf þe worlde ʒow hate now,
  Weteþ þat *he* me hated ar ʒow (253-4).

Here I cannot do better than quote Mr Skeat's remarks on the use of *Thou* and *Ye* before referred to. He says, "*Thou* is the language of a lord to a servant, of an equal to an equal, and expresses also companionship, love, permission, defiance, scorn, threatening; whilst *ye* is the language of a servant to a lord, and of compliment, and further expresses honour, submission, entreaty."[1] A careful examination of the pronouns used in this poem gives the same results. Thus, Christ addresses His Father as *Thou, Thee*—using ʒow once in the accusative (314)—or in the language of an "equal to an equal." The author addresses his reader in the same terms—*thou, thee.*

The Jews, in "scorn," address Jesus as *Thou* (436-8). John, as the beloved companion of Christ, uses *thee*—"who shal þe betrey?" (106). St Michael, who was sent from heaven to comfort the Saviour, uses at first the language of a "servant"—"for ʒow we (the angels) preyd" (382); but afterwards he uses that of love—*thee* (383). He again uses *thee*, but he seems to be repeating the Father's words (403).

Mary, using "the language of a servant to a lord," and expressing at the same time "honour, submission, and entreaty," in her prayer to the Father in heaven, uses *ye, you, youre*, with the plural verbs (457—469).

[1] *William of Palerne*, Intro. xlii.

The translator twice uses *you* when addressing Christ (579-80), and John uses *ye* to Mary (853).

IV. ADJECTIVES.

The comparative in *er* occurs in logher (133), and the superlative in *est* in ȝungest (56).

V. ADVERBS.

In adverbs we have *nygh* (90) and *ny* (418, 566) with the comparative *ner* (584). Once the adverb terminates in *lygh*, gladlygh (89); in all other instances in *ly*, as shamely (172), manly (398).

To conclude. The results of this examination show that

1. Verbs in the third person singular, present, indicative mood, end in *eth*. This termination is Southern and East Midland.[1]

2. Verbs in the third person plural, indicative mood, end in *eth* or in *en;* the number having the latter ending being eighteen, that of the former only eight : *eth* is the Southern ending ; *en* is the Midland ending.[2]

3. Verbs in the second person singular, indicative mood, end in *est*. This termination is Southern and East Midland.[3]

4. Verbs imperative, singular, end in *e*, except some few particularly mentioned above ; the imperative plural, second person, with one exception, in *eth;* (but note "þank we" and "gyn we" in ll. 1133, 1135, which are 1st pers. pl.)

5. The present participles end in *ing*, which is Southern,[4] but had spread over the Midland by 1310, as we see in the rimes in the *Handlyng Synne*.

6. Nouns plural end in *es*, *ys*, some few in *en*.

From all which we conclude the language is Midland, with some Southern forms, due, most likely, to the transcriber.

III. AUTHORSHIP, ETC.

The numerous translations of S. Bonaventura's *Vita Christi* which exist show how popular the work has always been. The partial translation here for the first time printed is probably the earliest in existence. The next in order would seem to be one

---

[1] *Specimens of E. E. Poetry*, xii.   [2] Ibid.
[3] Ibid. In the *Havelok* we find "Thou sittes."   [4] *Genesis and Exodus*, xxviii.

mentioned in Lowndes' *Bib. Manual* under the title of *The Myrrour of the blessyed Life of Ihesu Cryst*, translated into English in the year 1410, and printed by Richard Pynson.[1] In the British Museum are two copies, printed by Caxton in 1488, one on paper, the other on vellum. There is also in the Museum a copy printed by W. de Worde in 1525. The only copies of modern editions which I have seen are one published in London in 1739, translated and edited by "E. Y." and another published at Frome Selwood for the use of Members of the Church of England, so recently as 1868. This appears without translator's or editor's name.[2] "E. Y." speaks of an "Obsolete Edition" which he intended to copy, merely altering the orthography; but finding the "Editor (of this Obsolete Edition) having often through the whole omitted many Passages of the Saint, and inserted others in their Room, such as were either agreeable with his own Thoughts, or collected from other Authors, who have wrote on the same Subject," he determined on a new translation. To what "obsolete edition" he refers I cannot say, nor can I ascertain who "E. Y." was.

Robert Mannyng of Bourne, in Lincolnshire, was probably the translator of the *Medytacyuns*. In 1303 he translated *Le Manuel des Pechiez* under the title of *Handlyng Synne*. In the Harl. MS. our poem immediately follows the *Handlyng Synne*, and in the Bodleian the two also appear together. Between 1327 and 1338 Mannyng translated Peter de Langtoft's French *Chronicle* into English, and possibly he may, about this time, have made a translation of a portion of Bonaventura's *Meditationes Vitæ Christi*.[3]

As bearing upon the authorship, we may say it is well known that Mannyng used to take great liberties with his originals. A glance at Mr Furnivall's *Handlyng Synne* will show to how great an extent he introduced original stories to illustrate some point which he deemed of importance. The same thing will be found here. Among passages which do not appear in the Latin original may be noted the following:—

[1] Bohn's *Lowndes' Bib. Man.*, p. 234.
[2] The Catalogue says it is by the Rev. F. Oakeley.
[3] Mr T. L. Kington Oliphant thinks Manning wrote the *Handlyng Synne* from 1303—1310; and that he then began the present poem.

The opening part, consisting of 22 lines, is wholly the translator's own. Lines 130, 136, 138, and 170,

> þat þe lered men shulde teche the lewed,

are also interpolations.

Lines 212, 215, 217, and 218 are new, and noteworthy, as showing the opinion of the translator upon an important doctrine:—

> He þat þou seest yn þe prestes fest.   212
> He þat þou seest yn forme of brede,   215
> Hyt ys goddys sone quyk nat ded.
> With clene herte þou hym receyue,   217
> For elles þy soule þou wylt deceyue.   218

The expression "tyl þat he wax hote" (369), and that Christ suffered in His agony only in His Manhood and not in His Godhead (411-12), are also new; as are lines 477-8,

> Both bollers of wyne and eche a gadlyng
> Come oute for to se of Ihesus endyng;

and the exclamation (529-30),

> Almyȝty god! where art þou now?
> Þese houndes seme myȝtyer þan þou!

In the "third hour" the expressive lines (567-8) are due to the translator:—

> Þey punged hym furþe þurgh euery slogh,
> As an hors ys prykked þat goþ yn þe plogh.

As he went on the translator took greater liberties, and introduced more of his own matter, and generally with advantage. Thus, after l. 768 had said the Saviour's dying cry was heard in hell, we have added:—

> Þenk now, man, what ioye þere ys
> Whan soules ben broȝt from pyne to blys.
> A! how long þey haue þere lyne,
> To abyde here sauyour yn many a pyne;
> Þey cleped, and cryed, com goddes sone,
> How long shul we yn þys wo wone?

And further on, after l. 834, the following new matter is introduced:—

> To þe cros foote hastly she ran,
> And clypped þe cros faste yn here arme,
> And seyd, my sone here wyl y dey,
> Ar þou from me be bore aweye.

After the Saviour's death and the appearance of the water and blood, the translator breaks out (861-8):—

>   AA, wrong! aa, wo! aa, wykkednes!
>   To martyre here for here mekenes.
>   Þe sone was dede, he felte no smerte,
>   But certes hyt perced þe modyrs hert.
>   Þey wounded here, and heped harm vp on harmes;
>   She fyl, as for dede, yn maudeleyns armys.
>   A! Ihesu, þys dede ys ful wundyr to me,
>   Þat þou suffrest þy modyr be martyred for þe.

The line commencing "She fyl" only being in the original. Omitting the inserted lines 879-882 and 923-4, we arrive at a longer passage, which also seems worthy of being introduced here:—

>   Feyn wulde she ha bore more of here dere sone,
>   But grete sorowe here strengþe had ouercome.
>   Þat arme wepyng ofte she kyste,
>   She kolled hyt, she clypped hyt vp on here brest.
>   But euer whan she behelde þat grysly wounde,
>   For sorowe & for feyntnes she fyl to þe grounde.
>   Oftyn she seyd a, sone! a, sone!
>   Where ys now alle þat werk become,
>   Þat þou were wunt to werche with þys honde?
>   Feuers and syke men to brynge oute of bonde.
>   A, flesshe! a, fode! moste feyre and most fre,
>   Of þe holy goste conceyued yn me,
>   Why fadest þou? no fylþe yn þe ys founde,
>   For synneles y bare þe yn to þys mounde.
>   A! mannes synne dere hast þou bo3t,
>   With a gretter prys my3t hyt neuer be bo3t.—ll. 929-944.

The whole of the final Meditation, except the idea in ll. 1126-29, is due to the translator. Of other liberties, such as the expansion or condensation of the original, it would be too tedious to speak—the handling throughout has been free,—the translator following his own judgment wherever he deemed it best.[1]

R. Mannyng's desire to teach the lewed will be well remembered. He translated Langtoft's *Chronicle* into "*symple speche*" "*for the luf of symple men,*" and in "light lange" he it "beganne, *for luf of the lewed manne;*" and here, in the *Medytacyuns*, we have

>   A feyre monasshyng hys sermoun shewed
>   Þat þe lered men shulde teche þe lewed.[2]

One other parallel passage may be quoted. In *Handlyng Synne* we meet with this:—

>   Whan Iesu deyde thurghe passyun
>   Hys dyscyplys doutede echoun

---

[1] Miss L. Toulmin Smith read my proof with the Latin Original.
[2] ll. 169, 170.

> Whether he shulde ryse or noun.
> Alle that beleuede yn hym byfore,
> Alle here beleue was nyghe forlore
> Fro the fryday that he deyde
> To tyme that he ros, as he seyde.
> But hys modyr vyrgyne Marie,
> She bare the beleue vp stedfastly
> Fro the fryday at the noun
> Tyl alle the satyrday was doun,
> And alle the nyght tyle that he ros.[1]

With this compare ll. 1107, 1110 of the *Medytacyuns*. Addressing the weeping disciples, Mary says:—

> Beeþ of gode cumfort, for trustly y say,
> We shullen hym se on þe prydde day;
> Seþþen he haþ boght vs at so grete prys,
> Nedes from þe deþ he mote aryse.

Against these in favour of Mannyng being the translator we must place the undoubted difference of dialect between the *Medytacyuns* and the *Chronicle*. By the kindness of Mr Furnivall I have been supplied with some forward sheets of his forthcoming edition of Brunne's translation of Langtoft's *Chronicle*, and have made a careful examination of 2230 lines (all I had), or of a portion about twice the length of the *Medytacyuns*. I have shown in the grammatical notes to this poem[2] that the dialect is E. Midland. Availing myself of Mr Morris's tests I have obtained the following results respecting the dialect of the *Chronicle*:—

1. Verbs in the third person singular, indicative, end (with a very few exceptions) in *es*. This is the Northern or W. Midland form.[3]

2. Verbs in the third person plural, indicative, end in *s* or *es* (except one or two). This also is the Northern or W. Midland termination.[3]

3. Verbs of the second person singular, present, indicative, end in *es* and *est*, two of the latter to three of the former; again showing in favour of a Northern dialect.

4. Imperatives singular are but few, and show no partiality for any particular dialect; but the imperatives plural mostly end in *es*; that is, have a Northern or W. Midland ending.

5. Present or imperfect participles end in *and*, *ande*, and *yng*.

---

[1] *Handlyng Synne*, Furnivall's ed., p. 29.   [2] Ante, p. xii.
[3] These forms are also found in the E. Midland *Havelok*.

6. Nouns plural generally end in *es;* none I think in *en.*

There are other details which point strongly to a Northern rather than a Southern influence; such as the use of *hepen* and *þeþen*, which are said to be "unknown to the Southern dialect;"[1] the constant occurrence of *til* (to) as a preposition; and other forms which I need not specify. So marked a difference in dialect can only be accounted for, supposing the *Chronicle* and the *Medytacyuns* proceeded from the same man, by the liberties taken by transcribers with their originals. It was only natural that, when they copied a work, they should endeavour to adapt the language to the district in which it was to be used.

It is matter for regret that these *Meditations* have not been in the hands of subscribers and students earlier. I copied the MS., and this Introduction was written, some five years ago—want of funds on the one hand, and my absence from England on the other, have delayed its appearance until now. During my brief holiday I have done what little I could (imperfectly, I know) to finish Henry Brinklow's volume for the student of history, and these *Meditations* for those especially who care to go back to "The sources of Standard English."[2]

J. M. COWPER.

Watling Street, Canterbury,
February 23, 1875.

Mr T. L. Kington Oliphant has read the proof of the *Medytacyuns*, and has kindly made the following notes:—

"I think there is no doubt that the 'Soper' must have been compiled by Robert of Brunne. The following are expressions that also come in the *Handlyng Synne*:—

"Page (Soper) 30. God *ones* (olim) said; also, *sicyche, same, nat only, smert, afore, pens, tugge, holy* (omnino), *the which, ho* (quis), *wuld God, seced* (cessavit). There is the same fondness for *gh* instead of the old *h*, as *logher, syghyng, þogh, Myghel, þurgh, glad-*

---

[1] Morris's *Specimens, &c.*, xv.
[2] The title of Mr Oliphant's most useful book.

lygh. There is, in common with the Northern Psalter, *bis* (emere), *wicked* (with the *d* at the end), *thos* = *thes* (illi), p. 19, *them· which* (p. 9).

"*Astyte* is a regular Northern expression; *teit* comes in the Haveloc; so does *stone dead*.

"*Furthermore* is in the Tristrem. There are many expressions found in the Cursor Mundi (Northern Version, which I think Dr Morris dates about 1290). These are *tite*, p. 268; *rife*, p. 18; *put* (in the sense of *ponere*), p. 96; (Ormin's) *bad* (jussit), p. 108; *cole* (occidere), p. 166; *ha* instead of *have*, p. 22; *wunt*, p. 208; *you* for *thou*, p. 164; *cors* (corpus) is also used in both works. Stratmann gives none but Northern examples of this last.

"There are some new expressions in the Soper, such as *bring about*, *swoon* (the *n* at the end is here first found); *stuck*, from *stikien* (p. 29); *grub*, for pluck up; *hereupon*, *strait* to hell (p. 35); *by cause* (quia); *most* is used for the superlative, p. 15. We see *a by path*, 16, like Manning's *bi way*; *to lay on* (thrash), *own self* (line 680). The Northern *them*, not *hem*, comes in p. 12, and has not been altered by the transcriber. The East Anglian *clad* is found in p. 16. The 3 pers. sing. in *es* comes often, like *hangis* (pendet).

"The word *preyour* (p. 13) altered to suit the rime is odd. The Southern transcriber was most likely a Kentishman, for we find *a ver* (afar), p. 19. He has *teren* (lachryme), *some seyþ*, was *ibroke*, and many such.

"The different reading *nor* in p. 2 is a sure mark of the North; it is never found in the South East about 1360, which I suppose is the date of the transcription."

[*Harl. MS.* 1701, *leaf* 84, *col.* 1.]

Here bygynneþ[1] **medytacyuns of þe soper of oure lorde Ihesu. And also of hys passyun. And eke of þe peynes of hys swete modyr, Mayden marye. þe whyche made yn latyn Bonauenture Cardynall.**

Alle myȝty god yn trynyte,
   Now & euer wyþ vs be;   *God be with us,*
   For þy sones passyun
Saue alle þys congregacyun;   4
And graunte vs grace of gode lyuyng   *and grant us bliss.*
To wynne vs blysse wyþouten endyng.
Now euery man, yn hys degre,
Sey amen, amen, pur charyte.   8
Thou crysten creature, by goddes grace,   *Christian,*
Opone þyn herte and hyde þy face;   *open thy heart.*
For þou shalt chaunge þy chere a none,
Or elles þyn herte ys harder þan stone.   12
Y wyl þe lere a medytacyun   *I will teach thee*
Compyled of crystys passyun;   *a meditation of*
And of hys modyr, þat ys[2] dere,   *the Passion.*
What peynes þey suffred þou mayst lere.   16
Take hede, for y wyl no þyng seye
But þat ys preued by crystes feye,   *May be proved*
By holy wryt, or seyntes sermons,   *by Holy Writ or*
Or by dyuers holy opynyons.   20   *Saints' sermons.*

[1] bygynnen   [2] ys so

No fiend will annoy thee. [leaf 84, col. 2]	Whan þou þenkest þys yn þy þoȝt Thyr may no fende noye þe with noȝt.¹

Now of þe soper of oure lorde Ihesu.

God sent His Son to save mankind.	Comyng þe tyme of grete mercy, Whan god sent hys sone down² fro³ hy, 24 Of a mayden he wulde be bore, To saue mankynde þat was forlore.
He would not "buy" us with silver and gold, but with His blood.	But noþer with corupt syluer ne⁴ golde; But wyþ hys blode, by⁵ vs he wulde. 28 Whan tyme was come to suffre þys
He made a Supper for a memorial.	A soper he made to hys dycyplys; Are he were ded and shuld fro⁶ hem wende, A memorand þyng to haue yn mynde. 32
This Supper was real.	þys soper was real as þou mayst here, Foure real þynges cryst made þere.
Think upon it, and God will not let thee go fasting.	Ȝyf þou þenke weyl on þys fedyng, God wyl nat late þe passe fastyng. 36
Four things to be had in mind.	Foure þynges þou most haue yn þy þoȝt, þat yn þys soper cryst haþ wroȝt:
First, a bodily feeding.	þe fyrst ys a bodly⁷ fedyng,
Second, the feet washing.	þe secunde ys ⁸hys dycyples fete⁸ wasshyng, 40
Third, Himself in Bread.	þe þred yn brede hym self takyng,
Fourth, a Sermon.	þe fourþe a sermoun of feyre makyng.

The first "point."	## The fyrst poynt of þe soper. Now to þe fyrst :—take gode entent
He sent Peter and John to prepare the Supper. [leaf 84, back]	How petyr and iohne from hym he sent, 44 Yn to þe mounte of syon, To greyþe hys paske aȝens ne com.
On Thursday night He came with His disciples.	And on a þursday þedyr he lyȝt Wyþ hys dycyplys aȝens nyȝt. 48
The Supper was prepared by the 72 disciples.	þe soper was dyȝt, as y herd sey,

¹ oght   ² down *comes after* sent *in* B.   ³ from   ⁴ nor
⁵ bie   ⁶ from   ⁷ bodyly   ⁸ *om.*

By dyscyplys seuenty and twey;
Seynt Martyals legende wytnesseþ ryȝt,   S. Martial's legend.
With hem he was þe soper to dyȝt.   52
Whan þe soper was made redy,   When supper was ready,
Cryst sette hym down, and þey hym by;   Christ sat down;
Iohne þe euangelyst sate hym nexte,   John sat next to Him.
Al þogh he were of age ȝungeste;   56
To hym was none of hem echone   None so true as John.
So trusty and so trewe as was Iohne:
For fere wulde he nat fle hym fro,   He would not flee till Christ
Tyl he was ded and byryed also.   60 was buried.
Byholde now, man, and þou shalt se
How euery man sate yn hys degre.
Here table was brode and foure square, The table was four-square.
The maner of þat¹ cuntre was swych þare; 64
On euery syde sate of hem þre,   Three sat on each side and Christ
And cryst yn a corner mekely to se: in a corner.
So þat here by þou mayst lere   Hereby thou mayest learn how
þat of o dysshe þey etyn yn fere,   68 they could eat out of one dish.
þarfore þe myȝt nat vndyrstonde
Whan cryst seyd, "he þat hys honde
Yn my dysshe putteþ furþ ryȝt,
He shal betraye me þys nyȝt."   72
Thys table at rome men haue seyn,   This table men have seen at
Yn seynt Iohne chyrche þe latereyn.   Rome. [See Stacions of Rome, ed. Furnivall.]
A nouþer maner mayst þou vndyrstande,
þat þey stonde with staues yn honde, 76 They eat standing to fulfil Moses'
Etyng faste, and stondyng stylle,   Law,
Moyses lawe to fulfylle.
Cryst lete hem sytte, so semeþ best,   but Christ lets them sit.
For elles ne had Ione slept one hys brest. 80
When graces were seyd, and alle men sette, "Graces" said,
Here paske lombe rosted furþe was fette.
Thys lomb toke vp² cryst Ihesus,
A verry lombe slayn for vs,   84 [leaf 84, back, col. 2]

¹ om.   ² vp written over the line in MS.

Christ cuts the lamb into small gobbets. As a servant He sits with them.	Alle yn smale gobettes he hyt kytte; For vs as a scruaunt wyþ hem[1] he sytte, With hem he[2] ete ryȝt with glad chere, And cunforted hem to ete yn fere,	88
But they are afraid.	But euer þey dredde to ete gladlygh, For sum sorowe semed hem nygh. Whyles þey ete on þys manere,	
Christ says, "I have desired to eat this Passover with you.	Cryst seyd þese wurdes dere:— "Long haue y desyred with ȝow, y seye, þys paske to ete ar þat y deye: Forsoþe, þe soþe [3] to ȝow y[3] seye,	92
One of you shall betray Me."	One of ȝow shal me betraye." Byholde now, man, what sorowe and wo þe dycyplys toke[4] to hem þo;	96
This word pierces their hearts.	þys voys as a swerd here hertes persed, And to ete anone þey seced.	100
Each looks on other, and asks, "Lord, is it I?"	Eche loked on ouþer with grysly ye,[5] And seyd, "lorde wheþer hyt be y[6]?"	
Judas goes on eating.	þe treytur ete faste, and wulde nat blyn, As þogh þe[7] tresun come nat by hym.	104
John asks privily who should betray Him.	Pryuyly þan Ion to cryst gan prey, And seyd, "lorde, who shal þe betrey?" For specyal loue cryst hyt hym tolde, "Iudas skaryot," he seyd, "beholde."	108
John lays his head on Christ's breast.	þan Iohne þoȝte hys herte wulde breste, And leyd hys hede[8] on crystys breste. Ful mekely cryste lete hym lye stylle, And suffred hym do alle hys wylle.	112
Christ did not tell Peter.	Why cryst wulde nat to petyr telle, Yn austyns sermoun þou mayst hyt spelle;[9] Ȝyf cryst þys treytur hym had tolde, With nayles and teþ rent hym þey[10] wulde.	116
What meekness to hold His disciple on His breast!	Byholde what mekenes yn hym reste, To holde hys dycyple so on hys brest.	

[1] hem   [2] hem he written over in MS.   [3]–[3] I. wil ȝow
[4] token   [5] ie   [6] I   [7] þat   [8] heuede
[9] Homily on the Gospel for S. John's Day.   [10] he

A! how tendyrly þey loued yn fere,
Y¹ wys to loue, here mayst þou lere. 120
þenk, man, also a ruly poȝt,
What s[orow]e² hys dyscyplys ben yn broȝt. [leaf 85]
At cry[stys]³ wurde, beholde, a none
þey etyn no more but madyn here mone; 124 *The disciples cannot eat;*
Eche⁴ of hem loked vp-on⁴ ouþer,
But cunseyl coude none take of ouþer. *they know not what to counsel.*
Beþenke, and holde þys weyl⁵ yn þy mende,
How þys soper ys broȝt now to an ende. 128

The secunde poynt of the soper.

The secunde poynt, beþenke þe weyl,⁶ *The second point teaches meekness.*
For grete mekenes hyt wyl þe spelle.
Whan þe soper was do, cryst ros anone,
And with hym þey ryse⁷ vp euerychone; 132
To a logher place þey gunne þan to go, *they go into a lower room.*
þey þat þe hous haue sey seyn⁸ ryȝt so.
He made hem sytte downe yn þat stede; *Christ makes them sit.*
Beholde, and⁹ þenke weyl on crystys dede; 136
Hys cloþes he cast of swyþe sone,
Hys dycyplys wundred what he wulde done;
With a towel hym self he gert, *He girds himself with a towel.*
Watyr he badde brynge furþe smert, 140
He hyt yn a stonen bacyn put,
To wasshe here fete greued hym nat.¹⁰ *He washes their feet.*
Petyr refused al þat seruyse; *Peter refuses.*
Cryst bad hym suffre on alle wyse. 144
Beholde now, man, eche doyng,
And þenke þys mekenes with grete wundryng, *Think on the meekness of Christ.*
That þe hygh mageste aud myȝtyest eke,
Boweþ hym downe to a fysshers fete. 148
He stode krokyng,¹¹ on knees knelyng,
Afore hys cretures fete syttyng.

¹ I. ² Illegible in MS., but *sorowe* in B. ³ Illegible in MS.
⁴ fast vppon ⁵ *e* in *weyl* written over in MS. weil in B.
⁶ well*e* ⁷ rese ⁸ seie, seiin ⁹ now.*and* ¹⁰ not ¹¹ croked

	Wyþ hys handys hys[1] fete he wassheþ,	
	He wypeþ he cleppeþ,[2] and swetly[3] kysseþ.	152
A greater meekness yet: He does the same to Judas.	Of a more mekenes ȝyt mayst þou gryse,	
	þat he to hys treytur [4]dyd þe same wyse.[4]	
	O Iudas, sore a shamed þou be may,	
	So meke and to[5] myþe[6] a mayster to tray;	156
	þyn herte ys harder þan any hardnesse,	
	Aȝens swyche mekenes deþ for to dresse.	
[leaf 85, col. 2]	Whan cryst þys seruyse had alle ydone,	
They return to the place of supper.	To þe sopyng[7] place aȝen þan þey come.	160
	By þys ensample, and many ouþer,	
	He conforted[8] hem to do to[9] here broþer.	
Think of the ensamples of meekness which Christ showed.	Man, here beþenke, yn eche degre,	
	How feyre ensample cryst shewed to þe;	164
	Ensample of mekenes to þe he lete,	
	Whan he wysshe hys dyscyplys fete;	
	A grete ensample of mekenes[10] loke,	
	Whan he hys flesshe to þy fode toke.	168
	A feyre monasshyng hys sermoun shewed,	
The learned should teach the "lewed."	þat þe lered men shulde teche þe lewed.	
	Pacyens he suffred,[11] hys treytur suffryng	
	So shamely to þe deþ, as a þef hym bryng;	172
	Yn goyng to þe deþ, he shewed obedyens	
	Yn fulfyllyng[12] hys faders comoundemens.	
Learn to pray,	Stedfastly for to prey here mayst þou lere,	
for He prayed thrice ere He was heard.	For he preyd fyrst þryys ar hys fadyr wulde here.	
	By þese vertues folue hym, y[13] rede,	177
	And yn to hys blys þey wyl þe lede.	

The þrydde poynt of þe soper.

The third point	The þryd poynt, man, haue yn mynde,[14]	
	How derwurly,[15] afore hys ende,	180

[1] So in MS.; here in B.   [2] clippeþ   [3] sweteli hem
[4]—[4] dede þis seruise   [5] so written over in MS.   [6] miþi
[7] soupinge   [8] cumfortede   [9] to do to   [10] charite   [11] shewed
[12] fulli-fillinge   [13] I   [14] mende   [15] derwrþli

A derwurþ ȝyfte he wulde with þe lete,   *is the gift of Himself.*
Hym self al hole vn to þy mete.
Whan he hadde wasshe here al per¹ fete,
And seten aȝen þere as þey ete,   184 *When He had sat down again,*
A newe testament he gan sone,
þe olde sacryfyce to fordone;
A new sacryfyce hym self he fonde,
And toke vp brede yn hys holy honde,   188 *He took bread,*
And to hys fadyr lyfte vpp hys ye,
He blessed and made hys precyus body;   *and gave it to His disciples, and said,*
To hys dycyplys he hyt ȝaue, and seyd,
"þys ys my body for ȝow betrayed."   192 *"This is my Body." Also the chalice, saying, "This is my Blood."*
Also of the chalys drynke he hem bad,
"þys ys my blode þat shal be shad."
Yn a memorand of hym with outyn ende,
He seyd, "makeþ þys yn my mende."   196 [leaf 85, back]
Beholde, how trewly and how deuoutly
He comunde and conforted þat blessed meyny.
þys mete shulde, most of any þyng,   *This meat shall gladden thy soul.*
Glade þy soule yn euery werchyng;   200
þyn herte shulde brenne for grete loue,
Whan þou hyt² takest to þy³ behoue;
No þyng more profytable, ne more chere,
þan hym self ⁴ne myȝt he⁴ leue here.   204
þat sacrament, þat þou seest þe before,   *The Sacrament was born of a maiden.*
Wundyrfully of a mayden was bore,
Fro heuene he lyȝte for þe to deye,   *Came down from heaven,*
He ros fro deþ to heuene to stye;   208 *Rose from death, and is now at God's right hand.*
On goddys ryȝt honde he ys syttyng;
He made heuene and erthe and alle þyng;
He gouerneþ alle þyng swetly and best,
He þat þou seest yn þe prestes fest,   212 *He that thou seest in the priest's hand,*
Yn whos powere onely hyt ys
To ȝyue⁵ þe blys,⁶ or endeles blys;

¹ þer   ² him   ³ þin   ⁴—⁴ he ne mighte
⁵ ȝeue   ⁶ So in MS., but *pine* in B.

<small>in the forme of bread, is God's Son.</small>

He þat þou seest, yn forme of brede,
Hyt ys goddys sone, quyk and¹ dede.   216
Wíth clene herte þou hym receyue,
For elles þy soule þou wylt deceyue.

<small>The fourth point.</small>

The fourþe poynt of þe soper.

The fourþe [poi*nt*²] beholde and here,
A louesu*m* lessu*n* þou mayst lere.   220
Whan cryst hadde fed hem eue*r*ychone.

<small>Christ began a sermon,</small>

A feyre sermou*n* he began a none,
Ful of swetnes and ful of loue,
Ful of cumfort to oure behoue;   224

<small>of which I take five parts.</small>

Of whych wurdys su*m* mende to make,
Fyue pryncypals y þenke to take.

<small>1st. He told them of His parting from them.</small>

¶ The fyrst he tolde of hys partyng
   And cumforted hem ful feyre, seyyng,   228
"ȝyt a whyle y am wíth ȝow now,
But faderles y wyl nat leue ȝow;
Y go and come to ȝow aȝen,
Forsoþe eftsones y wyl ȝow sen;   232

<small>[leaf 33, back, col. 2]</small>

þan ȝoure hertys ioye shul make,
þat ioye shal no man fro ȝow take."

<small>His words cut them to the heart.</small>

Lyke to þese mo gan he moue,
þat kytte here hertys for grete loue.   236

<small>2nd. He commanded them to love one another.</small>

¶ In þe secunde þou mayst se
   How he enformed hem yn charyte;
Ofte he reherced þese wurdes dere,
"Thys y ȝow hote, þat ȝe loue yn fere;   240
ȝyf ȝe loue alle men shul knowe þys,
þat ȝe be my dere dyscyplys."
þus hertly of charyte he tagħ hem well,
As þou shalt fynde yn Iones gospel.   244

<small>3rd. He admonished them to keep His commandments.</small>

¶ The þrydde he tagħ hem by monasshyng
   For to kepe hys comandyng:

---

¹ So in MS., but *nat* in B.   ² Not in MS., but in B.

"Kepeþ my comandementys, 3yf 3e me loue,
3if 3e hem kepe, 3e dwelle in loue."¹   248
¶ The fourþe, he warned hem feyþfullye,   *4th. He warned them of the sufferings they should undergo.*
   What þey shulde suffre are þey shuld dye:
"3e shul here haue sorowes some,
But truly y haue þys worlde ouercome,   252
And 3yf þe worlde 3ow hate now,
Weteþ þat he me hated ar 3ow ;
3e shul be sorowful, þe wurlde shal ioye,
But 3oure sorow shal turne to ioye."   256
¶ The fyueþe, beþenke how cryst Ihesus   *5th. He prayed to His Father*
   To hys fadyr turned and preyd for vs .
"Fadyr, kepe hem whyche þou 3aue me,
For whyle y was with hem y kepte hem to þe ; 260
Now, holy fadyr, to þe y come,
For hem y pray, and nat for þys wone ;   *for them and for all men.*
And nat onely for hem, but for alle men
þat shul byleue yn me by hem.   264
Fadyr, y wyl where þat y be   *"Father, I will that where I am they may be with me."*
þey be with me, my blysse to se."
þese wurdys, and ouþer þat hem² tolde,
Kytte here hertys and made hem colde.   268
Beholde now þe dyscyplys yn here mornyng,³   *The disciples all stand sighing.*
How þey stonde alle heuy here hedys bowyng,
Mornyng,³ sorowyng, and ofte syghyng,
þat cryst wytnessed to hem seyyng,   272 [leaf 86]
"For y þese wurdes to 3ow haue seyd,
Sorwe 3oure hertes haþ alle be leyd."
Byholde how homely Ion lyþ slepyng   *Behold how "homely" John*
On crystys brest, as hys derlyng.   276 *lies on Christ's breast!*
þys sermoun at crystys⁴ brest slepyng he soke,
And toke hyt to vs yn holy boke,
Among al ouþer as cryst tagh hem.
He seyd, "aryseþ and go we hen."   280 *Christ says, "Arise, go we hence."*

¹ Line 248 is supplied from B.   ² he hem in B.
³ moreninge   ⁴ his. *crystys* written over in MS.

                                   A! what drede went yn hem þo,
                                   þey wyst nat whedyr for to go,
                                   For þey went, as y shal sey;
                                   Cryst endyd hys sermoun by þe wey.   284

As they go the   Behold þe dyscyplys, yn here wendyng,
disciples are like
chickens creeping   As chekenes¹ crepyn vndyr þe dame wyng;
under the hen's
wing.   Some go byfore, and some go behynde,
                        Hys blessed wurdes to haue yn mynde;   288
                        One þrest on hym, eftsones anoþer,
                        þat meke mayster ys neuer þe wroþer.

They go over the   Fast þey went, and come a none,
brook Cedron,   Ouer a broke men callen Cedron.   292

where Judas   Hys treytur he abode þere tyl he come,
awaits them.
                        And ouþer armed men, a grete summe.
                        Now foleweþ, yn þys medytacyun,
                        To trete of crystys passyun.   296

Here begynneþ þe passyun.

                        Now crystyn creature, take goode hede,
Prepare your   And do þyn herte for pyte to blede;
heart to bleed!
                        Loþe þou nat hys sorowes to se,
                        þe whych hym loþed nat to suffre for þe.   300
                        Beholde and þenke with ruly mone
What pains He   What peynes he suffred ar morowe none;
suffers!
                        Beholde hym yn an orcherd syttyng,
                        Hys treytur þere mekely abydyng;   304

He bids His   He byt hys dyscyplys pray and wake,
disciples watch,
                        þat none temptacyun ʒow ouertake;
and goes from   A stones kast þan from hem he went,
them a stone's
cast,   And to hys dere fadyr hys knees he bent.   308

[leaf 86, col. 2]   Now þenke how mekely and how reuerently,
and prays,   To hys swete fadyr he preyeþ an² hy:—

"My Father,   "My wurschypful fadyr, y pray to þe,
hear my prayer
and despise it not.   Bowe þyn eres and lestene to me,   312

                     ¹ The second *e* written over in MS.   ² on

Here my bone and dyspyse hyt noȝt,
For sorowe my soule haþ ȝow soȝt;
My spyryt ys anguyssed ful sore yn me,   *My spirit is anguished.*
Myn herte ys dysturbled, fadyr, now se;   316
þou sentest me hedyr, as þy wyl ys,   *Thou sentest me.*
To bye mankynde aȝen to blys;
To do þy wyl, y seyd ȝ go;   *I said, To do Thy will, I go.*
Yn þe bokes hede hyt ys wryte so;   320
Here haue y be and preched þyn helþe,   *Here have I preached Thine health.*
Yn pouert, yn trauayle & noþyng yn welþe:
Fadyr, þyn hestes y haue fulfylt,   *I have fulfilled Thine 'hests.'*
And more y wyl, ȝyf þou wylt;   324
þou seest what sorowe ys to me dyȝt,   *Thou seest my sorrow.*
Of my foos aȝens alle ryȝt,
Ȝyf any wykkednes ys yn me founde,   *If any wickedness is found in me,*
Or euyl for euyl haue ȝyue¹ astounde,   328   *then am I worthy of these pains.*
þan were y wurþy þese peynes to fong;
But, fadyr, þou wost weyl þey do me wrong;   *Father, Thou knowest they wrong me,*
Euyl for gode þey haue me ȝoue,
And also grete hate for my loue.   332   *and give me hate for love.*
My dyscyple, whych y haue chersed,²
Me to betraye hym haue þey hyred;   *They have hired my disciple to betray me.*
At þrytty pens my mede ys take,
þey haue me preysed my wo to awake;   336
My swete fadyr, y prey to þe,   *My Father, rise up to help me.*
Ryse vp redyly yn helpe of me,
For þogh þey wyte³ nat þat y am þy sone,   *They know not that I am Thy Son.*
Ȝyt, by cause þat y here wone,   340
Lyuyng with hem Innocent lyfe,
þey shulde nat shape me so grete stryfe.
þenk⁴ þat y stode afore þy syȝt,   *Think that I stand before Thee*
To speke for hem boþe gode and ryȝt,   344
To turne a waye ⁵from hem, fadyr,⁵ þy mode,⁶   *to turn away Thy wrath from them.*
But wheþer nat euyl be ȝulde for gode;

¹ ȝulde   ² chershed   ³ wete   ⁴ Thenke fader
⁵—⁵ fader from hem.   ⁶ wraþþe written over mode in B.

12 MEDITATIONS ON THE

[leaf 66, back] For þey to my soule deluyn a lake,
A vyleynys deþ to me þey shape; 348

Dear Father, let this death go from me; Wharfore, dere fadyr, ȝyf hyt mow be,
Y prey þat þys deþ mow go fro me;

If not, Thy will be done. ȝyf þou se hyt be nat so best,
þy wyl be ydo, ryȝt as þou lest. 352

I commend myself unto Thee." But, fadyr, myn herte y betake þe,
Kepe hyt and strenþe hyt how so hyt be."

To hys dyscyplys hys wey¹ þan he toke,

He finds His disciples sleeping. He fond hem slepyng and hem sone awoke:² 356
Here yen³ were slepy and heuy as clay,
He bad hem algates wake and pray.

He prays twice, thrice, the same orison. Aȝen to pray he toke hys pas,
Twyys, þryys, yn dyuers place. 360
þe same orysun þat he preyd byfore,
He preyd now and ded to more:

"Father, I am here to do Thy will. "Fadyr, ȝyf þys deþ mow nat fro me go,
Y am here, þy wyl be algates do. 364

I commend my mother and brethren unto Thee." My swete modyr, fadyr, y þe betake,
My breþren also, kepe hem fro wrake;
Y kepte hem þyrwhylys y⁴ was with hem,
My derwurþe fadyr, now kepe þou þem." 368

þus long he preyd tyl þat he wax hote,

For anguish His blood ran down as sweat. For anguys hys blode ran down ryȝt as swote.
Man, take ensample here at goddes sone,
Whan þou shalt pray of god any bone, 372
Prey so stedfastly tyl þat þou be herde,
For cryst preyd þryes ar þat he were herd.

While He prayed Whyles he þus preyd yn grete dolour

S. Michael came and said, Seynt myghel lyȝt a down fro heuene toure, 376
And hym cumforted and seyd þus:

"All hail! Thy prayer and bloody sweat I have offered to thy Father." "Alheyl, my lorde, cryst Ihesus!
Þy preyer and þy swote blody
Y haue offred to þy fadyr an hy, 380
Yn syȝte of alle þe courte of heuene;

¹ wel .   ² he woke   ³ eien   ⁴ þat L.

For ȝow we preyd alle with o steuene,
þat he shuld nat suffre þe dey¹ þus;
þy fadyr, by resun, answered vs,　　　　　384 He answered,
'My derwurþe sone wote þys ful weyl,　　　　[leaf 85, back, col. 2]
þat mannes soule, þat lyþ yn helle,　　　　"My Son knows if He will
May nat semely to blys be broȝt,　　　　　save souls He
But þey with hys blode be fyrst oute boȝt.　388 must die."
þarfore, ȝyf my sone wyl soules saue,
Nedes he mote for hem þe deþ haue.'"
þan cryst answered, with mylde state:　　　　Christ said,
"Soules saluatyun y wyl algate,　　　　392 "I choose death;
þarfore to dey raþer y chese,
þan we þe soules yn helle shulde lese,
þe whych my fadyr formed to hys lykenes:
Hys wyl be ydo, y wyll no lesse."　　　　396 His will be done."
þan seyd þe aungel to hym an hy:　　　　　The Angel said,
"Cumforte þe weyl and do manly;　　　　　"Comfort thyself and do manly.
Hyt ys semely to hym þat ys hyghest,
Grete þynges to do, and suffre mest;　　　　400
þy pyne shal sone be ouerpaste,
And ioye shal sewe euer for to last;
þy fadyr seyþ euer with þe he ys,　　　　　Thy Father is ever with Thee."
þy modyr he kepeþ and þy dyscyplys."　　　404
Cryst bade þe aungel, "go, grete þou² me
To my fadyr dere an hy yn hys cyte."
Beholde now, how mekely þys cumforte he toke
Of hys owne creature, as seyþ þe boke,　　　408
A lytyl from aungels he ys made lesse,　　　He was made little less than
Whyl he ys yn þys valey of dyrknes;　　　　the angels.
þys wo he suffred yn hys manhede,　　　　He suffered in His manhood,
But god suffred naght³ yn hys god hede.　　412 not in His God-head.
þe þryd tyme he ros from hys preyour
All be sprunge with blody coloure;
Beholde hym auysyly, þan shalt þou se
With oute grete dolour þys may nat be.　　416

¹ deio　² þou written over in MS.　³ noght

He returns to His disciples.	To hys dyscyplys went he, and seyd,	
	"He cumþ ny þat haþ me betrayd."	
Judas comes, and says,	Anone come Iudas, with hys cumpanye,	
	Cryst went aȝens hym ful myldely:	420
"Hail, Master!"	"Heyl, mayster!" he seyd, and to hym sterte,	
	He kessed hys mouþe with tresun yn herte.	
[leaf 57] They all fall upon Him.	Þo fyl vpp on hym alle þe touþer route,	
	For erst of knowlechyng þey were yn doute.	424
	Þe cursed houndes runne hym aboute,	
	And drowe hym furþe, now yn, now oute;	
Some bind, some blind, some spit upon, some buffet, some scorn Him.	Sum bynte hym, sum blyndyþ hym, & sum on hym spyt,	
	Sum boffeteþ hym, and sum seyþ, "telle who þe smyt;"	
	Sum scorneþ hym, and sum syngeþ of hym a song,	429
	Some axen questyons, to[1] do hym wrong;	
He says nothing.	But to hem no þyng answere he wulde.	
	Werse þo þan a fole of hem [2]he ys[2] holde,	432
"Where is Thy wisdom?"	Some seyd, "where ys now all þy wysdom?	
	Þou held þe wyser þan any ouþer man;	
	Of oure patryarkes & prestes þou haddest despyte,	
"Thou shalt die."	Þarefor [3]þou shalt[3] haue of vs þe deþ astyte;	436
"If Thou art God's Son, help Thyself."	Thou seyst þat þou art goddes sone,	
	Helpe þy self[4] ȝyf þou kone."	
Some seek false witness.	Sum seke aȝens hym fals wytnes,	
	Sum seyn on hym vnsekernes,	440
	Some tugge,[5] sum drawe[6] fro ce to ce,[7]	
Ah, how may this be!	A! lorde Ihesu, how may þys be?	
	Þyrwhylys he suffred þys[8] sorow & wo,	
The disciples run away.	Hys dyscyplys runne awey hym fro.	444
	To maudelens hous Ion went ful ryȝt,	
	Þere as þe soper was made þeke nyȝt;	
John tells Our Lady of her Son's punishment.	Oure lady he tolde and here felawshepe	
	Of here dere sonys shenshepe.	448
	Þenk, man, of þe dyscyplys doyng!	

[1] for to. to written over in MS. [2-2] is he [3-3] shalt þou
[4] þeself now [5] tugge him [6] drawe him
[7] place written over ce to ce in MS. [8] on.

þey wepe, þey weyle, here handys þey wryng,
Here mayster ys take, þat shulde hem kepe;
þey renne aboute as herdles shepe.   452
Oure lady wente here seluyn alone,   *She goes alone to pray.*
To þe fadyr of heuene she made þys mone:—
"My wurschypfullest fadyr, and moste meke,   *"My Father, my sweet Son*
Moste mercyable, and most helpyng eke,   456   *I commend to Thee.*
My swete sone y ȝow betake!
Derwurþe fadyr, kepeþ hym fro wrake,   *Keep Him from 'wrack.'*
Beþ nat cruel to my dere chylde,
For to alle men ȝe are ful mylde.   460
Fadyr, shal my chylde be dede, Ihesus,   [leaf 87, col. 2] *Shall He die?*
What haþ he mysdo to dey þus?
But, fadyr, ȝyf ȝe wyl mankynde   *Father, if Thou wilt save man-*
Be boȝt to blys withoutyn ende,   464   *kind,*
Y prey outher wyse doþ bye¹ hem now,   *do it in some other manner.*
For al þyng ys posyble to ȝow.
Lateþ nat, fadyr, my sone dede be;   *Let not my Son die.*
Y pray ȝow ȝeldeþ hym aȝen to me;   468
He ys so buxum to do ȝoure wyl,
þat he nat chargeþ hym self to spyl.
Helpeþ my sone fro cursed houndes;   *Help Him from cursed hounds."*
Dere fadyr, bryngeþ hym out from here hondes."   472
þenke, man, now & rewe on here syghyng,
For þys preyd she with watyr wepyng.

The medytacyun of þe oure of pryme.

On a colde mornyng, at pryme of daye,   *The priests prepare them-*
   The prestes and prynces gun² hem araye;   476   *selves.*
Both bollers of wyne and eche agadlyng   *Drunkards come to see Jesus.*
Come oute for to se of Ihesus endyng.
þey shokyn hym ³oute þan³ of hys cloþyng,   *They strip Him,*
And bonden hys handys fast hym behynd,   480
As a þefe among hem⁴ led furþe he was,   *lead Him to Pilate,*
Now to pylat, now to eroud, now to kayphas.   *thence to Herod and Caiaphas.*

¹ bie   ² gunne   ³—³ þan out   ⁴ hem written over in MS.
MEDITATIONS.   3

	þey cryde, "þou þefe, come to þy dome!"	
	And he, as a meke lambe, aftyr hem come.	484
His Mother goes to meet Him.	Hys modyr, Ion, and[1] ouþer kyn,	
	Wente by a bypaþ to mete with hym.	
	When þey hym saye so shamely ylad,	
	No tunge may telle what sorowe þey had.	488
	þenke, whan hys modyr fyrst hym byhelde,	
She swoons in the field.	Aswo[2] she fyl down yn þe felde :	
	þan cryst was turmented yn moste kare,	
	Whan he say hys modyr so pytusly fare.	492
	Beholde to pylat he ys furþe drawe,	
He is falsely accused. Pilate sends Him to Herod.	Falsly acused aȝens here lawe :	
	Pylat sent hym to eroude þe kyng,	
	And eroude þe kyng was glad of hys comyng ;	496
	A myracle he coueyted of hym for to se,	
[leaf 87, back]	But noþer myracle ne wurde hym shewe wulde he.	
	þan as a fole eroude hym hadde,	
Herod clothes Him with a white cloth, and sends Him again to Pilate.	And with a whyte cloþe y[3] skorne hym he clad,	500
	And sente hym aȝen to syre pylate :	
	And þo was made frenshepe þar arst was debate.	
	Nat onely a mysdoer now [4]he ys[4] holde,	
	But as a lewed fole he ys eke tolde :	504
	þey cryed on hym, as foules on owle,	
With wet and dirt they defile Him.	With wete and eke dung þey hym defoule.	
	Hys modyr þat tyme folwed hym longe,	
	And wundred þat he wulde suffre swyche wrong.	508
	þey broȝt hym to pylate, he stode ful feynt ;	
	Boldely þe[5] howndes pursewed here pleynt.	
	Pylate þoȝt to delyuer hym,	
	For no cause of deþ he fonde yn hym :	512
"Scourge Him, and let Him go."	"Y wyl vndyr neme hym, he seyd þo,	
	Do scurge hym weyl, and so late hym go."	
They bind Him to a pillar,	To a pylour fast þan þey hym bownde,	
	þey bette hym, & rent hym, wounde be[6] wounde.	516

[1] and his   [2] Aswowe   [3] in   [4] is he
[5] þo   [6] om.

PASSION OF OUR LORD JESUS.   17

Beholde now, man, a ruly¹ sy3t!   A rueful sight.
þy cumly kyng stant bounde vpry3t,
Alle forwounded for þe yn² mode;
Beholde how he wadeþ yn hys owne blode!   520
3yt þey bete hym and leyn³ on sore,   They lay on until they are weary.
Tyl þey be wery and mow no more.
þe pyler⁴ þat þey hym to bow[n]den⁵   The pillar shows the blood now.
3yt sheweþ þe blode of hys woundyn.   524
A, lorde Ihesu! how may þys be?
Ho was so hardy þat spoyled þe?
Ho more hardy þat þe bounden?
Ho moste hardy þat þe wounden?   528
Almy3ty god! where art þou now?   Almighty God, where art Thou?
þese houndes seme my3tyer þan þou!
But trewly, þou sone of ry3twysnes,
Withdrawest þy bemes ouer oure derkenes.   532
Whan þey hadde bete hym þus pytusly,
þey bro3t hym to pylate, & cryed an⁶ hy,
"Syre, þys fole kalleþ⁷ hym self a kyng!   "This fool calleth Himself a king!
Cloþe we hym þarfore yn kynges cloþyng."   536   [leaf 87, back, col. 2]
þenk þys was y do at þe oure of pryme: Clothe we Him in king's clothing!"
þe dowyng of⁸ þred now wyl y ryme.

The medytacyun of þe predde oure.

Wyþ purpyl þey cloþed hym alle yn skorne,   They clothe Him with purple.
   And syþen ⁹krounde hym with a crounе⁹ of
Yn hys hand a rede dyd þey take,   [þorne; In His hand they put a reed.
And manyone on hys hede þey brake;
þey sette hym opunly yn here seyng,
And knelyd, and seyd,¹⁰ "heyl, syre kyng!" 544   "Hail, Sir king!"
A Ihesu! þy pacyens may nat be tolde.
þou angry man, þy sauyour here beholde;
For þe he suffred þys pyne, þys shame,
And for a¹¹ lytyl wurde þou wylt men grame. 548

¹ rewli ² wiþ ³ leien ⁴ peler ⁵ bownden ⁶ on
⁷ kalled ⁸ of þe ⁹—⁹ corownde wiþ corowne : *croūne* in MS.
          ¹⁰ cride   ¹¹ o

18   MEDITATIONS ON THE

                Eftsones to pylate þey come cryyng,
                And seyd, "syre, saue Cesar, we haue no kyng;
                Who hym self a kyng wyl make

"Crucify Him! Crucify Him!"   By lawe þe deþ he most take."   552
                Tho seyd pylat, "what wyl ȝe with hym?"
                þey cryed, [1]"crucyfye, crucyfye[1] hym!"
                Pylat þan dredde for þe peples voys,

Pilate condemns Him.   And dampnede hys lorde to dye on þe croys.   556
                Ha, fals Iustyce! where fynst þou þat resun,
                So for to dampne an ynnocent man?[2]
                Whan he was dampned on cros for to hong,
                þe houndes wulde not tary hym long,   560

The houndes lead Him out at once.   But anone from pylat þey led[3] hym oute,
                And ioed[4] þat here malys was broȝt aboute.

A cros is fetched,   A cros [5]was fet furþ,[5] boþe long and grete,
                þe lengþe þerof was fyftene fete.   564

and put on His shoulders.   Vp on hys shulder þys cros þey kast,
                þat hys bak bent and wel ny to braste;

They hurry Him.   þey punged hym furþe þurgh euery sloghౖ,
                As an hors ys prykked þat goþ yn[6] ploghౖ.   568
                Beholde now, man, with wepyng herte,
                And late nat þy þoȝt lyȝtly a sterte.
                Cryst goþ krokedly þys heuy cros vndyr,
                And feyntly hyt bereþ, hyt ys no wundyr.   572

[leaf 88]   þey hye hym, and ho goþ withoutyn any stryfe,
                And bereþ hys owne deþ, and bereþ þy lyfe.

Yet more shame!   Ȝyt hym ys shape more shame and shenshepe;

Thieves are his companions.   þeuys be[7] broȝt to hym yn hys felawshepe!   576
                Ȝyt more, for cryste bereþ hys owne, Iuwyse,
                Y fynde nat þat þe þeues ded [8]þe same[8] wyse.
                A, Ihesu! what shame þey do to ȝow here,
                To make ȝow so vyleynsly[9] þese þeues fere.   580

The prophecy must needs be fulfilled.   But nedys þe prophecye mot be fulfylled,

[1]—[1] crucifige, crucifige: in the MS. is a mark over the final *e* which may be a very small *g—crucyfyge*.
  [2] moun   [3] ledden   [4] ioide   [5]—[5] furþ was fet
  [6] in þe   [7] ben   [8]—[8] on þat   [9] vilensli

þat seyd,¹ wit/¿ wykked men he ys spylled.   Isa. 53, 9.
Mary hys modyr folewed a ver,   Mary follows,
She myȝt for pres come hym no ner ;   584
A shorter wey for to chese þan bygan she,
To mete with here swete sone withoute the cyte ;
And þo she sayȝ hym þat grete tre bere,
Half dede she wax and swouned ³ryȝt þare ; ³   588   and swoons again.
Ful feyne she wulde hys peynes alyþed ;
She myȝt nat, so þese houndes hym hyed.
None of hem myȝt speke ouþer to,
For sorowe þat eche had of ouþer þo.   592
Furþe þey dryuen hym with hys berdoun,   –They drive Him till He faints.
Tyl he for feyntnesse fyl ny adoun.
For ouer long tyme þat cros he bare,
þe place weyl shewyþ, who so haþ be þare.   596
Thos howndes were lothe hys deþ for to tarye,
þey dredyn þat pylat hys dome wulde varye,   They are afraid Pilate will change his mind.
For euer hyt semed by hys wylle,
þat he was loþ Ihesu to spylle.   600
A man þey mette, and hym areyned,   They meet a man and lay the cross on him.
To bere þe cros þey hym constreyned ;
So furþe as a þefe, Ihesu þey nam,
Tyl þey to þe mounte of caluarye cam.   604

The medytacyun of⁴ syxte oure of⁵ none.

Thenk now, man, how hyt ys down   Think,
    Yn þe oure of⁴ syxte of⁵ none.
Beholde þe peynes of þy sauyour,
And crucyfye þyn herte with grete dolour.   608   and crucify thine heart.
Whan he to caluarye mounte was broȝt,⁶
Beholde what werkmen þere wykkedly wroȝt :   [leaf 88, col. 2]
Some dyggen, sum deluyn, sum erþe oute⁷ kast,
Some pycchen þe cros yn þe erþe fast ;   612   They pitch the cross.
On euery syde sum laddres vpp sette,   Ladders are set up.
Sum renne aftyr hamers, some nayles fette ;

¹ selþ   ² sagh   ³⁻³ þere   ⁴ of þe   ⁵ and of   ⁶ ibroght   ⁷ vp

MEDITATIONS ON THE

His clothes are rent off.	Some dyspoyle hym oute dyspetusly, Hys cloþys cleuyn on hys swete body; 616 þey rente hem of as þey were wode: Hys body aȝen ran alle on blode. A! wit*h* what sorow hys modyr was fedde, Whan she say¹ hym so naked and alle bled!² 620 Fyrþer more, þan gan she to seche, And say þat þey had left hym no breche. She ran þan³ þurgh hem, and hastyly hyde,
Mary wraps kerchiefs round Him.	And wit*h* here kercheues hys hepys she wryde. 624 She wulde do⁴ more, but she ne myȝt, For fersly here swete⁵ sone ys from her plyȝt.
They draw Him to the cross-foot.	To þe cros fote þey drowe hym hyyng. Se now þe maner of crucyfyyng. 628
Ladders are raised.	Twey laddres ben sette þe cros behynde, Twey enmyes on hem smartly gu*n* glymbe,⁶ Wit*h* hamers and nayles sharply whet: A shorte⁷ ladder before was fet.⁸ 632 þere as þe fete shorte⁷ weren, Beholde þys syȝte wit*h* ruly teren,
Christ goes up without urging,	Cryst Ihe*su* hys body vpp stey, By þat short ladder, þat cros an hy; 636 Wit*h*oute ȝenseyyng he gan vp wende, And whan he com to þe laddres ende, Toward þe cros hys bak he layde,
and extends His arms.	And hys real armes oute he dysplayde; 640 Hys fayre handys oute he streyȝte, And to þe crucyfyers oute⁹ he reyȝte;
He lifts His eyes and says, "Here am I, Father;	And to hys fadyr he kast¹⁰ hys yen,¹¹ And seyd, "here am y,¹² fadyr myn: 644 Vnto þys cros þou mekest me,
I offer myself for mankind:	Me for mankynde y offre to þe; My breþren and sustryn þou hast made hem;
[leaf 68, back]	For my loue, fadyr, beþ¹³ mercyable to hem; 648

¹ sagh   ² bebled   ³ þo   ⁴ ha do   ⁵ *om.*   ⁶ climbe
⁷ shorter   ⁸ So in MS; but *set* in B.   ⁹ hem   ¹⁰ caste
¹¹ ein   ¹² I. am   ¹³ be

Alle olde syñnes þou hem forȝyue,   be merciful unto them."
And grauñte hem blys with vs for to lyue :
Derwurþe fadyr, saue alle mankyñne,
Lo here y am offred for here synne."   652
Whyle he þus preyd¹ yn hys herte,
The too Iew a nayle yn hys hand gerte,   They nail Him to the cross.
þe touþer þey drowe tyl þe veynes braste,
And nayled þe touþer ²hand þer fyne² faste.   656
Anone þey com down with alle here gere,
And alle þe laddres þan remouede were.
Beholde, man, now a grete³ angwys!   Behold His anguish.
For by þe armes hys body alle hangys.   660
To hys fete anone þan þey straked,
þey haled hem harde, tyl þe cros kraked ;
Alle þe ioyntes þan brasten atwynne.
A, Ihesu! why suffrest þou⁴ þus for oure synne!   664
Hys fete þey nayled as tree to lede ;
þan myȝt ⁵nat he⁵ moue more but hys hede.   He can only move His head.
Beholde þese nayles beren alle hys lemes,
Loke, alle aboute hym renne blody stremes.   668   Bloody streams run all about Him.
He suffred sorowes byttyr and fele,
Mo þan any tunge may rede or telle.
Betwene þeues tweyn þey hange hym yn samen,
A, what wrong, what peyne, & also what shamen!   672
Some dyspyseþ hys lore, and seyþ,
"Fy! þat goddes temple dystroyþ!"   "Fy, Thou that destroyest the Temple!
Sum seyþ, "saue þy selfe, ȝyf þou kuñne ;⁶
Com adowne, ȝyf þou be goddes sone."   676   Come down, if Thou be God's Son."
Also þe Iewes, þat crucyfyed hym,
þe cloþes of hym þey parted⁷ atwynne.
Sum seyd, "ouþer coude he weyl saue,   "He could save others,
But now hym owne self⁸ may he nat saue."   680   Himself He cannot save."
þus whyl hys modyr þe cros stant nye,

¹ stilli preide   ²—² honde þere fin   ³ *a grete a grete* in MS.
    ⁴ þou   ⁵—⁵ he nat   ⁶ kone   ⁷ parteden
       ⁸ *hymowneself* in MSS.

MEDITATIONS ON THE

His mother stands near.
    Ruly on here sone she kast here ye.¹
    A! here sorow, here angwys, here pyne,²
    Y may sum þenk, but nat alle seyn ;   684
    Truly yn herte she ys crucyfyed,
[leaf 86, bk, col. 1]
    Ful feyn for sorow she wulde ha deyd.
    Here sones peyne was eke moche þe more,
    þat he here peynes say³ be so sore ;   688

He complains,
    And to hys fadyr stylly he pleynes :

"Father, seest Thou not my Mother?
I should be crucified, not she."
    "Fadyr! seest þou nat my modyr peynes?
    On þys cros she ys with me,
    Y shulde be crucyfyed, and nat she ;   692
    My crucyfyyng suffyseþ for alle mankynne,
    For now y bere alle here synne ;
    Yn to þy kepyng y here betake,
    Derwurþe fadyr, here peynes⁴ þou alake."   696

Also she prayed,
    Also she preyde, with byttyr wepyng,

"My Father, shall my dear Son die?"
    And seyd, "my fadyr, euer lastyng,
    Shal my dere sone deye algate?
    Hym now for to saue me þenkeþ to late.   700
    Se, fadyr, what angwys now yn hym ys,
    Y prey þe sumdele hys peyne þou lys."

By her stand John, the three Maries, James, Magdalene, and Cleophas [Salome in Lat. orig.].
    By here stant Iohne, and maryes þre,
    Iacobe, maudeleyn, and cleophe.   704
    Wundyr ys to telle what sorowe þey make,
    For here swete mayster ys from hem take.

The medytacyun of the wurdys þat cryst spak hangyng vpp on þe cros.

Christ speaks seven words.
    Thenk how⁵ cryst, hongyng on þe cros,⁶
    Seuene [wur]dys [seide⁷] with ful ruly voys.   708
    þe fyrst wurde þat he þere hongyng seyd,
    For hys crucyfyers mekely he preyd,

1. "Father, forgive them,
    "Fadyr, forʒyue hem here synnes sone,

¹ eye   ² pein   ³ sagh   ⁴ peine   ⁵ now how
⁶ crois   ⁷ not in MS.; *seide* in B.

For þey¹ wyte² nat wel what þey done."   712   they know not what they do."
Grete loue, grete pacyens, þys wurde shewyþ þe,
þat þou shust pray for hem þat þy foos be.
þe secunde wurde to hys modyr was mone :³
" Wo*m*man," he⁴ seyd, " beholde þy sone."   716   2. "Woman, behold thy son."
To hys dyscyple he seyd a nouþer,
And seyd, " beholde þy modyr, broþer."   "Behold thy mother, brother."
He wulde nat marye hys modyr clepe,
Lest for grete loue here herte wulde breke.   720
þe þred to þe þefe,—" forsoþe y seye þe,
To day yn blys þou shalt be w*ith* me."—   [leaf 59]
þe fourþe he cryed wyþ voys an hy,   3. "To-day shalt thou be in bliss with me."
" Eli, Eli, lamaȝabatany ! "⁵   724
þat ys, my god, my god, wharto   4. "My God, My God,
Hast þou forsake me yn my wo !   why hast thou forsaken me ?"
As who seyþ, þou me forsakest,
And for þys wurlde to day me betakest.   728
þe fyþe⁶ wurde he seyd, " y þryste :"   5. "I thirst."
þan þe hou*n*des wroȝtyn werste.
þey þoȝte to noye hym moste of alle,
And ȝaue hym to drynke aysel and galle.   732   They give Him gall.
He tastede su*m*dele hys þryst for to lyne :⁷
A ! A ! how strong was þat⁸ pyne.
þogh yt he expouñed yn a sermou*n*,
þat he þrysted soulys saluacyu*n*,   736
Ȝyt truly þe manhede þrysted on þe⁹ rode,
For he was ful drye for faute of blode.
The syxte wurde anone he spellede,
And seyd, " alle þyng ys now fulfylled."   740   6. "All things are now fulfilled."
As who seyþ, fadyr, fulfylled y haue
Alle þyn hestys, þy soules to saue :
Y haue be skurged, scorned, dyffyed,
Wou*n*ded, angred, and crucyfyed ;   744

¹ þey written over in MS.   ² wete   ³ nome
⁴ he written over in MS.   ⁵ lama sabatani   ⁶ fifþe
⁷ B has the gloss *slake*.   ⁸ þa*n* his   ⁹ *om*.

	Fulfylled y haue þat wrytyn ys of me,	
	þarfore, dere fadyr, take¹ me to þe.	
	ȝyf þou wylt more, y wyl hyt fulfylle,	
	For here now y hange to do þy wylle.	748
His Father said,	þan seyd hys fadyr, my derwurþe sone,	
"Come to my bliss;	Com to þy blys þere euer to wone;	
	Alle þyng fulweyl þou hast fulfylled,	
I will no more;	Y wyl no more þat þou be þus spylled,	752
soules thou hast brought from bond; come, sit on my right hand."	For soules þou haste² broȝt oute of bonde,	
	Come sone and sytte on my ryȝt honde.	
	Anone he traueyled as men done þat dyen,	
	Now shyttyng,³ now kastyng vpward, hys yen,	756
	þrowyng hys hede,⁴ now here, now þore,	
	For bodely strengþe haþ he no more;	
	þe seuenþe wurde ful loude þan he spake:	
[leaf 89, col. 2] 7. "Father, into thy hands I commend my spirit."	"Fadyr, yn þyn handys my spyryt y betake."	760
	He ȝelde vp hys goste, hys fadyr þankyng,	
	Toward hys brest hys hede⁴ hangyng.	
	þan to þat crye Centuryo turned sone,	
	And seyde, "forsoþe þys was goddys sone."	764
	For wyþ þat grete crye þe goste gan furþe go:	
	Ouþer men⁵ whan þey deye do nat so.	
This cry is heard in hell by those	þat crye was so grete, as y þe telle,	
	þat hyt was weyl herdo downe yn to helle.	768
	þenk now, man, what ioye þere ys	
	Whan soules ben broȝt from pyne to blys.	
	A! how long þey haue þere lyne,	
who there wait for their Saviour.	To abyde here sauyour yn many a pyne;⁶	772
	þey cleped, and cryed, "com goddes sone,	
	How long shul we yn þys wo wone?"	
	Here endeþ now crystys passyun,	
	Fulfylled yn þe oure of syxte and none.	776

¹ *t* not quite clear in MS.: *kal* in B.
² *haste* written over in MS. ³ shettinge ⁴ heued
⁵ *men* follows *deye* in B. ⁶ *apyne* in MS.

The medytacyun of þe sorowe þat oure Lady had for þe wunde yn here sone[1] syde.

Now gyn we a medytacyun
Of a swete lamentacyun,
þat mary, modyr meke and mylde,
Made for here derwurþe chylde.   780
Grete peynes she suffred here byfore,
But now she suffreþ moche more ;
For whan she say[2] hym drawe to ende,
Y leue she wax oute of here mynde ;   784
She swouned, she pyned, she wax half dede,
She fylle to þe grounde, and bette here hede.
þo Ion ran to here, and here vpbreyde.
Whan she myȝt speke, þese wurdes she seyd :   788
" A, my sone ! my socour ! now wo ys me :
Ho shal graunte me to deye wyþ þe ?
þou wrecched deþ, to me þou come,
And do þe modyr dye with þe sone ;   792
Aboue alle þyng y desyre þe :
Com deþ, and to my sone þou brynge me.
My fadyr, my former, my mayster, my make,
Why, swete sone, hast þou me forsake ?   796
þenk how we loued and leued to gedyr,
And late vs now, dere sone, deye togedyr.
Y may nat lyue here withoute þe,
For alle my fode was þe to se.   800
A sone ! where ys now alle my ioyyng,
þat y hadde yn þy furþe beryng ?
Y wys þat ioye ys turned to wo :
Symeon seyd soþ hyt shulde be so.   804
He seyd a swerd my soule shulde perce ;
Sertes,[3] swete sone, þys y[4] reherce."

Side notes: A lamentation that Mary made. She suffered great pains. She swooned. She cried, "Woe is me!" Come death. [leaf 89, back] Why, sweet Son, hast thou forsaken me? I cannot live without Thee. The joy I had at Thy birth is turned to woe."

[1] sones   [2] sagh   [3] Certes   [4] mai I.

                þan gan here felawshepe here sorowys¹ to aslake,²
                And softly and myldely aȝen she þo spake :   808

"Good womman, see if there be any sorrow like unto mine.
                " Now ȝe gode wymmen, seeþ, with ȝoure yen,
                Ȝyf þyr be any sorowe lyke vnto myn :
                My sone ys slawe here afore myn ye,
                þe whyche y bare wenles³ of my body.   812

Never womman bare such a child."
                þere was neuer womman bare swyche a chylde,
                So gode, so gracyus, so meke and so mylde ;
                Y feled no sorow yn hys beryng,
                Nedys þan mote⁴ yn hys deyyng.   816
                Myn owne gete⁵ ys fro me take,
                What wundyr ys þan þoȝ y wo make ?"
                Whyles she sate yn here lamentacyun,

An armed company comes to
                A cumpany armed she say⁶ fast come ;   820
                þe whych ware sent yn a grete reke,⁷

break the legs of the condemned.
                þe dampned mennes legges to breke ;
                To sley hem and kast here bodyes away,
                þat none shulde se hem hange yn þe halyday.   824
                A, mary, modyr, þy wo wexyþ newe !

Mary's martyrdom is renewed.
                Se, man, here martyrdom, and þeron rewe.
                For so oft she was martyred to day,
                As ofte as here sone turmented she say.   828

"What more will they do?
                She seyd, "my sone, what wul⁸ þey more do,
                Haue þey nat crucyfyed and slayn þe þerto ?
                Y wende þey had be all ful of þe.
                Now derwurþe sone, haue reuþe on me.   832

I may not help Thee, [leaf 59, bk, col. 2] but I will do what I can."
                Sone, y may helpe þe yn no degre,
                But ȝyt wyl y do þat ys yn me."

She runs to the cross, and says,
                To þe cros foote hastly she ran,
                And clypped þe cros faste yn here arme,   836

"Here will I die."
                And seyd, "my sone here wyl y dey,
                Ar þou from⁹ me be bore aweye."

The hounds come,
                Faste þese houndes come rennyng ryue,¹⁰
                And founde þe Iewes boþe alyue ;   840

    ¹ sorowe   ² slake   ³ wēles   ⁴ mote I.   ⁵ gete sone
    ⁶ sngh   ⁷ Glossed *haste* in B.   ⁸ mowe   ⁹ fro   ¹⁰ riue

þey brak here þyes boþe atwynne,
And founde a grete dyche and kast hem þer ynne.
Se¹ wende þey wulde so serue here sone,
And þoȝt with mekenes hem ouercome; 844
On knees she knelyd with here felawshepe,
And seyd, "seres, y prey ȝow of frenshepe,
Pyneþ² hym no more, brekeþ nat hys þees;³
Ȝyueþ hym me hole,⁴ for ded ȝe ⁵seeþ he⁵ ys; 848
Y wyl hym byrye my self and ouþer,
Haueþ reuþe on me, hys sory modyr."
Ey, lady! what do ȝe to knele wepyng
þus at þese houndes fete, socour⁶ sekyng? 852
Of salamons sawys ȝe are nat auysed,
þat meknes of proude men ys alle dyspysed.
þan longeus þe knyȝt dyspysed here pleynt,
þat þo proude was, but now, be⁷ mercy, a seynt. 856
A spere he sette to crystys syde,
He launced and opun[de]⁸ a wounde ful wyde.
þurgh⁹ hys herte he prened hym with mode,
And anone ran downe watyr¹⁰ and blode. 860
AA,¹¹ wrong! aa, wo! aa, wykkednes!
To martyre here¹² for here mekenes.
þe sone was dede he felte no smerte,
But certes hyt perced þe modrys hert. 864
þey wounded here, and heped harm vp on harmes;
She fyl, as for dede, yn maudeleyns armys.
A! Ihesu, þys dede ys wundyr to me,
þat þou suffrest þy modyr be martyred for þe. 868
þo Ion stert vp fresshly anone,
And seyd, "wykked men, what wul ȝe done?
Haue ȝe nat slayn hym with wrong and wo?
What wyl ȝe sle hys modyr also? 872
Goþ hens, for we wyl byrye hym anone."

and break the thieves' legs and cast their bodies into a ditch.

Mary kneels before them and says,

"Sirs, you see He is dead. I will bury Him. Have pity on me."

Eccius. xiii. 20.

Longinus pierces His side with a spear.

What wrong, to martyr her for her meekness!

She falls for dead into Magdalen's arms.

John cries, "Go hence, wicked men,

[leaf 90]

we will bury Him."

¹ She ² Peineþ ³ þes ⁴ hool ⁵ seþ his ⁶ secour
⁷ bi ⁸ de illegible in MS.; openede B. ⁹ Thurgh-out
¹⁰ boþe water ¹¹ Aa ¹² his moder

They go away ashamed.	Al ashamed þe houndes awey gun¹ gone.	
	Whan mary was waked oute of here swoun,	
	Aȝens þe cros she sate² here adowne;	876
	Pytusly she behelde þat grysly wounde;	
	Fro wepyng she ne myȝt stynte³ no stounde.	
What sorrow they all made no tongue can tell.	What sorowe made Ione, crystys derlyng,	
	What maudeleyn, with teres hys fete wasshyng,	880
	What Iacobe, what cleophe, and ouþer mo,	
	Y wys no tunge may telle here wo.	
	Ful feyn þey wulde Ihesu down taken,	
They cannot take the Body down.	But strengþe and ynstrumentys boþe þey lakkyn.	884
	Among hem þey kast þe best to done,	
	Sum seyd þe nyȝt wulde nyghe ful sone:	
	Ȝyf we here wake, deþ shul we þole,⁴	
	Ȝyf we go hens,⁵ þys body shal be stole.	888
They pray to God,	þey preyde to god sum socur hem sende,	
	For lyfe ne for deþ þey nolde þens⁶ wende.	
and then see men approaching with instruments.	A newe cumpanye þey say þo comyngge,	
	Instrumentys and oynementys with hem bryngyngge.	
	Oure lady dred sore þat þey were enmyes,	893
	Tyl Ihone on hem hadde sette gode aspyes;	
John recognises Joseph of Arimathea and Nicodemus.	"Beþe of gode cumforte," he seyde, "þey seme	
	Ioseph of barmathy and nychodeme."	896
	þys was here comyng; whan þey come þedyr	
They worship the cross.	þey wurscheped þe cros and salude to gedyr,	
	And þanked god þat þedyr hem sente:	
	Oure lady preyd hem to⁷ do here entent.	900

The medytacyun of þe oure of euensong.

	Now wyl y telle of euensong oure.	
	Se, man, a syȝte of grete dolo ure:	
Two ladders stand before the cross. Joseph and Nicodemus go up with pincers	Twey laddres afore⁸ þe cros now stonde,	
	Ioseph and nychodeme to clymbe þey fonde,	904
	With pynsours, pryuyly, and ouþer gere.	

¹ þan gun   ² sette   ³ stente   ⁴ B has the gloss *suffre*.   ⁵ hennes   ⁶ þennes   ⁷ om.   ⁸ before

Whan þey to þe hondes come were,
Pryuyly with here pynsours sore þey plyȝt,   to draw out the nails.
Lest marye shulde gryse sore of þat syȝte.   908
þey haled harde ar hyt wulde be,   [leaf 96, col. 2]
þe nayles stokyn so fast yn þe tre;
Ful faste þey wrastyn, no þyng þey wounden,
Nedes þey mote¹ brese foule hys honden;   912 They bruise His hands,
But ryȝtwus god accepteþ alle þyng   but God accepts a man according to his meaning.
Of eche man, mekely aftyr hys menyng.
Whan þey hadde drawe oute þe nayles with fors,
Ioseph bare vp þe precyous cors,   916.
Whyl hys felawe to þe fete wente,
And myȝtily þat nayle oute he hente.
Whan þe nayles were oute echone,
Nychodeme pryuyly toke hem to Ione.   920 The nails are given to John.
Anone runne to alle þat ²were þere,²   All help to carry the Body.
And hylpe þat precyus body to bere.   John bears the breast,
Ion bare hys breste and wepte ful sore,
For þeron he rested þe nyȝt before;   924
Hys fete bare maudeleyn and on hem weep,   Magdalen the feet,
For at hem here synnes she lette;³
þo þat were þere bare alle þe touþer,
Saue hys ryȝt honde bare marye hys modyr.   928 Mary His right hand.
Feyn wulde she ha bore more of here dere sone,
But grete sorowe here strengþe had ouercome.
þat arme wepyng ofte⁴ she kyste,   She kisses it,
She kolled hyt, she⁵ clypped hyt vp on here brest. 932
But euer whan she behelde þat grysly wounde,
For sorowe & for feyntnes she fyl to þe grounde.
Oftyn she seyd, "a, sone! a,⁶ sone!   and cries, "Ah, Son,
Where ys now alle þat werk become,   936 where is now Thy work?"
þat þou were wunt to werche with þys honde,
Feuers and syke men to brynge oute of bonde?
A, flesshe! a, fode! moste feyre and most fre,

¹ moten   ²—² þere were   ³ leet   ⁴ ful ofte
           ⁵ and   ⁶ om.

	Of þe holy goste conceyued yn me,	940
	Why fadest þou? no fylþe yn þe ys founde,	
	For synneles y bare þe yn to þys mounde.	
Thou hast bought man's sin dear."	A! mannes synne dere hast þou bo3t,	
	With a gretter prys my3t hyt neuer be bo3t."	944
They pray her to hinder them no longer. [leaf 96, back]	þys cumpany furþe þan þys cors gun¹ karye, And prayd² hys modyr no lenger hem tarye.	
	Wyþ oynementys and shetes þey wuldyn hyt dy3t,	
	And bery hyt anone for hyt was ny ny3t.	948
"I pray you," she said, "take Him not from me."	þan seyd she, "y pray 3ow a bone: Takeþ nat my sone³ fro me so⁴ sone,	
	Beryeþ me raþer with hym yn graue,	
	For, oþer dede or alyue, y mote hym haue."	952
	At þe laste she consented,⁵ so long þey pray ;	
They prepare to bury Him.	þan to byrye þys body þey hem aray.	
	þys body⁶ was leyde vpp on a shete,	
	To anoynte and sewe hyt downe þey sete;	956
His Mother sits at the head, and places it in her lap.	Marye hys modyr at þe hede⁷ sate ; She lyfte hyt, she leyd hyt feyre yn here lape,	
	She behylde hyt, how hyt was ybroke,	
	Prykket, and broysed⁸ wyþ many a stroke ;	960
	Shaue also boþe berde and hede,	
	With þornes ⁹þey rente,¹⁰ with⁹ blode alle rede.	
In a story it is said He was shaven:	Yn a story truly þys resun y nam, þat god ones seyd to an holy womman,	964
	Whan Iewes had dampned hym deþ for to haue,	
	Shamely ¹¹berde and hede¹¹ gun þey shaue.	
the Evangelists say nothing about it.	The euangelystys telle nat of þys doyng, For þey my3te nat wryte alle þyng.	968
	Of hys berde y fynde a resun,	
Isaiah said,	þe whyche seyd¹² Isaye yn goddys persone :	
My body I gave to the smiters and my cheeks to men grubbing."	"My body y 3aue to men smytyng, And also my chekes to men grubbyng."	972

¹ gun to   ² preiden   ³ swete sone   ⁴ þus   ⁵ consenteþ
⁶ body written over in MS.   ⁷ heued   ⁸ brissed   ⁹—⁹ irent of
¹⁰ for y rente   ¹¹—¹¹ his hede and berde   ⁹ seiþ

Fyrst, þan, marye, wiþ a swote cloute, *Mary wrapped His head in a cloth.*
Swaþed here sones hede alle aboute;
"Sone,[1] y was wunt þe swetly to wrappe,
Now swaþe y þe dede, here yn my lappe." 976
The touþer anoynted hym and closed þe shete, *The others anointed Him.*
Tyl þey com adowne ny to hys fete;
Maudeleyn prayd, þat hys fete she myȝt[2] dresse, *Magdalen prayed to dress His feet.*
For þer she gate of here synnes grace &[3] forȝyuenes :
She wepte, and wysshe hem wiþ many a tere, 981 *She washed them with tears.*
She keste hem, and wyped hem wiþ here feyre here.
Whan þe cors alle was [4]y dyȝt,[4]
To þe sepulcre þey bygan [5]to bere hyt ful[5] ryȝt. 984 *They carry Him to the sepulchre,*

The meditacyun of þe oure of cumplyn. [leaf 90, bk, col. 2]

Now ys þe oure y come of cumplyn : *and lay Him in it,*
þey leyn þe cors þer[6] hyt shal lyn,
Yn a new sepulcre and feyre y graue,
þat nycodeme made hym self for to haue : 988
þey shette hyt a boute wiþ a grete stone, *and prepare to leave.*
And arayde hem faste þen for[7] to gone.
"Abydeþ god breþren, marye gan seye, *Mary says, "Stay :*
Wharto hye ȝe so faste aweye ? 992 *why go so fast ?*
Ȝyf ȝe be ful[8] of my dere sone,
Goþ hens, and lateþ me here alone wone ;
Whedyr shulde y wende, to frende, ouþer kyn ? *Whither should I go?*
Y kan no whedyr go, but ȝyf[9] y had hym ; 996
He was my broþer, my mayster, my spouse ;
Now am y[10] wedew, helples yn house. *Now I am a widow.*
Wuld god ȝe wulde byrye me wiþ hym ! *Would God I were dead.*
For þan shulde we neuer departe[11] atwyn. 1000
Now certes my soule ys melted awey :
For ryȝt so[12] loue gan to me seye,

[1] And seide sone   [2] moste   [3] of   [4-4] ful weil idight
[5-5] hit to bere   [6] þere-as   [7] om.   [8] to ful
[9] ȝyf written over in MS.   [10] I. a   [11] departen
[12] A word partly erased here; apparently me or my : no word in B.

MEDITATIONS.   4

	'Y haue hym so3t, y fynde hym no3t,	
	Y haue hym clepyd, he answereþ no3t.	1004
I will abide here;	Y wyl a byde hym here yn fay,	
He said He would rise again."	For he seyde he wulde a ryse þe þryd day.'	
	But 3yf þat y hadde trust to hys seyyng,	
	Myn herte shulde ¹ha broste¹ at hys deyyng."	1008
John counsels her to go.	þan Ion cunseyled here, and seyd anone,	
	"Thys sabbat we mow nat wake² a lone :	
	3yf Iewes here vs take þey wyl vs spylle,	
	And þus was also 3oure sones wylle."	1012
She answers,	þan mary answered, myldely wepyng,	
"My Son gave me into thy keeping; I must do as thou biddest."	"My sone, Ion, toke me yn þy kepyng,	
	Y most³ nedys do as þou me byst:"	
	And ry3t with þat wurde aswyþe she ryst;	1016
	Afore þe sepulcre she kneled a downe,	
	And wepyng, she made þys lamentacyoun :	
With that she commends her Son to His Father in heaven.	"A, swete sone! now wo ys me,	
	þat y no lenger may byde with þe,	1020
	For nedys y mote now þe forsake,	
[leaf 91].	þy fadyr of heuene⁴ y þe betake ;	
	Oure felawshepe ys now dyuydyd,	
	For y may nat with þe be byryed ;⁵	1024
"My heart is buried with Thee.	But certes, swete sone, where so euer⁶ y be,	
	Holy myn herte ys byryed with þe ;	
If Thou rise up my heart shall rise also.	3yf þou ryse vp, as þou me behy3te,	
	Myn herte shal aryse with þe as ly3t ;	1028
If Thou rise not, I am stone dead.	3yf þou ryse nat vp on þe þrydde day,	
	Truly y am stonede⁷ dede ⁸for ay.⁸	
Arise, sweet Son.	þarfore, swete sone, aryse vp and come,	
	And kyþe weyl þat þou art of heuene goddys sone."	
	þe sepulcre swetly anone she kyst,	1033
	Se wente⁹ a boute and feyre she hyt blest,	
Sleep soft in ease ;	And seyd, "my dere sone, slepe softe yn ese,	

¹⁻¹ abroste   ² wake here   ³ mote   ⁴ final *e* written over in MS.
     ⁵ iberied   ⁶ om.   ⁷ stone
⁸⁻⁸ for ones *and* al.   eu*er* written above *ay* in MS.
     ⁹ She romede

For þy place ys made to þe yn pese." 1036 Thy place is in peace.
Eftesones þe sepulcre she kyst knelyng,
And cryde þys wurde with strong wepyng,
"A! sone, here may y no lenger lende, I may abide no longer.
Nedes from þe þou wylt me sende, 1040
Myn herte with þe y leue to wone,
Farwel, farewel, my derewurþe sone!" Farewell, my dear Son!"
With þat wurde certes ny swoned she had,
But Ion lefte here vp, and þens[1] here led. 1044 John leads her away.
Towarde þe cyte here wey þey toke,
Oftyn aȝenward marye gan loke.
Whan she come to þe cros, "abydeþ," she seyd; She stops,
"My sone, my sauyour, ryȝt now here deyd; 1048
Here vpp on he haþ boȝt alle man kynne,
Hys precyus blode haþ wasshe oure synne."
She wurschepyd hyt fyrst, & þan þey echone and they worship the Cross.
Towarde þe cyte here wey gun they gone. 1052
Are she shulde entre, þey kouerd here vysage.
As for a wedew þey dyd þat vsage.
þey kast where she herbored shulde be, They "cast" where she should be lodged.
Eche of hem seyd, "with me, with me." 1056 Each says, "With me, with me."
Now þe quene of heuene, modyr hyest,
Haþ nat where yn here hede for to reste.
She þanked hem, and seyd, "y am betake
To Ion, and þarfore y may nat hym forsake." 1060 [leaf 91, col. 2]
Ion seyd, "we wyl with maudeleyn a lyȝt, John said, "We will stay with Magdalen.
For þere rested oure mayster a whyle to nyȝt;
Also my breþren wyl come alle þedyr; The brethren will come thither."
þere wyl we reste and speke to gedyr." 1064
þey led here furþe þurgh þat cyte,
Wydewes and wyues of here had pyte. Widows and wives pity her.
Whan þey had broȝt here þere echone,
Some token here leue and wenten hom; 1068
Maudeleyn and martha were bysy þat nyȝu,
[2]To serue[2] here alle þat þey[3] myȝt.

[1] þennes [2-2] To ese here *and* serue [3] þey written over in MS.

She could not sleep, but wept and said,	þenke, man, how she myȝt no slepe slepe,	
	But sorowed, and syghed, and weyled, and wepe,	1072
"My dear Son!"	And euermore seyde, "my derwurþe sone,	
	For loue y anguysshe tyl þat þou come."	
Peter comes weeping, and salutes Mary and John.	Anone come petyr, with wepyng chere,	
	And salude Marye and Ion yn fere.	1076
The other disciples come,	Þan come þe dyscyplys, eche aftyr oþer,	
	For shame durst none loke on hys broþer.	
	Þey asked þe doyng of here dere lorde,	
and John tells them all.	Ion tolde hem þe processe euery aworde.	1080
"Woe is me," said Peter, "that I forsook Him."	"Wo me," seyd petyr, "me shameþ to loke,	
	For þat y my swete lorde and mayster forsoke,	
	Wheche loued and chersed me¹ so tenderly :	
	Wo me, a,² wreche, mercy, y cry."	1084
The others make their confession and weep.	Also þe dyscyplys here confessyun	
	Maden and weptyn with³ lamentacyun.	
	Þan crystes modyr, here mylde maystres,	
	Had grete compassyun of here heuynes ;	1088
Mary comforts them.	She comforted hem and seyd þus :	
	"Dysmay ȝow nat for my sone⁴ Ihesus,	
	For þus to hys deþ he wulde be bore,	
	To saue mannes soule þat was forlore ;	1092
	Þarto he com with moche stryfe,	
	Yn traueyle and yn pouert to leden hys lyfe.	
"No wonder you forsook Him, His Father did the same."	No wundyr þogh ȝe forsoke hym yn hys ende,	
	Hys fadyr forsoke hym socour to sende ;	1096
	Hymself he forsoke for oure mys dede ;	
[leaf 91, back]	Y preyd for hym, y myȝt no þyng spede ;	
	Certes y am sory for hys grete passyun,	
	But truly y glade for soules saluacyun ;	1100
	Þey shulden yn helle for euer be forlore,	
	But y hym to þys deþ had ⁵hym bore ;⁵	
	Ȝe weten weyl how benygne my dere sone was,	
	Lyȝtly to forȝyue al maner of trespas ;	1104

¹ *me* written over in MS. ; *me* follows *louede* in B.   ² aa
³ wiþ gret   ⁴ swete sone   ⁵⁻⁵ here ibore

Douteþ ʒe no þyng of hys grete mercy,
For largely he ʒyfþ þat cryeþ hyt hertly ;
Beeþ of gode cumfort, for trustly y say,
We shullen hym se on þe þrydde day ;   1108   "Be of good comfort; we shall see Him on the third day."
Seþþen he haþ boght vs at so grete prys,
Nedes from þe deþ he mote aryse."
"Certys," seyd patyr, " þys nyʒt at þe cene,[1]
He seyd eftsones we shuldyn hym sene,   1112   "Certainly," said Peter, "He said we should soon see Him, and that our sorrow should be turned to joy."
þan alle oure sorowe to ioye shulde come,
And þat ioye shulde nat from vs be nome."[2]
"A ! breþren !" seyd Marye, " y ʒow pray
þat swete sermoun ʒe wyl me say."   1116
A none Ion tolde here, for he coude best,
For slepyng he soke hyt at crystys brest.
þus þey dwel yn here medytacyun,
Tyl tyme was come of þe resurreccyun.   1120   Thus they dwelt until the resurrection.

The medytacyun how cryst ʒede to helle.

Thenk, man, and se cryst aftyr hys deþ :
    For þy synne streyght to helle he geþ,   For thy sin Christ goeth straight to hell.
Oute of þe fendys bonde to þe fre,
And þe fende bonde to make to þe.   1124
þenk, also, þe grete dede of hys powere :
He myʒt ha[3] sent an angel to saue vs here,   He might have sent an angel to save us.
But þan of oure saluacyun we shulde nat þanke hym,
But calle þe aungel sauer of alle man kyn.   1128
þarfor hys fadyr so hertly loued vs,   God so loved us that He gave us His Son.
He ʒaue vs hys owene gete sone Ihesus ;
þan we onely hym þanke and do hym onoure,
As fadyr, as former, socoure and sauyoure.   1132
þank we now oure sayoure, þat salue vs haþ broʒt,   Thank we now our Saviour,
Oure syke soules to saue, whan synne haþ hem soʒt.
Of hys grete godenes gyn we hym grete,   [leaf 91, bk, col. 2]
Seyyng þe wurde of sakarye þe holy prophete :   1136   saying the words of Zacharias,

[1] Glossed *soper* in B.   [2] Glossed *take* in B.
[3] haue

THE SONG OF ZACHARIAS.

"Blessed be the Lord God of Israel."
S. Luke i. 68.

"Lorde god of Israel, blessed mote þou be,
þy peple þou hast vysyted and boȝt hem to þe,
Whych setyn yn derkenes of deþ and dysese,
þou lyȝtest hem and ledest yn to þe wey of pese." 1140

To that "peace peerless" bring us. Amen.

To þat pes pereles we prey þou vs bryng,
þat leuyst and reynest *with* oute endyng. 1142
     Amen.

GLOSSARIAL INDEX.

A, 1084, 1115, ah.
And ther with al he bleynte / and cryde. *A.* *Chaucer,* 1078.
Adowne, 676, 1017, down.
Afore, 150, 180.
Agadlyng, 477, a gadling, a gadder about; a vagabond. Cp. "They ronne *agaddynge,* ye a whore hountinge after their false prophetes."—*The Lamentacyon of a Christian agaynste the Cyte of London,* leaf 4 (1545).
Al, Al hole, 182, all whole, entirely, wholly.
Algate, Algates, 358, 364, 392, 699, always, at all times, under all circumstances; in the last example it means certainly, of a truth, indeed.
Alheyl, 378, All hail!
Al thogħ, 56, although.
Alyþed, 589, have allayed, mitigated.
An, 310, 380, 397, on.
Angred, 744, angered, made sorry. "They *angered* Moses also in the tents."—Psa. cvi. 16, *P. B. Vers.*
Anguyssed, 315, pained.
Anguysshe, 1074, to pine, suffer.
Angwys, 659, 683, anguish.
Ar, Are, 31, 94, &c., ere, before.

Aray, 954, 990, to prepare, to make ready.
Areyned, 601, commanded.
Arst, 502, first, formerly.
Aslake, 807, to abate, to slake.
Aspyes, 894, spies.
Astounde, 328.
Astyte, 436, anon, quickly.
Aswyþe, 1016, quickly, immediately.
At, 371, of.
Atwyn, Atwynne, 663, 678, 841, 1000, asunder, "atwo," or in two.
Auysed, 853, informed, taught, advised.
Auysyly, 415, advisedly, carefully.
Awake, 336, arouse.
Aworde, every aworde, 1080, every word.
Axen, 430, ask.
Ay, 1030, ever.
Aysel, 732, vinegar.
Aȝens, 46, 48, "aȝens he com," "aȝens nyȝt," by, just before.
Aȝenward, 1046, backward.

Bacyn, 141, basin.
Bebled, p. 20, *note.*

Behoue, 224, behoof, advantage.
Behynde, 287.
Behyȝte, 1027, promised (compounded of 'be' and 'hight').
Benygne, 1103, benign, kind.
Berdoun, 593, burden.
Betake, 353, 365, 457, 695, 728, 760, bring to, give to, commend to.
Beþ, Beþe, 648, 895, be.
Beþenke, 127, 129, 163, bethink, remember.
Betraye, Betrey, 96, 106, betray.
Bie, p. 2, *note*.
Blyn, 103, to cease, to stop.
Bodly, 39, bodily, corporeal.
Boffeteþ, 428, buffet; *indic. plur.*
Bokes hede, 320, chapter (of a book).
"Brent sacrifise, and for synne thou askidest not; thaune I seide, Lo! I come. In the *hed* of the *boc* it is write of me that I do thi wil."—Psalm xxxix. 8, 9, *Wycliffe's Vers.*
"Thanne I seyde, Loo! I come; in the head, *or biȝynnyng*, of the book it is writyn of me."—Heb. x. 7, *Wycliffe's Vers.*
"In capite libri scriptum est de me."—*Vulgate.*
Bollers, 477, drinkers, drunkards, men who pass the bowl. See *P. Plow.*, C-text, Pass. x. 194, and note.
Bone, 313, prayer, petition, request.
Bone, 372, 949, boon, gift.
Bownden, 523, bound.
Breche, 622, breeches, covering.
Brenne, 201, burn.
Brese, 912, bruise.
Broysed, 960, bruised.
But, 666, only, except.
Buxom, 469, obedient.
Dy, Bye, 28, 318, buy, redeem.

By, "by þe wey," 284.
Byfore, 287.
Byhelde, 489.
Bynte, 427, bind. "The last word *bint* the tale."—Quoted in the *Journ. Sac. Lit.*, vol. i. (1865), p. 252.
Bypaþ, 486, by-path, a secluded way.
Byrye, 849, bury.
Byst, 1015, biddest, requestest.
Byt, 305, bade, warned.

Calle, 1128, call.
Ce to Ce, 441, place to place. Cp. "Cee, Mare, fretum, pontus."—*P. Parv.*, p. 64.
Cene, 1111, Fr. *Cène*, the Lord's Supper. Sp. *cena*, a supper.
Whan he sat with hem at the *cene*
. . . .
To swych he gaff hem alderlast Hys owne body.
MS. Cott. Vit. C. xiii., lf 69, bk.
Chalys, 193, chalice.
Chekenes, 286, chickens.
Chere, 11, 87, 1075, cheer, countenance.
Chere, 203, cheering, cheerful.
Chersed, 333, 1083, cherished.
Chese, 393, choose.
Clepe, 719, call.
Cleppeþ, 152, clippeth, embraceth.
Cleuyn, 616, ? clewe, fasten on, seize.
Cloute, 973, cloth.
Clypped, 932, embraced, pressed closely.
Compyled, 14, compiled.
Comunde, 198, communed, conversed with.
Conceyued, 940, conceived.
Constreyned, 602, constrained, compelled.

Cors, 916, 945, corse, a dead body.
Corupt, 27, corrupt.
Coude, 126, could.
Croys, 556, cross.
Crucyfyers, 642.
Cryeþ, 1106, asketh, demandeth.
Crysten, 9, christian, christened.
Cumplyn, 985, even-song, the last service of the day; compline.
Cumþ, 418, cometh.

Dame, 286, mother's.
Dampne, 556, 558, 559, condemn.
Day, 728, die.
Defoule, 506, defile, pollute.
Degre, 7, degree, condition in life.
Deluyn, 347, dig, delve.
Derkenes, 1139, darkness.
Derlyng, 276, dearling, darling.
Derwurly, 180, cheerfully, willingly, honourably.
 þe sculen biwiten þene king!
 durewurþliche þurh alle þing.
   Laȝamons Brut., ii. 210.
 þise were diȝt on þe des, & *derwarþly* scrued.
   Sir Gawayne, 114.
Derwurþ, Derwurþe, 181, 368, 385, 651, precious, very dear.
Deye, 94, 207, die.
Do, 131, "was do," was done.
Done, wuld done, 138.
Dresse, 158, prepare.
Drye, 738, dry, thirsty. "Dry fro moysture. *Siccus.*"—*P. Parv.*
Dung, 506.
Dyffyed, 743, defied, rejected, despised. "*Dyffyyn*, or vtterly dyspysyn. *Vilipendo, floccipendo, sperno, aspernor, aporio.*"—*P. Parv.* 115.
Dyggen, 611, dig.
Dyrknes, 410, darkness.

Dysese, 1139, disease, trouble.
Dyspetualy, 615, angrily, without pity.
Dysplayed, 640, displayed, extended, spread out.
Dyspoyle, 615, despoil, spoil, undress.
Dysturbled, 316, disturbed, troubled. "*Dysturbelyn, Turbo, conturbo.*"—*P. Parv.* 123.
"And thei . . . . weren *distourblid*, seyinge, For it is a fantum."—S. Matt. xiv. 26. "He began for to be *distourblid* and sory in herte."—S. Matt. xxvi. 37, *Wycliffe.*
Dyȝt, 49, 325, prepared, made ready.

Echone, 57, all, each one.
Eftesones, Eftsones, 549, 1037, 1112, immediately.
Eke, 506, also.
Enformed, 238, informed, taught.
Entent, 43, "Take gode entent," give good heed.
Erst, 424, before, formerly: *arst* in l. 502.
Ese, 1035, ease, rest.
Euerychone, 132, every one.
Expouned, 735, expounded, explained.
Ey, 851, eh?

Fare, 492, suffer, endure.
Fay, 1005, faith, confidence.
Fedyng, 35, 39, feeding.
Felawshepe, 447, 576, company, companions.
Fele, 669, many.
Fere, 68, 88, 119, 240. In fere, together, in company, one with another; l. 240, "loue yn fere," love one another. "This is my

comåundement, that ȝe loue *to gidere.*"—S. John xv. 12, *Wycliffe.*
Fere, 580, a companion.
Fersly, 626, fiercely.
Fest, 212, fist, hand.
Fette, fet, 82, 563, 614, fetched.
Feye, 18, 86, faith, belief.
Feyn, 686, fain, gladly, willingly.
Feynt, 509, faint, weak.
Feyntly, 572, faintly, weakly.
Feyntnesse, 594.
Feyre, 164, 169. In l. 164 the Lat. orig. has *five*.
Feyre, 1034, fair.
Folue, 177, follow.
Fond, 356, found.
Fonde, 187, founded, instituted.
Fong, 329, to endure, suffer.
For, 273, because.
Fordone, 186, destroy, do away with. *Fordone* is properly the participle of *for-do*.
Forlore, 26, utterly lost.
Former, 795, Maker, Creator.
Forwounded, 519, much wounded.
Fresshly, 869, fiercely, briskly.
Furþe, 802, "furþe beryng," birth, bringing forth.
Fyne, 656, perfectly, quite.
Fynst, 557, findest.
Fyrþer more, 621.
Fyþe, 729, fifth.
Fyueþe, 257, fifth.

Gan, 185, began.
Gere, 657, 905, gear, tools.
Gert, 139, girded, girt.
Gerte, 654, pushed, drove.
Gete, 817, 1130, gotten, begotten.
Geþ, 1122, goeth.

Gladlygh, 89, gladly, cheerfully.
Glymbe, 630, climb.
Gobbettes, 85, morsels, bits.
Gone, 1052, "gan gone," began to go.
Graces, 81, prayers before meat.
Grame, 548, to anger.
Graue, y graue, 987, dug.
Grete, 1135, greet, address.
Greyþe, 46, prepare, make ready.
Grubbyng, 972. In Wycliffe's translation this passage (Isa. l. 6) stands thus: "My bodi I ȝaf to the smyteres, and my chekes to the pulleris; my face I turnede not awei fro the blameres, and the spitteres in me."
Gryse, 153.
Grysly, 101, sorrowful.
Grysly, 877, 933, terrible, frightful.
Gun, 630, 945, 966, gan, began.
Gunne, 133, began.
Gyn, 777, 1135, begin.

Ha, 686, 929, 1126, have.
"He wolde *ha* men · as lord to hym loute."
See *Gospel Stories, Man who made a Supper* (p. 6).
Haled, 662, pulled.
Halfdede, 588, half dead.
Hardy, 526.
He, 254.
Hem, 259, "hem whyche."
Hen, 280, hence.
Hente, 918, drew.
Hepys, 624, hips.
Herbored, 1055, lodged.
Herdles, 452, herdless, without a shepherd.
Here, 63, their.
Here by, 67.

Hertly, 243, 1106, heartily.
Hestes, hestys, 323, 742, commands, behests.
Ho, 528, 790, who.
Ho, 573, he.
Hole, 182, "al hole," wholly, entirely.
Holy, 1026, wholly.
Hom, 1068.
Homely, 275. Will the reader supply a word which will convey the sense as well as this does?
Hote, 240, command.
Hyde, 623, hye, 573, hyed, 590, hyyng, 627, to hurry, hurried, hurrying.
Hylpe, 922, helped, assisted.
Hyt, 102, it.

Instrumentys, 892, instruments.
Ioed, 562, joyed.
Iuwyse, 577, I-wis.

Kast, 643, lifted, raised.
Kast, 885, 1055, cast, considered.
Kercheues, 624, kerchiefs.
Knowlechyng, 424, knowledge.
Kolled, 932, embraced, clasped.
Kone, 438, can.
Kouerd, 1053, covered.
Kraked, 662, cracked, broke.
Krokedly, 571, crookedly.
Krokyng, 149, crooking, bending.
Kunne, 675, can.
Kynne, 1049, man kynne, mankind.
Kyþe, 1032, know.
Kytte, 85, 236, 268, cut, pierced. It *kittiþ* myn herte as with a knyf. *Pol., Rel., and Love Poems*, p. 205, l. 10.

Lake, 347, a pit.

Lakkyn, 884, lack.
Lamaȝabatany, 724. See St Matt. xxvii. 46.
Lape, 958, lap.
Lateþ, 467, 994, let, allow, permit.
Launced, 858, lanced, pierced with a lance.
Lede, 665, ? lead, the metal.
Lemes, 667, limbs.
Lende, 1039, remain, tarry.
Lere, 13, 16, 67, 120, learn.
Lered, 170, learned.
Lese, 394, lose.
Lestene, 312, listen.
Lete, 165, 181, } left, ? leave.
Lette, 926,
Leue, 784, believe.
Lewed, 170, ignorant.
Leyd, 274, "be leyd," laid low, overcome.
Leyn, 521, "leyn on," lay on, thrash.
Leyn, 986, lay.
Logter, 133, lower.
Loke, 167, see, behold.
Lone, 1010, "a lone," alone.
Lore, 673, learning, knowledge, doctrine.
Louesum, 220, lovely, loving.
Lyn, 986, lie, remain.
Lyne, 733, slake, stop.
Lyne, 771, lain, remained.
Lys, 702, ease, relieve, lessen.
Lyȝt, 1061, "a lyȝt," remain, stay.
Lyȝt, 47, remained, tarried.
Lyȝt, 207, alighted, came down.
Lyȝtly, 1104, willingly, quickly, commonly.

Make, 795, mate, companion, equal.

Manly, 398, manfully.
Many one, 541.
Mede, 335, value, worth.
Mekest, 645, humblest (verb).
Memorand, 32, memorable.
Memorand, 195, a memorial.
Mende, 127, mind.
Mende, 196, memory.
Mercyable, 456, mercyful.
Mest, 400, most.
Meyny, 198, company.
Mode, 345, 859, wrath, anger.
Monasshyng, 169, 245, admonishing, admonition.
Mone, 454, moan, supplication.
Mone, 715, told, said, made. Qy. moaned? But B. has *nome*, took.
Moste, 199, 528.
Mot, Mote, 390, 581, must.
Mounde, 942, the earth, the world.
Mow, 349, 350, 363, may.
Mow, 522, might, could, were able (to do).
Mysdo, 462, misdone, done amiss.
Mysdoer, 503, a wrong-doer.
Myþe, 156, mighty. See *myhthy* in Prompt. Parv. (? *mild*.)

Nam, 603, 963, took.
Nat, 590, not.
Nayles, 116, nails.
Neme, 513, "vndyr neme," ? examine, punish.
Ner, 586, nearer.
Nolde, 890, ne would, would not.
Nome, 1114, taken.
Noþer, 27, neither.
Noye, 22, annoy.
Noʒt, 22, "with noʒt," in any manner, in anything.

Ny, 418, nigh, near.
Nygh, 90, nigh, near.
Nyghe, 886, come, approach.

O, 68, 382, one.
Ones, 964, once.
Onoure, 1131, honour.
Opone, 10, open.
Opunly, 543, openly.
Opynyons, 20, opinions.
Orcherd, 303, orchard, garden.
Orysun, 361, orison.
Oute, 615; "*oute* dyspetusly," without pity.
Owne, 817, 1130, "owne gete," only begotten.
Oynementys, 892, 947, ointments.

Pas, 359, "toke hys pas," went his way.
Paske, 82, paschal.
Paske, 94, passover.
Pens, 335, pence.
Pereles, 1141, peerless.
Pese, 1036, 1140, peace, rest.
Pleynes, 689, complains.
Pleynt, 510, plaint, complaint, indictment.
Plogh, 568, plough.
Plyʒt, 626, plucked, taken away.
Plyʒt, 907, pulled.
Pouert, 1094, poverty.
Prened, 859, pierced, pricked.
Preued, 18, proved.
Preyour, 413.
Preysed, 336, appraised, valued.
Processe, 1080, the manner in which an act was done; details, particulars.
Pryme, 475, 537, prime; six o'clock in the morning.

Pryncypals, 226, heads of a discourse.
Pryuyly, 105, privily, secretly.
Punged, 567, pricked, goaded.
Pur, 8, for.
Put, 141.
Pycchen, 612, pitch, throw, or let fall.
Pyler, pylour, 523, 515, pillar.
Pyne, 401, 547, pain, grief.
Pyneþ, 847, punish, torture, *imperat. plur. 2nd pers.*
Pynsours, 905, pincers.
Pytusly, 533, grievously. Cp. "*Pytyows*, or rufulle yn syʒhte. *Dolorosue, penosus.*"—*P. Parv.* 402.

Real, 33, 34.
Reke, 821, hurry, haste.
Rent (verb), 116, rend.
Reuþe, 832, 850, pity, compassion.
Rewe, 473, 826, to regret, be sorry for: to rue.
Reyʒte, 642, raught, reached.
Riue, note to l. 839.
Route, 423, a company.
Ruly, 121, 301, 517, 634, rueful. "*Ruly, idem quod* ruful (ful of ruthe and pyte)."—*P. Parv.* 439.
Ryme, 538 (verb).
Ryst, 1016, arose.
Ryue, 839.
Ryʒtwus, 913, righteous.

Salude, 898, 1076, saluted.
Salue, 1133, salve, salvation.
Samen, 671, "yn samen," in company, together.
Sauer, 1128, saver, Saviour.
Sawys, "Salamons sawys," sayings, proverbs.
Sum *sawes* of Salomon · y shall you shew sone.
The Crowned King, l. 44.

The passage is, "As the proud hate humility: so doth the rich abhor the poor."—Ecclus. xiii. 20.
Say, 587, 688, saw.
Scorneþ, scorned, 429, 743.
Se, 843, 1034, she.
Seced, 100, ceased.
Seche, 621, ? to look, to observe.
Secunde, 40, second.
Seluyn, 453, "here seluyn," herself; owne self, 680.
Semely, 387, properly, becomingly, justly.
Sen, 232, see (*1st pers. indic. fut.*).
Setyn, 1139, sit.
Sewe, 402, ensue, follow.
Sewe, 956, to sew.
Sey, 134, seen.
Seyn, seyd, 134, 553, say, said.
Seyth, "sum seyth," 675.
Seyyng, 228, saying.
Shamely, 966, shamefully.
Shape, 575, "hym ys shape," for him is prepared, or intended; devised.
Shaue, 966, shave; 961, shaven.
Shenshepe, 448, 575, punishment.
Shete, 955, Shetes, 947, sheet, sheets.
Shokyn, 479, shook.
Shulder, 565, shoulder.
Shullen, 1108, shall.
Shust, 714, shouldest.
Shyttyng, 756, shutting.
Slake, 696, mitigate.
Slogh, 567, slough, a dirty place.
Smert, 140, smart, quick, quickly.
Soper, 30, 33, supper.
Sopyng place, 160, supping place.
Specyal, 107, special.
Spelle, 114, learn, read.

44 GLOSSARIAL INDEX.

Spelle, 130, teach.
Spelled, 739, uttered, said.
Sprunge, 414, "be sprunge," besprinkled.
Spyl, spylle, spylled, 470, 582, 600, 752, 1011, spoil, destroy, punish.
Stant, 681, stands.
State, 391, manner.
Stede, 135, place.
Sterte, 421, hurried, went forward.
Sterte, 570, "a sterte," start away, turn away, wander.
Steuene, 382, voice.
Stey, 635, "vpp stey," raised, elevated.
Stilly, 689, softly, silently.
Stokyn, 910, stuck.
Stonede dede, 1030, "stone dead."
Stonen, 141, of stone, of earthenware.
Story, 963, history, legend.
Stounde, 878, a moment, a short space of time.
Straked, 661, proceeded, went.
Streyght to helle, 1122.
Streyȝte, 641, stretched.
Stye, 208, to ascend.
Stynte, 878, stint, stop, cease.
Sum, 684, somewhat, partly.
Sumdele, 702, 733, somewhat, a little.
Sustryn, 647, sisters.
Swaþe, 974, 976, wrap.
Swote, 370, 379, sweat.
Swouned, 785, swooned.
Swycho, 508, 813, such.
Swyþe, 137, "swyþe sone," very soon. See *Anoyþe*.
Syghyng, 271.

Syre, 501, 535, sire, sir.
Syxte, 606.

Tagh, 243, 279, taught.
Tary, 560, 597, tarry, delay.
Tendyrly, 119, tenderly.
Teren, 634, tears.
Teþ, 116, teeth.
þe, 69, they.
þees, 847, thighs.
þeke, 446, that.
þeron, 924.
þeuys, 576, thieves.
þo, 98, 423, 432, then, at that time.
Thogh, 104, "as þogh," though.
þole, 887, suffer.
þore, 757, there.
þred, 41, 538, third.
þrest, 289, thrust.
þryd, þrydde, 179, 245, third.
þryst, 733, thirst.
þrysted, 736, desired.
þrysted, 737, thirsted.
þrytty, 335, thirty.
þryys, 360, thrice.
þurgh, 623, 859, through.
þyes, 841, thighs.
Thyr, 22, there.
þyrwhylys, 367, 443, therewhiles, during that time.
To, 362, two, or twice.
To braste, 566.
Toke, 168, 278, 1014, gave.
Too, 654, two.
Toure, 376, tower.
Touþer, 656.
Tray, 156, betray.
Trewe, 58, true, faithful.
Trustly, 1107, confidently, truly.

Trusty, 58, trustworthy.
Tugge, 441, pull violently.
Twey, 50, 629, two.
Twyys, 360.

Varye, 598, alter, change.
Ver, 583, "a ver," afar, at a distance.
Verry, 84, true, real.
Vnder neme, 513, ? examine.
Vnsekernes, 440.
Vpbreyde, 787.
Vsage, 1054.
Vyleynsly, 580, villanously.
Vysage, 1053, visage, face.

Wadeþ, 520, wades.
Wake, 305, 358, 887, watch.
Wax, 369, 784, grew.
Wenles, 812, wemless, spotless.
Werche, 937, to work, perform.
Werchyng, 200, deed, undertaking.
Weren, 633, were.
Wete, 506, wet, water.
Weten, 1103, know.
Weyle, 450, wail.
Wharto, 725, whereto, for what purpose.
Whet, 631, whetted, pointed.
Whyle, 1062, "a whyle," a-while, for a time.
Witnesseþ, 51, bears witness.
Wode, 617, mad.
Wo me, 1081.
Wone, 262, dwelling place, world.
Wone, 750, to dwell.

Wrake, 366, 458, destruction, mischief, harm.
Wrappe, 975.
Wrastyn, 911, wrest, strain, pull.
Wraþþe, 345, (glossed) wrath.
Wroþer, 290 (a comparative), more angry.
Wryde, 624, wrapped, covered.
Wul, 829, would, will.
Wuld, "wuld God," 999.
Wuldyn, 947, would (*plur.*).
Wunt, 937, 975, wont, in the habit of (doing).
Wykked, 870.
Wynne, 6, gain, obtain, win.
Wyse, 144, "alle wyse."
Wysshe, 166, washed.
Wyte, 339, wete, knew.

Y, 102, I.
Y, 500, in.
Y, 120, 882, "y wys," I-wis, truly, certainly.
Ye, *plur.* yen, 101, 357, 643, eye.
Ylad, 487, led.
Ynstrumentys, 884, instruments.

ȝede, went, p. 35.
ȝenseyyng, 637, opposition, strife, gainsaying.
ȝoue, 331, given, rewarded.
ȝow, 314, thee.
ȝulde, 346, given, rewarded.
ȝungeste, 56, youngest.
ȝyfte, 181, gift.
ȝyfþ, 1106, giveth.
ȝyueþ, 848.

JOHN CHILDS AND SON, PRINTERS.

Thomas of Erceldoune.

BERLIN: ASHER & CO., 53 MOHRENSTRASSE.
NEW YORK: C. SCRIBNER & CO.; LEYPOLDT & HOLT.
PHILADELPHIA: J. B. LIPPINCOTT & CO.

The Romance and Prophecies of
Thomas of Erceldoune

PRINTED FROM FIVE MANUSCRIPTS;

WITH

Illustrations from the Prophetic Literature

OF THE 15TH AND 16TH CENTURIES.

EDITED, WITH

INTRODUCTION AND NOTES,

BY

JAMES A. H. MURRAY, LL.D.

LONDON:
PUBLISHED FOR THE EARLY ENGLISH TEXT SOCIETY,
BY N. TRÜBNER & CO., 57 & 59, LUDGATE HILL.

MDCCCLXXV.

JOHN CHILDS AND SON, PRINTERS.

PREFATORY NOTE.

IN printing the complete text of the 15th-century "Romance and Prophecies of Thomas of Erceldoune," with lengthy illustrations from the prophetic literature of that and the following century, it seemed desirable to give in the Introduction a summary of all that History, Legend, and Tradition have to tell of Thomas and his alleged sayings. Since the subject was taken up by Mr (afterwards Sir) Walter Scott in the Minstrelsy of the Scottish Border, it has been touched upon by numerous writers, who have pointed out additional historic references, discussed the authenticity of the works attributed to the Rhymer, or contributed to the Folk-lore of the question by collecting rhymes and traditions associated with his name. The present Editor begs to acknowledge his indebtedness to all these his predecessors, of whose writings he has made free use. At the same time no statement has been taken at second hand which was capable of verification by original reference. In particular, all the documentary evidence has been examined afresh, and the quotations from MSS. verified, leading in some cases to the correction of important errors, which have passed current from writer to writer for seventy years. The inferences which the Editor has drawn from these data, and the theories which he has founded upon them, are of course his own; as is the view which he has taken of the origin and development of the prophetic literature generally. He has also given an independent investigation to the scenery and *locale* of the Romance, in which he has been zealously assisted by the local researches of his friends, Mr Andrew Currie of Darnick, the well-known Sculptor and Border Antiquary, and T. B. Gray, Esq., late of Hawkslie, who has had the good fortune to seize and fix an almost obliterated local tradition of the site of "Huntlee Bankis." The Editor has also to acknowledge the valued kindness and help of Henry Bradshaw, Esq., of the University Library, Cambridge, both during a visit to that Library in 1874, and on numerous occasions since; of the Rev. H. O. Coxe, M.A., for the kindness with which he made several searches among the MSS. in the Bodleian; and of the Rev. Dr Bennett, Chancellor of Lincoln, for his arrangements to facilitate the Editor's access to the Thornton MS. in 1874.

PREFATORY NOTE.

Acknowledgments are also due to the Rev. W. W. Skeat, for many a timely service, to James Tait, Esq., of the *Kelso Chronicle*, and Charles Wilson, Esq., of Rhymer's Lands, Earlstoun, for investigation of local matters; and to the Rev. Dr R. Morris, F. J. Furnivall, Esq., and David Laing, Esq., LL.D., for assistance on special points.

The following works touch in one way or another on Thomas and his prophecies:

Lord Hailes (David Dalrymple). Remarks on the History of Scotland. Edin., 1773.
John Pinkerton. Ancient Scottish Poems never before in print. London, 1786.
Sir Walter Scott. The Minstrelsy of the Scottish Border. 1st Edition. Kelso, 1802. (Reprinted, London, 1869.)
Sir Walter Scott. The Minstrelsy of the Scottish Border. 5th Edition, 3 vols. Edin., 1821.
Sir Walter Scott. Sir Tristrem, a metrical Romance of the 13th century. 2nd Ed. Edin., 1806.
Robert Jamieson, F.A.S. Popular Ballads and Songs from Tradition, Manuscripts, and scarce editions. Edin., 1806.
David Laing, LL.D. Select Remains of the Early Popular Poetry of Scotland. Edin., 1822.
Thomas Warton, D.D. The History of English Poetry. (Edited by R. Price, with the additional Notes of Ritson, Ashby, Douce, and Park.) London, 1840.
History of the Berwickshire Naturalist's Club. Part for 1837 contains "The Popular Rhythmes of Berwickshire," by Mr Henderson; Part for 1866 contains "Earlston," by James Tait, Esq.
J. O. Halliwell, Esq. Illustrations of the Fairy Mythology of "A Midsummer Night's Dream." The Shakespeare Society. London, 1845.
Robert Chambers, LL.D. The Popular Rhymes of Scotland. 3rd Edition. Edin., 1858. New Edition, much enlarged; London, 1870.
David Irving, LL.D. History of Scotish Poetry. Edin., 1861.
Professor F. J. Child. English and Scottish Ballads. London, 1861.

After research has done its utmost, the facts as to Thomas are still few and scanty. When we have summed them all up, we can appropriately adapt the words of the minstrel who first told his tale, and like him conclude:

<blockquote>
" Of ' man or woman yet' walde I here,
That couthe mare telle of swilke ferly !
Ihesu, coroúnde with crowne of brere,
Thow brynge us to thy heuene on hye !
        Amen."
</blockquote>

Mill Hill School, Nov. 1875.

CONTENTS.

	PAGE
INTRODUCTION (FOR PLAN, SEE COMMENCEMENT)	ix
"TRADITIONAL" BALLAD OF THOMAS AND THE QUEENE OF FAERIE ...	lii
DESCRIPTION OF THE MSS. AND EDITIONS	lvi
COLLATION OF MSS.	lxiv
NOTES TEXTUAL AND EXPLANATORY	lxix

TOMAS OFF ERSSELDOUNE:

FYTTE I	2
FYTTE II	18
FYTTE III	32

APPENDIX:

I. THE [SCOTTISH] PROPHECIE OF THOMAS RYMOUR (1515—1548) ...	48
II. THE [ENGLISH] "PROPHISIES OF RYMOUR, BEID, AND MARLYNG" (1515—1525)	52
III. ENGLISH PROSE PROPHECY OF GLADSMOOR, SANDEFORD, AND SETON AND THE SEE (1549)	62

INTRODUCTION.

1. *Documents fixing the existence and date of Thomas of Erceldoune* ... page ix
2. *His family, and name* ... xi
3. *Historical (?) notices of Thomas personally* ... xiii
4. *Thomas as a prophet—early citations of his prophecies* ... xvii
5. *Thomas as a poet—testimony of Robert of Brunne—Sir Tristrem* ... xx
6. *The Romance of Thomas and the Queen, Outline of* ... xxiii
7. *Its date and authorship* ... xxiii
8. *The 2nd fytte of prophecies historical—written after the event* ... xxiv
9. *The 3rd fytte of prophecies legendary—their Arthurian origin* ... xxvii
10. *Subsequent prophetic literature connected with Thomas* ... xxix
11. *"The whole prophecies of Scotland, &c.," 1603, examined* ... xxx
12. *Influence of Thomas the Rymour at the Union, 1603* ... xl
13. *Credit during the Jacobite risings—Lord Hailes* ... xli
14. *English Prophecies attributed to Thomas* ... xlii
15. *Local traditions of the Rymour and his prophecies* ... xliii
16. *Eildon Tree and Huntlee Banks; the "Rhymer's Glen"* ... l
17. *The "traditional" Ballad of Thomas and the Queen* ... lii

Description of the MSS. of Thomas of Erceldoune ... lvi
Printed editions ... lxi
Plan of the present Text ... lxii
Collation of the five MSS. ... lxiv

Notes textual and explanatory ... lxix

---

1. THOMAS OF ERCELDOUNE, commonly known as the Rhymer, occupies a more important place in the legendary history of Scotland than in the authentic annals, though the few notices of him which occur in the latter are sufficient to prove his personality and to fix the age in which he lived. The name of *Thomas Rymor de Ercildune* occurs along with Oliver, Abbot of Dryburgh; Willelm de Burudim; Hugh de Peresby, Viscount of Rokysburgh; and Will. de Hattely, as witnessing a deed whereby Petrus de Haga de Bemersyde (on the Tweed) binds himself and his heirs to pay half a stone of wax (*dimidiam petram cere*) annually to the Abbot and convent of Melrose, for the chapel of Saint Cuthbert at Old Melros.[1] This

---

[1] The following copy of Petrus de Haga's Charter is taken from the Cartulary of Melrose MS. Harl. No. 3960, leaf 109 a. It is also printed in the *Liber de Melros* (Bannatyne Club).
Carta Petre de Haga de dimidia petra Cere.
Omnibus hoc scriptum uisuris uel audituris. Petrus de Haga dominus de Bemerside, salutem in domino. Noueritis vniuersi. quod cum olim conuenissem cum viris religiosis Abbate et Conuentu de Melros pro quibusdam transgressionibus eisdem per me & meos illatis. quod eisdem singulis annis ego & heredes mei decem salmones quinque videlicet recentes. & quinque veteres in perpetuum solucrimus; Tandem ijdem religiosi pietate ducti perpenderunt

document has no date, but the grantor, Petrus de Haga, is himself witness to another charter, by which Richard de Moreville, Constable of Scotland (from 1162 to 1189), granted certain serfs to Henry St Clair. It thus defines Thomas's age to the extent of showing that he was a contemporary—a junior one doubtless—of one who was himself at least old enough to witness a document in 1189. In the year 1294 (November 2nd), *Thomas de Ercildoun filius et heres Thomæ Rymour de Ercildoun*, conveyed by charter, to the Trinity House of Soltra, all the lands which he held by inheritance in the village of Ercildoun.[1]

hoc esse in exheredacionem mei & heredum meorum. mediantibus viris bonis consenciente & concedente Johanne filio & herede meo cum dictis Abbate et Conuentu taliter conueni. scilicet quod ego et heredes [mei] tenemur & presenti scripto in perpetuum obligamur ipsis Abbati & Conuentui soluere singulis annis dimidiam petram Cere bone & pacabilis ad Capellam sancti Cuthberti. de veteri Melros die beati Cuthberti. in quadragesima uel triginta denarios. sub pena triginta denariorum singulis mensibus soluendorum ad luminare dicte Capelle. quibus in solucione dicte Cere aut triginta denariorum predictorum fuerit cessatum post diem & terminum memoratos. Subiciendo me & heredes meos Iurrisdiccioni & potestati domini Episcopi sancti Andree. qui pro tempore fuerit. ut me & heredes meos per censuram ecclesiasticam qualemcumque possit compellere ad solucionem dicte Cere. aut triginta denariorum predictorum vna cum pena si committatur. Renunciando pro me & heredibus meis iu hoc facto omni accioni defencioni & accepcioni. & omni legum auxilio canonici. & civilis. beneficio restitucionis in integrum. & omnibus aliis que michi & heredibus meis prodesse potuerunt iu hoc facto & dictis Abbati & Conuentui obesse. quo minus solucio fieri valeat dicte cere. aut triginta denariorum predictorum. una cum pena si committatur. In cuius rei testimonium presenti scripto sigillum meum. vna cum sigillo domini Oliueri tunc Abbatis de Driburgh est appensum. Testibus domino Oliuero Abbate de Driburgh domino Willelmo de Burudim. milite Hugone de Perisby tunc vicecomite de Rokysburgh Willelmo de Hatteley Thome Rymor de Ercildune & aliis.

[1] The following is a transcript of Thomas de Ercildoun's Charter, from the Cartulary of the Trinity House of Soltra, Advocate's Library, W. 4. 14 :—

Ersylton

Omnibus has literas visuris vel audituris Thomas de Ercildoun filius et heres Thome Rymour de Ercildoun, Salutem in domino. Noueritis me per fustum & baculum in pleno iudicio resignasse ac per presentes quietum clamasse pro me & heredibus meis Magistro domus Sancte trinitatis de Soltre, & fratribus eiusdem domus totam terram meam cum omnibus pertinentis suis quam in tenemento de Ercildoun hereditarie tenui Renunciando de cetero pro me et heredibus meis omni iuri & clameo que ego seu antecessores mei in eadem terra alioque tempore de preterito habuimus siue de futuro habere poterimus. In cuius rei testimonium presentibus literis sigillum meum apposui Data apud Ercildoun die Martis proximo post festum Sanctorum apostolorum Symonis & Iude Anno Domini millesimo et nonogesimo quarto.

Although this document has been printed half-a-dozen times, and its date quoted twenty times at least, the latter has been given by every editor as 1299, and in the *Border Minstrelsy* it is actually printed *nonagesimo nono*, which looks like an attempt to evade the chronological difficulty it offers. Mr Skeat kindly points out that the Sunday letter for 1294 was C, and Easter the 18th April, so that St Simon's and St Jude's, the 28 Oct. (the old day for electing mayors, &c., advanced by New Style to 9th Nov.) fell on Thursday, and the next Tuesday after (die Martis proximo post) was 2nd November.

"The superiority of the property called 'Rhymer's Lands,' now owned by Mr Charles Wilson, Earlstoun, still belongs to the Trinity College Church in Edinburgh. It would almost appear as if Thomas had held his lands not direct from the Crown, but from the Earls of Dunbar; for his name does not appear in any State document of that period. Nor does it appear that

Contemporary documents thus fix Rymour's existence between the end of the twelfth and end of the thirteenth century; and, as will be seen in the sequel, he is further historically identified, on sufficient, though not contemporary, evidence, with the latter part of this period, by his connexion with events in the year 1286, and (though less authentically) 1296. From 1189 to 1296 is, of course, more than a century; but, as has been shown by Sir Walter Scott, these dates involve no difficulty, for supposing De Moreville's charter to have been granted towards the end of his career in 1189, and De Haga to have been then about 20, the grant of the latter was probably not made before the end of his life, say between 1230 and 1240. If Erceldoune was about 20 when he witnessed this, it would fix his birth somewhere between 1210 and 1220, so that he would be between 66 and 76 in 1286, and may, so far as this is concerned, have outlived the latter date by several years. The *prima facie* purport of the charter of 1294 is that Thomas is already dead, and his son in possession of the paternal property, which he in his turn gives away. Considerations at variance with this inference will be noticed further on.

2. Of his family, or how much was actually implied by his surname, *de Erceldoun*, we know nothing. The latter was, however, evidently derived from the village of Ercheldun, Erceldoune, Ersyltoun, in Berwickshire, on the banks of the Leader, a northern tributary of the Tweed, from which, in still earlier times, there had emerged a shepherd boy, destined to become the apostle of his native Northumbria, St Cuthbert. Ercheldoun, in the twelfth and thirteenth centuries, seems to have been a place of considerable importance, and is connected both with the family of Lindesey, and the Earls of March. A *Carta Wilheimi Linseia, de Ecclesia de Ercheldoun* to the priory of Coldingham, dating to the reign of David I. or Malcolm the Maiden (1124—1163) is preserved in the Durham archives, and a *Carta W. de Lindessi de Fauope iuxta Ledre*, ante 1165, to the monks of Melros, is also in existence, witnessed among others by Arosine de lindeseia, Swano de Ercedun, and Cospatricio de Ercedun. The Lindesey family do not appear ever to take the surname de Erceldoun, which is borne by that of Cospatric, Earl of March (called often, from his chief residence, Earl of Dunbar). The Earls of March are said to have had a castle at the east end of the village, which was probably the scene of the royal visits in the reign of David I., when various documents, including the Foundation Charter

---

the lands were of large extent, for through old deeds the dimensions of the lands can be observed unaltered for the last three centuries back at least."—*James Tait, Esq., in 'History of Berwickshire Nat. Club,'* vol. v. p. 264. The actual area of *Rhymer's Lands*, as I learn by letter from Mr Wilson, is only 9½ acres, and no other land in Earlstoun or its neighbourhood owns the superiority of Trinity College Church.

of Melrose Abbey in June 1136, and its confirmation by his son Prince Henry in 1143, were subscribed *apud Ercheldon.*

Whether Thomas de Erceldoune was related to the family of March, as might perhaps be assumed from the way in which his name appears more than once in connexion with the Earl and Countess of that house, or whether his relations with them were those of a vassal, or of a neighbour merely, cannot be ascertained. Of a tower, traditionally pointed out as his, the ruins still exist at the west end of the village, though the family connexion with it must have ceased in 1294, when, as already stated, the patrimonial estate in Erceldoune was conveyed to the religious establishment at Soltra. The Earl's Tower at the other end of the village continued to be an important fortress, and, according to popular belief, to it is due the corruption of the old name of Ercheldoun or Ersyltoun, to the modern spelling of *Earlstoun,* which railway and postal authorities contract to *Earlston.*[1]

Thomas is not known to any of the older authorities by any surname save his territorial one of *Erceldoune,* or that of *Rymour,* derived, it is generally supposed, from his poetic or prophetic avocations; " though even this is uncertain, for Rymour was a Berwickshire name in those days, one John Rymour, a freeholder, having done

[1] My friend, Andrew Currie, Esq., of Darnick, to whom I am indebted for much local information as to the Rhymer, and who is himself, I believe, a native of Earlstoun, considers that Erceldoun, or Ersyltoun, has not been altered into Earlstoun, but supplanted by it. He thinks that the original village of Erceldoune is represented by the hamlet of thatched houses at the west, on the road to Lauder, and immediately to the north of Rhymour's Tower, and that the hamlet which rose nearly a mile to the east round the Earl's Tower, was distinguished as the Earl's Town; and this having in process of time become the main village, and absorbed the more ancient Erceldoune, gave its name to the whole. But Erceldoune was originally the general name, as the Earl was *Cospatric de Erceldun,* so that the " Earl's Town," if it existed, would be the " Earls-town at *or* in Erceldoun." *Rhymer's Lands,* beside the ruins of Thomas's Tower, also contained an ancient water-mill, of which Mr Currie says: " Rhymer's Mill was renewed by me in 1843. The old one had a stone in the gable with the words in antique letters, **Rhymer Mill**; I think this stone was replaced in the new mill above the water-wheel. The site of the Earl's Tower, a much more extensive structure than Rhymour's Tower, is now occupied by the Gasworks. I remember seeing hewn pavement, &c., turned up on the spot some forty years ago, besides large chiselled blocks, which had been part of the original walls and foundations. A little to the west of this, and by the burn-side, is a knowe or moraine, which still bears the name of *the Hawk's Kaim,* and is traditionally remembered as the site of the Falconry of the Earls of Dunbar. A long level strip of ground between it and the burn is still called *The Butts,* and said to have been the archery practice ground. Of Rhymer's Tower, the decay has proceeded rapidly within my memory; about 1830, the fireplace was still entire, with massive red stone lintel and corbels from the free stone of the Black Hill behind Cowdenknowes. A curious discovery was made, when clearing out the brushwood of this old quarry, of a corbel nearly finished, identical in pattern and size with those remaining in Rhymer's Tower. This is now preserved at Cowdenknowes. There is no male inhabitant of Earlstoun now claiming descent from the Rhymer, since the death of the last of the Learmonts, an old bachelor, Robert by name, and a weaver by trade, from whom I learned many traditions of Erceldoun, some 35 years ago." (See some additional particulars at end of the *Notes.*)

homage to Edward I. in 1296." The inscription on the front wall of the church at Earlstoun, which marks the traditional place of his sepulture,

"Auld Rymer's race
Lies in this place,"

seems to point to Rymour as the name of the family.[1] But Hector Boece or Boyce (1527) gives him the surname of Leirmont;[2] and Nisbet, the Herald, in a work written 1702, styles him Sir Thomas Learmont of Earlstoun in the Merss, in which he is followed by later writers; and, according to Sir Walter Scott in 1804, "an unvarying tradition corresponds to their assertion." A tradition of the eighteenth century, however, corresponding to a statement which has passed current in books since the sixteenth, has no independent value; and as Nisbet quotes as evidence for Thomas's surname "charters of an earlier date" which no one has ever seen, we may dismiss the subject with a mere mention of the hypotheses suggested by David Macpherson and others to account for Boyce's and Nisbet's nomenclature, such as "that Thomas, or his predecessor, had married an heiress of the name of Learmont, and occasioned this error," or that "some family of that name may have traced their descent from him by the female side." For us, it will be sufficient to know him as he was known to Barbour, Fordun, and Robert of Brunne, as Thomas of Erceldoune, otherwise Thomas Rymour.

3. The incident by which he is associated with the year 1286 is his so-called prediction of the calamitous death of Alexander III.; the earliest notice of which is found in the Scotichronicon of John of Fordun, or rather his continuator Walter Bower (born 1385, wrote about 1430). According to this account, on the night before the king was killed, by being thrown over the precipice at Kinghorn; "Thomas of Erseldon, visiting the castle of Dunbar, was interrogated by the Earl of March, in the jocular manner which he was wont to assume with the Rymour,

---

[1] Mr Tait, in the Berwickshire Nat. Transact. already quoted, says, "Tradition says the stone was transferred from the old church, which stood some yards distant from the present edifice. In 1782 the ancient inscription was defaced by some senseless fellow in a drunken frolic, but the clergyman compelled him to replace it in the same words as before. The defaced characters were very ancient, the present are quite modern, and the spelling also is modernised. The right of sepulture is still claimed there by persons named *Learmont*, an indication that if Thomas did not bear that surname, it was adopted by his descendants," [or some who claimed to represent him]. "The church itself," says Mr Currie, "may not be more than 150 years old. It stands on the site of an older one which was a vicarage of Coldinghame. In the east gable is built a red stone bearing a dagger-shaped cross, the well-known symbol of the Knights Templars. (See additional particulars at end of the *Notes*.)

[2] *Boece* lib. xiii. f. 291 a (Parisiis, 1575). Tradunt scriptores pridie quàm Alexander fate functus esset, comitem merchiarum percunctatum sub noctem insignem quendam vatem ac praedicendi arte haud saepe fallentem, Thomas Leirmont nomine, vtrùm aliquid in posterum diem noui euenturum esset.

what another day was to bring forth. Thomas, fetching a heavy sigh from the bottom of his heart, is said to have expressed himself to this effect: 'Alas for to-morrow, a day of calamity and misery! Before the twelfth hour, shall be heard a blast so vehement that it shall exceed all those that have yet been heard'in Scotland: a blast which shall strike the nations with amazement, shall confound those who hear it, shall humble what is lofty, and what is unbending shall level to the ground.' In consequence of this alarming prediction, the Earl and his attendants were induced to observe the state of the atmosphere next day; but having watched till the ninth hour without discovering any unusual appearance, they began to deride Thomas as a driveller. The Earl, however, had scarcely sat down to dinner, and the hand of the dial pointed the hour of noon, when a messenger arrived at the gate and importunately demanded admission; they now found that the prediction was fatally verified; for this messenger came to announce the intelligence of the king's death."[1] Bower's story is repeated by Mair (Joannes Major Scotus), and Hector Boece (Boethius) (see note 2, p. xiii), the former adding, "To this Thomas our countrymen have ascribed many predictions, and the common people of Britain yield no slight degree of credit to stories of this nature; which I for the most part am wont to treat with ridicule." Bellenden also, in his vernacular version of Boece, tells the story in more moderate language than Fordun:

"It is said ye day afore ye kingis deith, the Erle of Merche demandit ane propheit namit Thomas Rimour, otherwayis namit Ersiltoun, quhat weddir suld be

[1] "Annon recordaris quod ille vates ruralis, Thomas videlicet de Erseldon, nocte praecedenti mortem regis Alexandri, in castro de Dunbar, obscure prophetando, de occasu ejus dixerat comiti Marchiarum interroganti ab eo, ut solitus quasi jocando, quid altera dies futura novi esset paritura? Qui Thomas attrahens de imo cordis singultuosum suspirium, sic fertur comiti coram aulicis palam protulisse: 'Heu diei crastinae! diei calamitatis et miseriae! quà ante horam explicite duodecimam audietur tam vehemens ventus in Scotia, quod a magnis retroactis temporibus consimilis minime inveniebatur. Cujus quidem flatus obstupescere faciet gentes, stupidos reddet audientes, excelsa humiliabit, et rigida solo complanabit.' Propter cujus seria affamina comes cum aulicis crastinum observantes, et horas diei usque ad nonam considerantes, et nullum vestigium in nubibus vel signis ventosis coeli auspicantes, Thomam tanquam insensatam reputantes, ad prandium properarunt. Ubi dum comiti vix mensae collocato, et signo horologii ad meredianam horam fere approximato, affuit quidam ad portam, importunis pulsibus aures comitis concutiens, aditum sibi ocius fieri flagitavit. Intromissus igitur advena, et de novis impetitus, 'Nova,' inquit, 'habeo, sed nosciva, toto regno Scotiae deflenda, quia inclitus, heu! rex ejus finem praesentis vitae hesterna nocte apud Kingorn sortitus est, et haec veni nunciare tibi.' Ad hanc narrationem, quasi de gravi somno excitatus, comes una cum familiaribus tutuderunt pectora, et dicti Thomae experti sunt credibilia nimis facta fore vaticinia." Bower, Scotichronicon, lib. x. c. 43. "The local tradition," according to Mr Currie, "has it that the prophecy was delivered in the Earl of Dunbar's castle at Erceldoune, the royal herald announcing his arrival by a bugle blast from the Corse-Hill Head, on the Huntshaw road, to the north of the village. The spot is still called, if my memory serves me right, The Trumpet or Bugle Knowe."

on ye morrow. To quhome answerit this Thomas, that on the morrow afore noun, sall blaw the greatest wynd that euir was herd afore in Scotland. On ye morrow, quhen it wes neir noun, ye lift appering loune but ony din or tempest, ye Erle sent for this propheit and repreuit hym that he pronosticat sic wynd to be and na apperance yairof. Yis Thomas maid litel answer, bot said, noun is not ȝit gane. And incontinent ane man come to the ȝet schawing y't the king was slain. Yan said ye propheit, Zone is the wynd yat sall blaw to ye gret calamite and trouble of all Scotland. Yis Thomas was ane man of gret admiration to the people, and schew sindry thingis as they fell. Howbeit yai wer ay hyd vnder obscure wourdis."

Divested of the grandiloquence of its monkish chroniclers, "the story," says Sir Walter Scott, " would run simply that Thomas presaged to the Earl of March that the next day would be windy—the weather proved calm, but news arrived of the death of Alexander III., which gave an allegorical turn to the prediction, and saved the credit of the prophet. It is worthy of notice that the rhymes vulgarly ascribed to Thomas of Erceldoune are founded apparently on meteorological observation. And doubtless before the invention of barometers, a weather-wise prophet might be an important personage."

Whatever the foundation of the story, and however explained, it may be taken, at least in conjunction with the documentary evidence already given, as showing that Thomas was alive in 1286. According to Harry the Minstrel he survived also to 1296, when he was identified with a critical passage in the life of Wallace.

Towards the beginning of that hero's career, as reported by his minstrel biographer, he was seized in the town of Ayr, by the soldiers of the English garrison under Lord Percy, whose steward, amongst several others, Wallace had slain in a market brawl. While lying in prison awaiting his trial, the rigour of his treatment and filthiness of his dungeon brought on dysentery, under which he sank, and was found by the jailor apparently dead. His body was cast over the walls upon a " draff myddyn," whence it was begged by an old nurse, who desired to do the last rites to the corpse. While washing the body, however, she noticed faint signs of animation, and by dint of careful nursing, secretly restored him to life and health, while observing all the outward show of mourning for his death.

thomas Rimour in to *the* faile[1] was *t*han,	The peple demyt of witt mekill he can;
With *the* mynystir, quhilk was a worthi man :	And so he told, *th*ocht at *th*ai bliss or ban,
He wsyt offt to *th*at religiouss place.	Quhilk hapnyt suth in many diuerss cace,

---

[1] The *Faile* or *Feale*, a priory of the Cluniacenses in the neighbourhood of Ayr, which was still flourishing in the sixteenth century.

xvi   INTRODUCTION.

I can nocht say, be wrang or rychtwisnas,
In rewlle of wer, quhethir thai tynt or wan;
It may be demyt be diuisioun of grace.
Thar man that day had in the merket bene,
On Wallace knew this cairfull cass so kene.
His master speryt, quhat tithingis at he saw.
This man ansuerd; "of litill hard I meyn."
The mynister said; 'It has bene seildyn seyn,
quhar scottis and Ingliss semblit bene on Raw,
Was neuir ʒit, als fer as we coud knaw,
Bot other a scot wald do a sothroun teyn,
Or he till him, for awentur mycht faw.'
"Wallace," he said, "ʒe wist tayne in that
    steid ;
Out our the wall I saw thaim cast him deide,
In presoune famys[i]t for fawt of fude."
The mynister said with hart hewy as leid,
'Sic deid to thaim, me think, suld foster
    feid ;
For he was wicht and cummyn of gentill blud.'
Thomas ansuerd " thir tythingis ar noucht
    gud ;
And that be suth, my self sall neuir eit breid,
For all my witt her schortlye I conclud.
' a woman syne of the Newtoun of Ayr,
Till him scho went fra he was fallyn ther ;
And on her kneis rycht lawly thaim besocht,
To purchess leiff scho mycht thin with him
    fayr.
In lychtlyness tyll hyr thai grant to fayr.
Our the wattyr on till hir houss him brocht,
To berys him als gudlye as scho mocht.'
ʒhit thomas said " Than sall I leiff na mar,
Gyff that be trew, be-god, that all has wrocht."
the mynister herd quhat thomas said in playne.

He chargyt him than "go speid the fast
    agayne
To that sammyn houss and werraly aspye."
The man went furth, at byddyng was full
    bayne ;
To the new town to pass he did his payn,
To that ilk houss ; and went in sodanlye,
About he blent on to the burd him bye.
This woman raiss, in hart scho was [nocht]
    fayn.
quha aw this lik, he bad hir nocht deny.
"wallace," scho said, " that full worthy has
    beyne,"
Thus wepyt scho, that pete was to seyne.
The man thar to gret credens gaif he nocht:
Towart the burd he bowned as he war teyne.
On kneis scho felle, and cryit : ' For marye
    scheyne,
Lat sklandyr be, and flemyt out of ʒour
    thocht.'
This man hir suour "be him that all has
    wrocht,
Mycht I on lyff him anys se with myn eyn,
He suld be saiff, thocht Ingland had him
    socht."
scho had him wp to Wallace be the dess ;
He spak with him ; syne fast agayne can press
With glaid bodword, thar myrthis till amend.
He told to thaim the first tithingis was less.
Than thomas said : " forsuth, or he decess,
Mony thousand in feild sall mak thar end.
Off this regioune he sall the sothroun send ;
And scotland thriss he sall bryng to the pess :
So gud off hand agayne sall neuir be kend."

This incident, if authentic, could not have taken place before 1296 or 1297 ; and it is at once evident that it conflicts with the idea that Thomas was already dead in 1294, when *Thomas de Ercildoun filius et heres Thomæ Rymour de Ercildoun* devised the paternal estates. It is easy, of course, to say that, the charter being undoubted, Harry's story must be set aside as a mere fable. But I am not disposed to treat the Minstrel's circumstantial narrative quite so lightly ; and I would suggest that it is not impossible that Thomas, wearied and dispirited with the calamities under which his country was sinking, may before his death have transferred his estates, and retired to end his days in the priory of the Faile. If Harry is to be trusted in saying that Thomas " usyt offt to that religiouß place," we may even have a key to those temporary disappearances from his home, which popular superstition accounted for by visits to Fairyland ; and a final retirement while still alive may really be the fact concealed under the legend of his sudden disappearance from the world. Then, are we correct in assuming that the charter in question is granted by Thomas's son, and not by Thomas himself? If Rymour was the family surname, the latter is not impossible. It is at least a pleasing fancy to picture Thomas, the last mayhap of his line, after setting his house in order and disposing of his worldly goods, retiring from earthly cares and pursuits, and leaving his neighbours to marvel at his departure, and attribute it to the powers of another world, who could spare him to "middle-erd" no longer. Many a myth has gone farther astray from its simple basis. Patrick Gordon, in his rhymed History of Robert Bruce (Dort, 1615), says Rymour survived to 1307; but as he gives us no authority for the statement, his evidence is of very doubtful value.

4. Such are the only notices which refer, or purport to refer, to Thomas in his lifetime. They seem to point to him as a man of sagacity and foresight, who, veiling his observations "under obscure wourdis," had already before his death attained to the repute of something like prophetic power. As a patriot, and one who had lived during the palmy days of the old Scottish monarchy before

> Alysandyr owre kyng wes dede
> That Scotlande led in luve and le,

he must have keenly felt the sorrows which overtook his country in his last years, and if he understood the temper of his countrymen, he may well have expressed his hope and confidence of their final triumph in tones which fell from the lips of the "old man eloquent" with all the weight of inspiration. That his reputed sayings were so quoted early in the course of the struggle, and within a few years after his own death, is abundantly evident from various references. One of these occurs in Barbour's Bruce, where, after Bruce had slain the Red Cumyn in the Grey Friars church at Dumfries in 1306, news of the event reached amongst others the patriotic Bishop of St Andrews :

> The lettir tauld hym all the deid,
> And he till his men gert it reid,
> And sythyn said thaim, "sekyrly
> I hop Thomas prophecy
> off hersildoune sall weryfyd be
> In him; for, swa our lord help me!
> I haiff gret hop he sall be king,
> And haif this land all in leding."

Andro of Wyntown also in his "Orygynale" (Book VIII, chap. 32), referring to the battle of Kilblane, fought by Sir Andrew Moray against the Baliol faction in 1334, says :—

> Of this fycht qwhylum spak Thomas
> of Ersyldoune, that sayd in derne,
> There suld mete stalwarthe,[1] stark, and sterne.   [1 MS. stalwartly]
> He sayd it in his prophecy;
> But how he wist it was ferly.

ERCILDOUN.   b

INTRODUCTION.

At a still earlier period the prophetic renown of Thomas is alluded to by the author of the *Scalacronica*, a French chronicle of English History, compiled by Sir Thomas Grey, constable of Norham, during his captivity in Edinburgh Castle in 1355. One of the *Notabilia*, extracted by Leyland from the unpublished part of this chronicle, is headed : "William Banestre and Thomas Erceldoune, whose words were spoken in figure, as were the prophecies of Merlin." [1]

Most of these writers, however, lived a century after Thomas, and it might of course be, that their references to the notoriety of his prophetic powers represented rather the current opinion of their own age than of that of which they wrote; that Barbour, for example, in making Bishop Lamberton quote "Thomas' prophecy," described what he was very likely to do himself, though he might have no ground either in tradition or history for imputing it to the Bishop of St Andrews But this is sufficiently met by the fact that a MS. of the beginning of the fourteenth century not only credits Thomas with oracular powers, but preserves what purports to be one of his prophecies, in the following form (*MS. Harl.* 2253, *lf* 127, *col.* 2):

> La countesse de Donbar demanda a Thomas de Essedoune qua*nt* la guere descoce prendreit fyn. e yl la repoundy e dyt,
> When man as mad akyng of a capped man ;
> When mon is leuere oþermones þyng þen is owen ;
> When londyonys forest, ant forest ys felde ; [2]
> When hares kendles oþe herston ;
> When Wyt & Wille werres togedere ;
> When mon makes stables of kyrkes, and steles castles wyþ styes ;
> When rokesbourh nys no burgh [3] ant market is at Forwyleye ;

---

[1] The Rev. W. W. Skeat has been so kind as to find the original of Leyland's extract in the manuscript in the library of Corpus Christi Coll. Cambridge (No. 133, leaf 60, back). He says: "It is a long paragraph, in which the name of 'Merlyns' occurs repeatedly; some remarks at the end imply that he spoke so much 'en figure' as to render the interpretation of his meaning very doubtful. It is remarked that much is said about boars, dragons, bears, eagles, lions, asses, moles, trees, and brooks; and that the object seems to have been to make the prophecies obscure—'ne purra estre determyne en certayne, si fussent, en le hour de lescriuer de cest cronicle, passe ou auenir. pusq*ue* tauntes des Roys sount passez. tancom durerent les Regnes des .vij. reaulmes Saxsouns. en queux la g*ra*nt bretaigne estoit deuise. et des autres puscedy Engles & Norma*n*des. pur quoy ne agreast a le deuisour de cest cronicle plus dez p*ar*olis de Merlyne de soy entremettre. ne dez autres queux hom disoit en le houre p*re*destino*ur*s. com de Willa*m* Banastre. ou de Thom*as* de Erceldoun. les parolis de queux furount ditz en fig*ure*. od diuers entendement*z* aptez a lestimacioun de les comentours. q*ue* en cas p*ur*roint deascorder.'"

[2] The letters þ and y are in the MS. only distinguished by the y having a dot, which is often omitted; n and u also are indistinguishable; *londyonys* or *loudyonys* may be *London is* or *Loudyon*, i. e. "*Lothian* is forest, and forest is field." *Forest* may refer to the old name of Selkirkshire, or Etterick *Forest*.

[3] Roxburgh, the ancient county town of Roxburghshire, and one of the "four great burghs" of Scotland, the remains of whose castle still crown the promontory between the Tweed and Teviot at their confluence, has been "no burgh" since 1547, and not a stone of the once great town now remains *in situ*.

EARLY CITATIONS OF THOMAS'S PROPHECIES.

> When þe alde is gan ant þe newe is come þ' don (or dou) noþt
> When bambourne is dongeð Wyþ dedemen;
> When men ledes men in ropes to buyen & to sellen;
> When a quarter of whaty whete is chaunged for a colt of ten markes;
> When prude prikes & pees is leyd in prisoun;
> When a scot ne may hym hude ase hare in forme þ' þe englysshe ne sal hym fynde;
> When ryþt ant Wrong ascenteþ to gedere;
> When laddes weddeþ louedis;
> When scottes flen so faste, þ' for faute of ship, by drowneþ hem selue
> Whenne shal þis be? Nouþer in þine tyme ne in myne;
> ah comen & gon wiþ inne twenty wynter ant on.

This is in a southern (or south-midland) dialect, and doubtless by an English author. The effect of it seems to be that many improbabilities will happen, and in especial that many calamities will happen to Scotland, before the war with that country shall end, which shall not be in the time of either Thomas or his interrogator, but within twenty-one years after. (See further at end of the *Notes*.)

Mr Pinkerton, who first printed the lines in the "List of the Scotish Poets," prefixed to his "Ancient Scotish poems never before in print" (London, 1786, Vol. I, p. lxxviij), and Sir Walter Scott, who quoted it from Pinkerton (very inaccurately, and with loss of one line), in the "Border Minstrelsy," assume that the *Countesse de Donbar* is the heroic Black Agnes, daughter of Randolph, so celebrated for her defence of Dunbar Castle in 1337, and also referred to in the following poem. But as Mr Bond says the MS. is undoubtedly before 1320, this is not possible; and by the Countess is no doubt meant the wife of the Earl to whom Thomas predicted the death of Alexander III, and with whom, as already said, he seems to have been a familiar visitor. *Bambourne* is evidently Bannockburn, and the reference to its being "donged with dede men," leads one to infer that the prediction was composed *after*, or or least on the eve of that battle, in 1314. But there was no time between that battle and 1320, or even Bruce's death in 1329, when a prophecy that "the Scots should hide as hare in form," would suit events or even distant probabilities; and I am inclined therefore to suppose that it was actually composed on the eve of the Battle of Bannockburn, and circulated under Thomas's name, in order to discourage the Scots and encourage the English in the battle. It is well known that Edward II felt so sure of gaining that battle, and finishing the war at a blow, that he held a council in the camp on the previous day, and drew up statutes and ordinances for the disposal of Scotland and its inhabitants, which were found in the English camp after his defeat. Counting back from 1314, "twenty wynter ant on" would bring us to 1293, when Thomas was, as we have seen, still alive.

That prophecy formed an important weapon on both sides during the wars between England and Scotland appears from many sources, and a passage in Higden's Polychronicon (as translated by Trevisa) referring to this very period says:

"The Scottes waxed stronger & stronger thyrty yeres togyder, vnto Kyng Edwardes tyme the thyrde after the Conquest, and bete down Englyshemen ofte, and Englyshe places, that were nygh to theyr marches. Some seyd that that myshappe fell for softnesse of Englyshemen; and some seyde, that it was goddes own wreche, *as the prophecye said*, that Englyshemen sholde be destroyed by Danes, by Frenshemen, and by Scottes."

The prophetic powers of Thomas of Erceldoune seem thus to have been sufficiently credited to give importance to predictions purporting to be his within the twenty years that followed his own life-time; and it is noteworthy that all these early references agree in attributing to his utterances the "derne," "obscure," and "figurative" character so well exemplified in those still preserved as his; also, that the writers who quote them agree in their doubts as to the quarter whence Thomas derived his inspiration, while making no doubt of the inspiration itself.

5. We have equally early authority for his poetical abilities. Robert Mannyng of Brunne, who was actually a contemporary of Thomas, since his "Handlyng of Synne" was written in 1303, appears in his English Chronicle, written about 1330, to celebrate him as "the author of an incomparable romance of the story of Sir Tristrem." After stating his intention of telling his Story of England in the simplest speech, and without using intricate rhymes, since he has observed that such artificial compositions, though they may exhibit their authors' talent, are most spoiled by readers, Mannyng adds as an illustration of this:

I see in song in sedgeyng tale
of Erceldoun & of Kendale,
Non þam says as þai þam wroght,
& in þer sayng it semes noght;
þat may þou here in sir Tristrem;
ouer gestes it has þe steem,
Ouer alle þat is or was,
if mene it sayd as made Thomas;
But I here it no mane so say,
þat of som copple som is away;
So þare fayre sayng here beforne
is þare trauayle nere forlorne;

þai sayd it for pride & nobleye,
þat non were suylk as þei;
And alle þat þai wild ouerwhere,
Alle þat ilk wille now forfare.
þai sayd in so quante Inglis,
þat many one wate not what it is.
þerfore [I] henyed wele þe more
In strange ryme to trauayle sore;
And my witte was oure thynne
So strange speche to trauayle in;
And forsoth I couth[e] noght
so strange Inglis as þai wroght.

It is not certain whether the "Thomas" here is Thomas of Erceldoun or Thomas of Kendale; nor indeed that the first four lines refer to the same subject as those that follow: Sir Tristrem may, for anything that appears, be a third example, in addition to the works of Erceldoun and Kendale, of the liability of "quante

Inglis" to be marred by reciters, and its author "Thomas" may not be the Erceldoun of the second line, especially as the earlier German versions of Sir Tristrem quote as their authority one Thomas von Brittanien, or Thomas of Brittany, who must have lived, whoever he was, long before Thomas of Erceldoun. On the other hand, the Romance of Sir Tristrem in the Auchinleck MS., supposed to have been transcribed about the middle of the fourteenth century, and which, though it has been altered by a Southern transcriber, is demonstrably a copy of an earlier Northern one, begins by claiming Thomas of Erceldoune as the authority for its information, in terms which have induced Sir Walter Scott and others to consider the romance as his own production:

<pre>
I was at Erþeldoun¹   & who was bold baroun
    Wiþ tomas spak y þare   As þair elders ware
þer herd y rede in roune   bi ȝere
    Who tristrem gat & bare   tomas telles in toun
Who was king wiþ croun   þis auentours as þai ware.
    & who him fosterd ȝare
</pre>

In stanzas 37-38 Thomas is mentioned, at the point where Tristrem found himself left on an unknown shore by the mariners who had carried him off from home:

<pre>
þo tomas asked ay   In o robe tristrem was boun,
    Of tristrem trewe fere,   þat he fram schippe hadde brouȝt;
To wite þe riȝt way,   Was of a blihand broun,
    þe styes for to lere ;   þe richest þat was wrouȝt;
of a prince proude in play   As tomas telleþ in toun ;
    Listneþ lordinges dere ;   He no wist what he mouȝt,
Who so better can say,   Bot semly set him doun,
    His owhen he may here,   & ete ay til him gode þouȝt,
            As hende   Ful sone
of thing þat is him dere   þe forest forþ he souȝt
Ich man preise at ende.   When he so hadde done.
</pre>

In Fytt III, stanza 45, the authority of "Tomas" is quoted again:

<pre>
Beliagog þe bold   Adoun he fel y fold,
    As a fende he fauȝt;   þat man of michel mauȝt,
Tristrem liif neiȝe he sold,   & cride
    As tomas haþ ous tauȝt   "Tristrem, be we sauȝt,
Tristrem smot, as god wold,   & haue min londes wide."
    His fot of at a drauȝt ;
</pre>

Notwithstanding that in all these passages, the author professes to have learned his tale from "Thomas," Sir Walter Scott, in editing Sir Tristrem, assumed it as

---

¹ This word is cut through in the MS. by some former possessor who cut out the illuminations; but the catchword at foot of preceding leaf (280) has "y was at erþeldoun" (not erseldoun), and the lower part of the word including the þ is quite clear in the folio itself. *Erþeldoun* for *Ertheldoun* may be the scribe's error for *Ercheldoun* in his original.

undoubtedly the genuine work of Erceldoune, committed to writing by some one who had learned it from him personally; and started a theory that Thomas had himself collected the materials from the Britons of Strathclyde, and that his work, being thus original in its character, was the source of the numerous versions in continental languages which quote one "Thomas" as their authority. Dr Irving, in his History of Scottish Poetry, also considered it as "not altogether absurd to suppose that he was nevertheless the real author, and had recourse to this method" [*i. e.* quoting his own name as his authority] "of recording his own claims," and so preventing reciters from claiming the romance as their own composition. But in the additions to Warton's *History of English Poetry* (editions of 1824 and 1840) it is shown that not only did the romance exist in several European languages long before the days of Erceldoune, but that the "Thomas" quoted in some of the French and German poems was the writer of one of the French versions of the story, who must have lived before 1200; that this French version was apparently the original of the English translation in the Auchinleck MS., and that while it is doubtful whether the latter be the work referred to by Robert of Brunne, it is still more doubtful whether it is the production, either directly or indirectly, of Erceldoune. Mr Garnett, in summing up his review of the subject, considers it proved, " 1. That the present Sir Tristrem is a modernized [rather a *southernized*, it cannot well be a *much* more modern] copy of an old[er] Northumbrian romance, written probably between 1260 and 1300. 2. That it is not, in the proper sense of the word, an original composition, but derived more or less directly from a Norman or Anglo-Norman source. 3. That there is no direct evidence in favour of Thomas of Erceldoune's claim to the authorship of it, while the internal evidence is, as far as it goes, greatly adverse to that supposition. It is however by no means improbable that the author availed himself of the previous labours of Erceldoune on the same theme. The minstrels of those days were great plagiarists, and seldom gave themselves the trouble of inventing subjects and incidents when they found them ready prepared to their hands." Later criticism is still more adverse to the claims of Erceldoune. Mr Wright thinks it most probable that the person who translated the Auchinleck version from the French original, finding a "Thomas" mentioned therein, and not knowing who he was, "may have taken him for the Thomas whose name was then most famous, viz. Thomas of Erceldoune, and thus put the name of the latter to his English edition." I must confess that, looking at the way in which the name and authority of Erceldoune were afterwards affixed to productions with which he had no connexion, Mr Wright's theory seems to me most probable, especially as this English version must have been originally by a northern writer who would be well acquainted with Thomas's name, and probably wrote soon after his death, so that the southernized transcript in the Auchinleck MS. could be made before the middle of the 14th century. But the Early English Text Society has *Sir Tristrem* in its list for early reprinting, when the question of the origin and authorship of the romance will of course be fully discussed. At present we have only to note that, however the opinion was founded, Thomas of Erceldoune at least passed in popular estimation as a poet of renown within thirty years after his own death.

6. In the twofold character of poet and prophet, thus attributed to him from the earliest period, the name of Thomas of Erceldoune continued to be venerated for many centuries, and numerous compositions claiming to be his, or at least to derive their authority from or through him, are still preserved. The earliest of these is the poem printed in the following pages, the completion of which, from internal evidence, must be placed shortly after 1400, or about a hundred years after Thomas's death. It represents Thomas as meeting " a lady gaye," who is described as the Queen of a realm not in heaven, paradise, hell, purgatory, or on middel-erthe, but " another cuntre " from all these, answering to the Faërie or Fairy-land of later tales, but nowhere so called in the poem itself. Thomas makes love to her, and is transported by her power to her own country, where he dwells for three years and more. On his dismissal, necessary to prevent his seizure by a foul fiend of hell, who is coming next day for his tribute, he asks a token from the lady, and, in compliance with his repeated request to abide and tell him some ferly, she proceeds to give an outline in prophetic form of the wars between England and Scotland from the time of Bruce to that of the death of Robert III, with a mysterious continuation, which must still rank as " unfulfilled prophecy," and ending with a reference to Black Agnes of Dunbar, whose death is predicted. After an affectionate farewell, in which she promises to meet Thomas again at the same spot, the lady leaves him and takes her way to Helmsdale.

7. In regard to the professed authorship of this poem, we meet with even greater difficulty than in *Sir Tristrem*, the narrator passing from the first to the third person, and from the third to the first again, with the most sudden transition, so that it is difficult to say whether it even claims to be the work of Thomas. Thus in the first 72 lines (including the prologue), the writer describes himself as lying on Huntly banks himself alone, and seeing the lady, whose array he describes as a professed eye-witness ; but in line 73 it is :

> *Thomas* laye & sawe that syghte
> Vndir-nethe a semly tree :
> *He sayd*, &c. &c.
>
> Gyff it be *als the storye sayes*
> *He* hir mette at Eldone Tree,

and so on for 200 lines, the author describing Thomas and his actions as if he himself had them only by hearsay, till in l. 273 we have again the sudden transition to the first person :

> Thomas duellide in that solace
> More than j ȝowe saye parde ;
> Till one a day, so hafe I grace,
> *My* lufly lady sayde *to mee ;*
> Do buske the, Thomas, the buse agayne, &c. &c. ;

but this is only a momentary interruption, for the narrator immediately speaks of Thomas again in the third person, a style which he continues to the end of the narrative. In the prophecies from l. 317 to 672 the speeches of Thomas and the lady are merely quoted without even as much as an introductory " he said " or " she said," so that nothing can be determined as to the professed narrator. The conclusion, however, ll. 673—700, is very decidedly narrative in the third person :

> Scho blewe hir horne on hir palfraye,   Of swilke an hird mane wold j here
> Lefte Thomas vndir-nethe a tre ;   That couth Me telle of swilke ferly.
> To Helmesdale scho tuke the waye ,   Ihesu, corouned with a crowne of brere,
> And thus departede scho and hee !   Brynge vs to his heuene So hyee !

where, even if with the Cambridge MS. we read *woman* for *hird mane*, it is clearly the wish of a third party that he had such an experience as Thomas had, and not of Thomas himself.

8. But, whoever the professed author, I have said that the poem in its present form bears evidence of being later than 1401, the date of the invasion of Scotland by Henry IV, or at least 1388, the date of the Battle of Otterbourne, the last of the historical events " hyd vnder obscure wourdis " in Fytt II. For the whole of the events described in that Fytt are really historical and easily identified, preserving, with a single important exception, the chronological order; and this part of the poem must have therefore been composed after the last of them had happened. But of the events predicted in Fytt III, after the second, which seems to refer to Henry IV's invasion of the country in 1401, I cannot make any such sense, and I prefer to consider these as real predictions or expectations of the future. Moreover, the oldest MS. of the poem, the Thornton, itself clearly not an original, dates to 1430—1440, some time before which the poem must have existed in its present form, so that we have the period between 1402 and 1440, with strong reasons in favour of the earlier date, for its completion. But portions of it may have been

THE SECOND FYTTE OF THE PROPHECIES HISTORICAL. xxv

earlier even than this, for it is clearly possible that the prophecies may have been altered, added to, and interpolated, from time to time, since each incident of them is separate, and easily detachable from the context. There seems indeed to be evidence of very early treatment of this kind in Fytt II, in examining which it will be seen that the events therein "predicted" are

The failure of Baliol's party in the struggle with David Bruce	1333
the battle of Halidon Hill	1333
The battle of Falkirk	1298
the battle of Bannockburn	1314
the death of Robert Bruce	1329
the invasion and partial success of Edward Baliol, who lands at Kinghorn	1332
the battle of Dupplin and occupation of Perth . .	1332
the English withdraw to the French war . . .	1337
David Bruce fetched from France	1342
he invades England, is captured at Durham, and led to London	1346
Scotland again invaded by Baliol	1347
Scotland heavily taxed for the ransom of King David . .	1357
Robert Stewart made king	1370
Douglas invades England, and slain at Otterbourne . .	1388

Excluding the two first entries, we have here an outline of the chief events in Scotland from the Battle of Falkirk under Wallace to that of Otterbourne under Robert II, references being specially numerous to the period of the Second War of Independence under David Bruce. But the prediction of the eventual ruin of Baliol's party, and the battle of Halidon Hill—a battle "that shall be done right soon at will," come out of order and quite apart from this chronological list, as if they had no connexion with it, while they are also intimately connected with the introduction of this Fytt, and Thomas's request to the lady—

> Telle me of this gentill blode
> Wha sall thrife, and wha sall thee,
> Wha sall be kynge, wha sall be none,
> And wha sall welde this northe countrie?—

a question as to the conflicting claim of the Bruce and Baliol families scarcely likely to be made after 1400, when the latter line was extinct. I am inclined to suppose, then, that this part, with perhaps Fytt I, the conclusion, and an indefinite portion of Fytt III, which is in all probability a *melange* of early traditional prophecies, may have been written on the eve of Halidon Hill, with a view to encourage the Scots in that battle; in which the oldest text, it will be observed, makes the Scots win with the slaughter of six thousand Englishmen, while the other texts, wise after the fact, make the Scots lose, as they actually did.

The question has been asked before, whether the "fairy tale" contained in Fytt I is not distinct from the "prophetical rhapsody" to which it serves as an introduction, and collectors of ballads have generally answered the query in the affirmative; thus Jamieson, in editing the poem in his "Popular Ballads and Songs," is of opinion that "In the introduction to the prophecies, there is so much more fancy and elegance than in the prophecies themselves, that they can hardly be supposed to be the composition of the same person. Indeed, the internal evidence to the contrary almost amounts to a proof that they are not." Professor Child, also, in his "English and Scottish Ballads" (London, 1861), vol. I, p. 95, says, "the two 'fytts' of prophecies which accompany it (the ballad) in the MSS. are omitted here, as being probably the work of another, and an inferior, hand." Although diffident of venturing an opinion at variance with that of poets and poet-editors, I can hardly think that Fytt I stands alone. Some of the prophecies may be later than others, but I think that, *as a whole*, they flow so naturally from the tale, as a response to Thomas's request for a token of his intercourse with the Lady, without any trace of patching or awkward joining, as to preclude the suspicion of having been afterwards tacked on. As to their style, they could not well, from their nature, be rendered so interesting or lively as the ballad; yet the introduction to them, as well as their conclusion and the parting of Thomas and the Queen, seem not inferior in execution to any part of Fytt I.

On the other hand, it must be granted that, artistically considered, the tale of Thomas and the Lady is far too long and minute to have been invented as a mere introduction to the prophecies, and I willingly admit that the story, perhaps even in a poetic dress, may have existed some time before it was caught up and told anew as an introduction and passport to the predictions. The reference in line 83,

<blockquote>
Gyff it be *als the storye sayes*,
He hir mette at Eldone tree,
</blockquote>

implies that there was in existence an older tale of Thomas and the Queen, which fixed the place of their meeting. If we are to suppose that part of the work as it now exists is as old as Halidon Hill, we are taken to a date little more than thirty years after Thomas's own time, a fact, so far as it goes, in favour of the idea of those who think that this older tale may have been composed by Thomas himself, and

THE THIRD FYTTE OF THE PROPHECIES LEGENDARY. xxvii

that the first-personal style of parts of the existing ballad may have been transferred from his narrative.

If modern editors despise the prophecies, and look upon them as a rubbishy addition to the ballad, it is very clear, that early scribes thought otherwise, and that it was to the respect which the prophecies inspired, that we owe so many MS. copies of the poem as have come down to us; we may be glad that their appreciation of the relative merits of the parts did not lead them all to do like the scribe of the Sloane MS., who omits Fytt I, and dignifies the prophecies alone' with a place in his pages. In addition to this MS. four others preserve the poem more or less perfectly, and with considerable differences, as exhibited in the following text. These MSS. and the peculiarities of their texts will be described hereafter; it is only necessary here to note that the poem appears to have been originally by a Scottish author, though all the copies of it now exist in English MSS., and that the strongly northern character of the language as preserved by Robert Thornton, who, as a northern Englishman, would leave it nearly as he found it, is more or less modified in the others, especially in the Lansdowne and Sloane, which are also comparatively late in their transcription. The various modifications introduced by southern or midland transcribers may be well seen in lines 357—372. In these repeated transcriptions also the proper names of Scottish families, and of battles, have suffered so much at the hands of scribes to whom they were devoid of meaning, as often to become quite unintelligible. The results of the battles also are often altered in the different texts, doubtless because the transcribers in many cases did not understand the application of the predictions, and perhaps patriotically changed their burden, in accordance with their own wishes or hopes.

9. I look upon the greater part of the predictions in Fytt III as in reality adaptations of legendary prophecies, traditionally preserved from far earlier times, and furbished up anew at each period of national trouble and distress in expectation of their fulfilment being at length at hand. The origin of these effusions takes us back to the period of Arthur himself, and the expiring efforts of the Britons against Saxon conquest. It is well known that the flush of enthusiasm and hope which swelled the breasts of his countrymen, during Arthur's series of victories over the pagan invaders, was too fondly cherished to be willingly renounced on his premature removal from the scene. Their hero could not be really dead, he had only withdrawn from them for a while—gone on a pilgrimage to a far-off land, retired to some desert sanctuary, or fallen asleep with his warriors in some secret cavern,—and would yet return to rule "broad Britaine to the sea" and scatter

the Saxons to the winds of heaven.[1] "*Hic jacet Arturus, rex olim rexque futurus*" —Here lies Arthur, king of yore and king to be,—reported to have been found inscribed on his coffin at Glastonbury, represented, it is certain, the sacred belief of his people. That belief was common to all the relics of the Cymric race, from Strathclyde to Cornwall, and the shores of Armorica, and was preserved not least faithfully in that Northern land, which, according to all early authority, had witnessed alike Arthur's most splendid achievements and his death. The belief in the "kyd conqueror" yet to come must have cheered the Cumbrian Britons during the long struggle which ended in their incorporation with the Scottish monarchy, and fusion into the mingled stock which produced the later Scottish nation. Even after that fusion, and the loss of their ancient tongue, the loss even of all memory of the actual events to which these expectations and beliefs and dreams of the "good time coming" originally referred, the dreams and prophetic aspirations themselves survived, as dim mysterious legends of the future, foreboding great national crises, perils, and deliverances. Hence the legends of "a bastard in wedlock born, who should come out of the west," "a chieftain unchosen that shall choose for himself, and ride through the realm and Roy shall be called," "a chiftane stable as a stone, stedfast as the christull, firme as the adamant, true as the steele, immaculate as the sun, without all treason," whose "scutifers shal skail all the faire South, fra Dunbertane to Dover, and deil al the lands—he shall be kid conqueror, for he is kinde lord, of al Bretaine that bounds to the broad sea—" against whom in vain

> the Saxonys shall chose them a Lord
> That shall make them greatly to fall vnder.
> The ded man shall rise: and make them accord
> And this is much wonder and slight,
> That he that was dead and buried in sight
> Shall rise again and live in the land;—

---

[1] A similar belief was cherished by the Britons as to Cadwaladyr, son of Cadwallawn, who, a century and a half after Arthur, "waged, in conjunction with Penda, a successful war against the Angles of Northumbria. For one year he had actually been in possession of that kingdom, and his successful career of upwards of twenty years roused the courage and hopes of the Cymry to the highest." When Cadwaladyr died in the pestilence of 664, his countrymen could not realize that he was gone; "the death was denied, and he was said to have retired to Armorica, whence the Cymry looked for him to return, and re-establish their supremacy over the Angles."—Skene: The Four Welsh Books, vol. I, p. 75. It is interesting to see that this British legend also had been preserved in the north. "The prophecy of Merlin," afterwards quoted, has

> When the Calualider of Cornwall is called
> And the Wolfe out of Wales is wencust for ay.

who should conquer "Gyane, Gaskone, and Bretane the blyth," and

> turne into Tuskane but trety or true,
> And busk him ouer the mountaines on mid winter euen,
> And then goe to Rome and rug downe the walles,
> And ouer all the region Roy shall be holden ;

who should ride with pride over England and Scotland, and overthrow all false laws, and establish righteousness, till

> "bothe the londes breton shal be ;"

who should finally, like a true Christian knight, die in the Holy Land—

> For euerie man on molde must de—
> But end he shall in the land of Christ
> And in the valle of Josaphat buried shall be.

The resemblance of many of these expressions, and actual identity of many of the epithets, with those to be found in the old Northern "Morte Arthur," and other kindred works, is very notable.

10. During the wars between England and Scotland, under the three Edwards, and after, down even to the reign of Henry VIII, these scraps of old traditional prophecy were eagerly called to mind, and their dim light anxiously sought for in each successive crisis, the English, as we may suppose, dwelling specially on any passages which brought the "kyd conqueror" out of the south, or spoke of his ruling from "Cornwall to Caithness all Britain the broad," the Scots finding encouragement in the promise that he should finally extirpate the "Saxons," a name which, from its being used by their Celtic fellow-subjects as equivalent to "English" in a linguistic or ethnological sense, the Lowlanders now adopted as equivalent to "English" in the political sense. Strictly speaking, they also were "Sasunnach," or Saxon, to the Celts; but the effect of the struggle with England was to make them disclaim all "Saxon" connexion, and to use the term only of their enemies of England. Prior to the death of Alexander III, Scotland had enjoyed peace and tranquillity for many generations, and no wonder that the sudden outburst of calamity, with which the country was then assailed, stirred deeply the minds of the people, and led them to anticipate that the mighty overturnings, which were the mysterious burden of these ancient saws, were at length at hand.

Is it too much to suppose that Thomas of Erceldoune may, from his literary tastes, have been a repository of such traditional rhymes, and himself have countenanced the application of their mysterious indications to the circumstances of his country, and thus to some extent at least given currency to the idea of his own prophetic powers? It is certain at least that many of these ancient fragments were mixed up with the prophecies attributed to him, even as fragments of the latter were from time incorporated in, and blended with, later "prophecies" or prophetic compilations, which continued to be supplied whenever the demand arose, down to the union of the Kingdoms, and to be reverenced and consulted even as late as the Jacobite risings in the '15, and the '45. In these the name of Thomas Rymour is associated with those of Merlin, Bede, Gildas, and others; and collections of this mystic literature, such as the Sloane MS. 2578, and Lansdowne 762 in the British Museum, from which two of the following texts are printed, and Rawlinson C. 813 in the Bodleian, already existed in the fifteenth and sixteenth centuries when Sir David Lyndesay entertained the boyhood of James V with

The prophisies of Rymour, Beid, and Marlyng,

and the author of the "Complaynt of Scotland" in 1529 found it necessary to warn his countrymen against "diuerse prophane prophesies of merlyne, and vther ald corruptit vaticinaris, the quhilkis hes affermit in there rusty ryme, that scotland and ingland sal be vndir ane prince," to which "the inglismen gifis ferme credit." Merlin, whose name takes us back to the Arthur period itself, was evidently the oldest of these "vaticinaris," and at one time the most venerated, but in Scotland the fame of Thomas Rymour gradually outshone that of all his rivals, so that his pretended sayings were interpolated, and even his authority quoted, to give greater authority to theirs. This is well seen in a collection of these occult compositions printed in Edinburgh in 1603, and since then constantly reprinted down to the beginning of the present century, some of the contents of which must have been written as early as the reign of the Scottish James I (died 1437), while of others, MS. copies are in existence belonging to the same century.

11. The oldest printed edition yet discovered bears the following title: "The Whole prophecie of Scotland, England, and some part of France and Denmark, prophesied bee meruellous Merling, Beid, Bertlington, Thomas Rymour, Waldhaue, Eltraine, Banester, and Sibbilla, all according in one. Containing many strange and meruelous things. Printed by Robert Waldegraue, Printer to the King's most Excellent Maiestie. Anno 1603." To the goodly fellowship of Prophets here exhibited the later editions add "Also Archbishop Usher's wonderful prophecies."

As several of the pieces in this collection quote Thomas by name, and illustrate the subject of this volume, it seems desirable to give some account of them. The first piece is, like all the older ones, in alliterative verse, and begins, without any title:—

"THE WHOLE PROPHECIES OF SCOTLAND."—MERLIN.

Merling saies in his booke, who will reade right,
Althoght his sayings be vncouth, they shalbe
    true found
In the vij. chap. reade who so will

One thousand and more after Christes birth
When the Calualider of Cornwall is called
And the Wolfe out of Wailes is win cust for ay
Then many ferlie shall fall & many folke die.

As to the long-expected return of Calualider, or Cadwaladyr, see p. xxviii, note. This article really consists of three distinct compositions, of which the first predicts that a "Freik fostered farre in the South" shall return to the "kyth that he come from" with much wealth and worship, on whose arrival in Albanie many shall laugh; but his severity will soon give others cause to weep:

At his owne kinde bloode then shall he begin
Choose of the cheifest and chop of there heads,
Some haled on sleddes, and hanged on hie
Some put in prison & much pain shal byde.
In the month of Arrane an selcouth shal fall,

Two bloodie harts shall be taken with a false
    traine,
And derflie dung downe without any dome.
Ireland, Orknay, and other lands manie
For the deth of those two great dule shall
    make—

in which we see a description of the return of James I. from his detention in England, and his severity against the family of his uncle who had prolonged his captivity. The latter part of this passage was a century later quoted in connexion with the execution of the Regent Morton. "When that nobleman was committed to the charge of his accuser, captain James Stewart, newly created Earl of Arran, to be conducted to his trial at Edinburgh, Spottiswoode says that he asked 'Who was earl of Arran?' and being answered that Captain James was himself the man, after a short pause, he said, 'And is it so? I know then what I may look for!' meaning, as was thought that the old prophecy of the Falling of the heart (the cognizance of Morton) by the mouth of Arran should then be fulfilled. Whether this was his mind or not, it is not known; but some spared not, at the time when the Hamiltons were banished, in which business he was held too earnest, to say that he stood in fear of that prediction, and went that course only to disappoint it. But if it was so, he did find himself now deluded; for he fell by the mouth of another Arran than he imagined."—*Spottiswoode*, 313. In all ages, it would appear, it has been orthodox to wrest a verse of prophecy from its context and circumstances, and find a fulfilment for it in spite of these.

    The second and third sections of this piece are found in a much older form in the Cambridge University Library MS., Kk. i. 5, whence they were printed for the E. E. T. S. by Rev. J. R. Lumby in 1870. (Bernardus de cura rei familiaris; with some Early Scottish Prophecies, &c. p. 18.) This MS. is late fifteenth century, but the character of the language shows it to be a copy of one belonging to the first half of that century. The order of the two divisions is here reversed, the *first* part of the poem in the Cambridge MS., lines 1—72 of the E. E. T. S. edition being the *third* in the edition of 1603, and following lines 73—139, which forms the second part in the Edinburgh prophecy. This second part quotes a figure found also in "Thomas of Ersseldoune," and recurring in almost all the prophecies, which thus appears in the older copy (line 103 of Mr Lumby's copy).

> In his fayre forest sall ane ern bygye,
> And mony on sall tyne *th*ar lyff in the mene tyme;
> They sall founde to the felde, and *th*en fersly fyght,
> Apone A brode mure *þ*ar sall A battell be,
> Be-syde a stob crose of stane *th*at stand*is* on A mure:
> It sall be cou*e*ret wyth corsis all of a kyth,
> That the craw sall nocht ken whar the cross standis.

Compare lines 567—576 of Thomas; both are evidently borrowed from some traditional prophecy:—

A Raven shall comme ouer the moore,	Bot wiete wele, Thomas, he sall find nane.
And after him a Crowe shalle flee,	He sall lyghte, whare the crose solde bee
To seeke the moore, without(en) rest	And holde his nebbe vp to the skye;
After a crosse is made of stane	And drynke of gentill blode and free;
Ouer hill & dale, bothe easte & weste;	Thane ladys waylowaye sall crye.

This section does not quote or name Thomas; it ends with a reference to the legend of "wily Vivien."

> For bed*is* buke haue I seyn, & banysters[1] als;
> And m*e*rwelus merlyn*e* is wastede away
> Wyth A wyked*e* womane—woo mycht sho bee !—
> Scho has closede him in a cragge of cornwales coste.

The third part is in rhyme, with much alliteration, and begins—

Qwhen the koke in the northe halows his nest,	Then *th*e mone shall Ryse in the northwest
And buskys his birdys and bunnys to flee,	In A clowde als blak as the bill of A crawe;
Th*a*n shall fortune his frende *th*e ʒatt*is* vp-caste,	Then shall the lyonne be lousse, the baldest & best
And Rychte shall haue his Free entree;	That euer was in brattane sen in Arthuris daye.

It was one of the most popular prophecies of the fifteenth and sixteenth centuries, and besides forming, as already mentioned, the first half of Mr Lumby's "Ancient Scottish prophecy" from the Cambridge Kk. MS., it occurs in two of the MSS. that contain "Thomas of Erceldoune"—viz. in Lansdowne 762, fol. 65, with the title "Brydlington," and twice over in Sloane 2578 (leaves 15 *b* and 100 *b*). It names Thomas's prophecy as an authority, and mentions several of the mysterious episodes of the third fytte of our romance; thus :—

[1] "William Banister, a writer of the reign of Edward III. The *Prophecies of Banister of England* are not uncommon among MSS."—*Warton*. Among the contents of Rawl. C. 813 is "*Pars visionis Domini Willielmi Banistre, milytis*" (leaf 142 *b*).

"THE WHOLE PROPHECIES OF SCOTLAND."—DEDE.

> At Sandyfurde, for-suthe, in the south syde,
> A pruude prunce in the prese lordly sall lythe,
> Wyth balde bernes in bushment t*h*e batell sall mete ;
> T*h*ar sall profecy proffe t*h*at thomas of tellys, &c.
>
> Betuix Setone and t*h*e See sorow sall be wrought.
>
> T*h*en the lyonne wytht t*h*e lyonisses efter t*h*at sall Reigne ;
> T*h*us bretlington*e* buk*is* and ba*n*estre us tellis,
> Merlyne and mony moo t*h*at men*e* of may men*e*,
> And t*h*e exposit*o*ris Wigythtoun*e* & thomas wytht-all tell*is*.

In the printed edition of 1603 the two last lines run :—

> Merling & many more that with meruels melles
> and also Thomas Rymour in his tales telles.

What follows is also reproduced in many later prophecies :—

Sone at t*h*e Saxonis shall chese þame a lorde,	He that is dede ande beryde in syght
And full sone bryng hyme at vnd*er*,	Sall Ryse ayane, and lyffe in lande,
A dede ma*n* sall make [thame] A-corde	In comforte of A yhong knyght
And t*h*at sall be full mekyl wond*er*.	T*h*at fortoune has schose to be hir husbande.

The "prophecie of Beid," the second in the collection, appeals to Thomas for confirmation, and mentions Sandeford, as in l. 624 of our Romance :—

> Who so trusts not this tale, nor the tearme knowes,
> Let him on Merling meane, and his merrie words,
> And true Thomas tolde in his time after
> At Sandeford shall be seen example of their deeds.

Bede died five hundred and fifty years before True Thomas ; but clearly the support of the latter was too valuable to be sacrificed to a trifling question of dates !

His prophecy is specially directed to Berwick-on-Tweed, formerly the first of the four great burghs of Scotland, but now, alas ! in the grip of the English :

> Though thou be subiect to the Saxons, sorrow thou not,
> Thou shall be loosed at the last, belieue thou in Christ !

The year MCCCCLXXX is indicated by a method of which many imitations occur after, for the prophets had on the whole but little original genius, and when one of them started game, however poor, the rest all followed in the chase till it was done to death :—

> Who so doubts of this dead or denyes heereon,
> I doe them well for to know, the dait is deuised,
> Take the formest of midleird, & marke by the selfe   [M]
> With foure crescentes, closed together,   [CCCC]
> Then of the Lyon the longest see thou choose   [L]
> Loose not the Lyones, let her lye still,
> If thou castes through care, the course of the heauen,
> take Sanctandrois Crose thrise   [XXX]
> Keep well these teachments as Clarkes hath tolde
> thus beginnes the dait, deeme as thou likes,
> thou shall not ceis in that seit assumed in the text.

ERCILDOUN.

The year 1480 was that in which James III allowed himself to be enticed by the King of France into breaking the truce with Edward IV, as a result of which Berwick was captured by the English in 1482, and in spite of the prophecy, which was no doubt composed or compiled soon after, was never again recovered by Scotland. As to the influence which pretended prophecies had upon the conduct of the king at this very time, see Tytler's History of Scotland, p. 214. Nor was the belief in such occult agencies less powerful in England: see Greene's History of the English People, p. 268.

"The prophecie of Merlyne," which follows, after 16 lines of alliterate rhyme, beginning—

It is to fal when they it finde	The Beare his musal shal vpbinde,
that fel on face is faine to flee	And neuer after bund shal be
That commed are of strodlings strinde,	Away the other shal waxe with winde
Waxing through the worke of winde	And as they come so shall they flee—

introduces an ancient alliterative poem of marked Arthurian cast, which I have reprinted in my Introduction to the "Complaynt of Scotland," p. xlvi. From its contents, I am inclined to think that it may have been compiled shortly after the death of Alexander III, and I think the description of the "kid conqueror" and "kind lord of all Bretaine that bounds to the broad See," is clearly derived from obscure legends of the expected return of Arthur.

"The prophecie of Bertlington"—the Brydlyngton,[1] to whom the Lansdowne MS. attributes the "Cok in the North" prophecy—is a medley of older fragments of various ages, some alliterative, some in rhyme, some in both, and some in neither, ingeniously adapted and fitted together, and interpolated with others here first met with, about the son of a French wife, a descendant of Bruce within the ninth degree, who should unite England and Scotland in one kingdom. This, which became in the sequel by far the most famous of all the prophecies, was skilfully analyzed by Lord Hailes in his "Remarks on the History of Scotland" (Edin., 1773), and shown to have been intended originally for John, Duke of Albany, son of Alexander, brother of James III and his French wife, the daughter of the Count of Boulogne, who came to Scotland, after the death of James IV in the Battle of Flodden, and from whose regency great things were hoped. Lord Hailes, however, has inadvertently accused the author of inventing many things, which he really found in prophecies of the preceding century, and transferred, as they were still

---

[1] "John Bridlington, an Augustine Canon of Bridlington in Yorkshire, who wrote 3 books of '*carmina vaticinalia*,' in which he pretends to foretell many accidents that should happen to England. MSS. Digby, Bibl. Bodl. 89 and 186. He died, aged 60, in 1379, and was canonized."—*Warton.*

unfulfilled, to his own prediction, honestly believing, no doubt, that they were now to be accomplished. Such were the prediction that Albany should land in the Forth (which he did not), and the "thrice three" years after '13, given him for the performance of his doughty deeds (which he utterly failed to do). He starts with alliterative verse :—

> When the Ruby is raised, rest is there none,
> But much rancour shal rise in River & plane.
> Throw a tretie of a true,[1] a trayne shal be made,
> That Scotland shal rew, and Ingland for ever,
> For the which Gladsmoore, & Gouan mure gapes thereafter.

Then, an adaptation of some lines in the prophecy of Merlin introduces the new prediction :—

Betwixt Temptallon & the Basse
thou shall see a right faire sight,
Of barges & bellingars, and many broad saile,
With iij Libertes and the flourdelice hie vpon hight
And so the dreadful Dragon shall rise from his den
And from the deepe doughtelie shall draw to the height.
Of Bruce's left side shall spring out a leif,
As neere as the ninth degree,
And shall be flemed of faire Scotland
In France farre beyond the see;

And then shall come againe riding
With eyes that men may see,
At Aberladie he shall light
With hempen halters & hors of tree ;
On Gosforde greene it shall be seene,
On Gladsmoore shall the battle be.
Now Albanie thou make the boun,
At his bidding he thou prompt, [? yare]
He shal deile both towre and towne,
His guiftes shal stand for euer more.
[? mare]
Then boldly boun tho thereafter.

The original of this is in the "Ancient Scottish Prophecy," No. 1 in E. E. T. S., No. 42, edited by Mr Lumby, already referred to :—

> Fra bambrwgh to the basse on the brayde See,
> And fra farnelande to the fyrth salbe a fayr syght
> O barges and ballungerys, and mony brod sayle :
> and the lybberte with the flurdowlyss sall fayr ther apon.
> Thar sal A huntter in bycht come fra the Southe.
> Wyth mony Reohis on Raw Rewleyd full Ryght.

Then the stob-cross and the crow, the dead man rising, and Gladsmoor, as before :—

Upon a broad moore a battle shal be,
 Beside a stob crose of stone,
Which in the Moore stands hie,
It shal be clearly cled ouer with corps of knights,
That the crow may not find where the crose stoode,
Many wife shal weepe, and Sice shall vnder,
the ded shal rise, and that shal be wonder,

And rax him rudely in his shire shield,
For the great comfort of a new King.
Now hye the powok with thy proud showes,
Take thy part of the pelfe when the pack opens.
It shall not be Gladsmoore by the sey
It shall be Gladsmoore where euer it be
And the little lowne that shall be
Is betuixt the Lowmond and the sea.

---

[1] *True, trew*, the proper singular of *trewis, trewes, truce,* now treated in English as a singular ; Fr. *trève*, pl. *trèves.*

Then,—after much alliterative matter about a hound out of the south, an Egle out of the north, a Ghost out of the west, and the bastard in wedlock born, as in Thomas, to do doughty deeds, and bring all to peace again,—comes a clearer delineation of Albany, several quotations from Thomas and Merlin, and appeals to them and Bede for confirmation, ending appropriately with an Arthur bit to clench all :—

> How euer it happen for to fall,
> The Lyon shal be Lord of all.
> The French wife shal beare the sonne,
>   Shal welde al Bretane to the sea,
> And from the Bruce's blood shall come.
>   As near as the ninth degree.
> Meruelous Merling that many men of tells,
> And Thomas sayings comes all at once
> Thogh their sayings be selcouth, they shal be suith found.
>   And there shal all our glading be,
>   The Crowe shal sit upon a stone
>   And drink the gentle blood as free
>   Take of the ribes, and beare to her birdes,
>   As God hath said, so must it be,
>   Then shal Ladies laddes wed,
>   And brooke Castles, and Towers hie.
> Bede hath breued in his booke, and Banister also,
> Meruelous Merling, and al accordes in one,
> Thomas the trew, that neuer spake false
> Consents to their saying, & the same terme hath taken,
> Yet shall there come a keene Knight ouer the salt sea,
>   A keene man of courage, and bolde man of armes,
>   A Duke's son doubled, a born man in France,
>   That shal our mirthes amend, and mend all our harmes,
> After the date of our Lord 1513, & thrise three there after,
> Which shal brooke al the braid Ile to him selfe,
> Betwixt xiij. and thrise three the Threip shal be ended,
> the Saxons shal neuer recouer after,
> He shal be crowned in the kith, in the Castle of Douer,
> Which weares the golden garland of *Julius Cæsar*
> More worship shal he win, of greater worth,
> Than euer Arthur himselfe had in his daies,
> Many doughtie deedes shal he doe there after,
> Which shal be spoken of many dayes better.

I have treated this composition at greater length, because it illustrates very clearly the history of the prophecies generally, which were formed by compiling the unfulfilled portions of older predictions already current, and giving them point and application to events now in view or expectation. The prophecy of the French wife's son was a very striking one, and was fondly cherished by the nation. After miserably failing in its original application to Albany, it was served up again and again in new combinations all through the sixteenth century.

It reappears in the next piece in the collection of 1603, "the prophecie of Thomas Rymour" himself, which, from its nominal connexion with the subject of this work, I print entire in the Appendix. Although unconnected with the older poem, it bears a considerable resemblance to it in imagery. There is a vision of a lady on a "louely lee," whose mount and array is fully described, and several lines and couplets are actually taken from the older Thomas. It seems originally to have appeared shortly after the battle of Flodden, referring in lines 109—125 to the doubtful fate of James IV, and in

> The sternes three that day shall die,
> That beares the harts in silver sheen,—

to the death of the heir of the house of Douglas.

But it seems to have been interpolated to suit the time of the battle of Pinkie, which is cleverly identified with the "Spyncarde clow" in line 496 of our Romance. Now also the prediction of "the French Wife" and her son was added to the prophecy, being awkwardly interpolated into an inquiry as to the narrator's name, at the close. The origin of this prediction, forty years before, being now quite forgotten, it was accepted as a genuine deliverance of the Rymour himself, and continued to be held in the highest credit as his. It was applied to Queen Mary, as having been the wife of a French prince, by the poet Alexander Scott in his "New Year's Address to the Queen," and finally, when her son James VI actually succeeded to the English throne, the renown of Thomas as the accredited author of the prophecy filled all Britain, and excited attention even beyond the seas.

"The prophecie of Waldhaue,"[1] which comes next, is in fine alliterative measure, reminding one in its commencement of "Piers Plowman":—

> Upon Loudon Law a lone as I lay
> Looking to the Lennox, as me leif thought,
> The first morning of May, medicine to seeke
> For malice and melody that moued me sore.

While in this situation the author "hears a voice which bids him stand to his defence; he looks round, and beholds a flock of hares and foxes pursued over the mountains by a savage figure, to whom he can hardly give the name of a man. At the sight of Waldhave, the apparition leaves the object of his pursuit, and assaults him with a club. Waldhave defends himself with his sword, throws the savage to the earth, and refuses to let him rise till he swear, by the law and leid he lives

---

[1] St Waldhave or Waltheof, the most famous of the early abbots of Melrose (1148—1159), was grandson of the great Earl Waltheof, by his daughter Matilda, wife of Simon de St Liz, earl of Northampton, and afterwards of David I. His life, full of miraculous legends, was written by Josceline, a monk of Furness Abbey.

upon, 'to do him no harm.' This done, he permits him to rise, and marvels at his strange appearance :—

> He was formed like a freike, all his foure quaters
> And then his chin and his face haired so thick,
> With haire growing so grime, fearful to see.

He answers briefly to Waldhave's inquiry concerning his name and nature, that he 'drees his weird,' *i. e.* endures his fate, in that wood; and having hinted that questions as to his own state are offensive, he consents to tell 'the fate of these wars,' and concludes with—

> Go musing upon Merlin if thou wilt
> For I mean no more, man, at this time."

The whole of this scene is exactly similar to the meeting of Merlin and Kentigern as related by Fordun. Merlin's prophetic outpourings consist chiefly of short apostrophes to the principal towns and fortresses of Scotland; for example :—

> What Jangelst thou Jedburgh, thou Jages for nought,
> there shal a gyleful groom dwel thee within,
> The Towre that thou trustes in, as the truth is,
> Shal be traced with a trace, trow thou non other.

The next piece,—" Here followeth how Waldhaue did coniure this Spirit to shew much more of sindrie things to come, as foloweth,"—seems to be a later compilation, made up of pieces from the older prophecies in the name of Merlyne and true Thomas. The transactions of "the Lillie, the Lyon, and the Libbart," form its immediate burden, but it quotes the legend of the dead man rising again,—

> 'as meruelous Merling hath said of before.'

There are also many references to Thomas :—

> The first roote of this war shal rise in the north,
> That the Iles and Ireland shal mourne for them both,
> And the Saxons seased into Brutes landes.
> This is a true talking [takyn] that Thomas of tells,
> that the Hare shal hirpil on the hard stones,
> In hope of grace, but grace gets she non,
> Then Gladsmoore and Gouane shal gape there after.

The "token" here alluded to is in the very ancient prophecy of Thomas to the Countess of Dunbar, in the Harleian piece already quoted (p. xviii). The date fixed on seems to be 1485, and the prophecies of Merling, Bede, Thomas and Waldhave, are quoted as already existing :—

> When the Moone is dark in the first of the number,   [M]
> With foure Crescentes to eik forth the daies   [CCCC]
> And thrise ten is selcouth to see,   [XXX]
> With a L. to lose out the rest of the number,   [L]
> Syne let three and two Threipe as they will   [V]
> This is the true date that Merling of tells,
> And gaue to King Uter, Arthures father:
> And for to mene and muse with there merrie wordes,
> For once Brittaine shal be in a new knightes handes,
> Who so hap to byde shall see with his eies,
> As Merling and Waldhaue hath said of before,
> And true Thomas told in his time after,
> And Saint Beid in his booke breued the same,
> Mute on if ye may, for mister ye haue,
> I shal giue you a token that Thomas of tells,
> When a lad with a Ladie shal goe ouer the fields,
> And many faire thing weeping for dread,
> For loue of there dear freindes lies looking on hilles,
> That it shal be woe for to tel the teind of there sorrow.

The token of the "Lad," or man-servant and "the Lady," is found both in the old Harleian piece and our Romance; in the former, among the paradoxical things to happen before the war's end—

> When ryȝt and wrong ascenteþ to gedere,
> When laddes weddeþ levedies;

in the latter, l. 651, as a result of the carnage in the last battle at Sandyford,

> ladys shalle wed laddys ȝyng,
> when þer lordis ar ded away.

See the same figure repeated in the "Prophecie of Bertlington," already cited, p. xxxvi.

Waldhave's pieces are followed by "the Scottes prophesies in Latine," and "the prophesie of Gildas," seemingly directed against reformation in the church. Older still than Bede by three centuries, Gildas, to do homage to Thomas, still more daringly defies chronology:—

> Prepare thee, Edinburgh, & pack up thy packes,
> thou shalt be left void, be thou leif or loath,
> Because thou art variant, and flemed of thy faith
> throgh Envie & couetousnes that cumbered thee euer.
> True Thomas me told in a troublesome time
> In a haruest morning at Eldound hilles.

Passing "the prophecie of the English Chronicles," an extract from Higden, we come to "the prophecie of Sibylla and Eltraine," which appears to refer to the troubles during the regency of the Earl of Arran in the minority of Mary:—

xl   INTRODUCTION.

When the Goate with the gilden horne is   And the longest of the Lyon,   [L]
    chosen to the sea   Foure Crescentes under one Crowne   [CCCC]
The next yeare there after Gladsmoore shal be   With Saint Andrews Crose thrise,   [XXX]
Who so likes for to reade,   then threescore and thrise three,   [LX.IX]
Mereuelous Marling and Beid,   Take tent to Merling truly,
In this maner they shal proceede,   Then shal the warres ended be
Of thinges unknowne   And neuer againe rise.
    the truth now to record,   In that yeare there shal ring
And that from the date of our Lord,   A Duke and no crowned king.
Though that it be showne,   Because the prince shall be young
take a thousand in Calculation   [M]   and tender of yeares.

"The date above hinted at seems to be 1549, when the Regent, by means of some succours derived from France, was endeavouring to repair the consequence of the fatal Battle of Pinkie. Allusion is made to the supply given to the Moldiwarte [England] by the faiued hart [the Earl of Angus]. The regent is described by his bearing the antelope; large supplies are promised from France, and complete conquest promised to Scotland and her Allies."

>   Thus shall the warres ended be   And who so likes to looke,
>   Then peace and pollicie   The description of this booke,
>   Shall raigne in Albanie   This writes Beid who will looke.
>   Still without end,   And so doth make an end.

"Thus was the same hackneyed stratagem repeated, whenever the interest of the rulers appeared to stand in need of it."

Happily the need was not to last for ever. That Union, so long expected, and so oft deferred, of England and Scotland, under one sovereign was at length accomplished. To add lustre to it, the Queen of Sheba and the Cumæan Sibyl are rolled into one, and furnish the crowning "prophecy" of the book :—

"Heere followeth a prophesie pronounced by a Noble Queene and matron called Sibylla Regina Austre. That came to Solomon throgh the which she compiled foure bookes at the instance and request of the said King Solomon and others diuers, and the fourth booke was directed to a noble King called Baldwine, King of the broade Ile of Bretaine : of the which she maketh mention of two Noble princes and Emperours the which is called Leones of these two shall subdue and ouercome all earthlie princes, to their Diademe & Crowne, and also be glorified and crowned in the heauen among Saints. The firste of these two, Is, Magnus Constantinus that was Leprosus, the Son of S. Helene that found the Croce. The second is, the Sixte King of the name of Steward of Scotland the which is our most Noble King!"

12. It was in the year that James VI ascended the English throne that the prophecies, having at length been accomplished, were in greatest credit and renown. Robert Birrell, in his Diary, tells us that "at this time all the haill commons of Scotland that had red or understanding, wer daylie speiking and

exponing of Thomas Rymer hes prophesie, and of vther prophesies quhilk wer prophesied in auld tymes." John Colville, in his funeral oration on Queen Elizabeth, mentioned the "carmina" of Thomas the Rhymer, which as a boy he had heard quoted by *balathrones ceraulas*, and then looked upon as only subjects for laughter, but now recognized as serious and authentic; though, like his predecessor Wyntown, he was equally in doubt whether the inspiration of Thomas was Delphic or divine. Sir William Alexander, Earl of Stirling (1580—1640), in dedicating his "Monarchicke Tragedies" to King James, refers to the same belief:—

> Ere thou wast borne, and since, heaven thee endeeres,
> Held back as best to grace these last worst times;
> The world long'd for thy birth three hundreth yeeres,
> Since first fore-told wrapt in propheticke rimes.

Nor does his more celebrated contemporary, William Drummond of Hawthornden (1585—1649), neglect to offer to his royal patron the same flattering incense:—

> This is that king who should make right each wrong,
> Of whom the bards and mysticke Sibilles song,
> The man long promis'd, by whose glorious raigne
> This isle should yet her ancient name regaine,
> And more of Fortunate deserve the stile
> Than those where heauens with double summers smile.
>
> *Forth Feasting*, Edin., 1617.

Archbishop Spottiswood (1565—1639) was a firm believer in the authenticity of these compositions. In his "History of the Church of Scotland" he says, "the prophecies yet extant in Scottish *Rithmes*, whereupon he was commonly called Thomas the Rhymer, may justly be admired, having foretold, so many ages before, the union of England and Scotland, in the ninth degree of the Bruce's blood, with the succession of Bruce himself to the crown, being yet a child, and other diuers particulars which the event hath ratified and made good. . . . . . Whence or how he had this knowledge, can hardly be affirmed; but sure it is, that he did divine and answer truly of many things to come." (Spottiswoode Society's Ed., Vol. I, p. 93. Edin., 1851.)

13. These alleged revelations received considerable attention even during the Jacobite rising in 1745. It appears that the final accomplishment of the unfulfilled parts of Thomas's predictions was now expected. The Duke of Gordon, one of the friends of the Stuart cause, was recognized as the "Cock of the North;" and in the flush of triumph at their easy victory of Prestonpans, within six miles of the parish church of Gladsmuir in East-Lothian, and not a third of that distance

from Seaton, a village about a mile from the sea, on the line of the railway between Edinburgh and Dunbar, the Jacobites identified it with the great Armageddon of the prophecies, the "Battle of Gladsmoor" itself. Hamilton of Bangor sang—

As over Gladsmoor's blood-stained field, Scotia imperial goddess flew, Her lifted spear & radiant shield, Conspicuous blazing to the view;	With him I plough'd the stormy main, My breath inspir'd the auspicious gale; Reserv'd for Gladsmoor's glorious plain, Through dangers wing'd his daring sail.

* * * * *

while in other songs we find—

>Cope turn'd the chace, & left the place;
>The Lothians was the next land ready;
>And then he swure that at Gladsmuir
>He would disgrace the Highland plaidie.

The battle of Gladsmoor, it was a noble stour, And weel do we ken that our young prince wan; The gallant Lowland lads, when they saw the tartan plaids, Wheel 'round to the right, and away they ran.	For Master Johnnie Cope, being destitute of hope, Took horse for his life & left his men; In their arms he put no trust, for he knew it was just That the king should enjoy his own again.

It was no doubt in reference to the use thus made of them, that Lord Hailes, in his Remarks on the History of Scotland (Edin., 1773), thought it necessary to give a serious refutation of the alleged prophecies of Thomas the Rhymer; "for, let it be considered," he says, "that the name of Thomas the Rhymer is not forgotten in Scotland, nor his authority altogether slighted, even at this day. Within the memory of man, his prophecies, and the prophecies of other Scotch soothsayers, have not only been reprinted, but have been consulted with a weak, if not criminal curiosity. I mention no particulars; for I hold it ungenerous to reproach men with weaknesses of which they themselves are ashamed. The same superstitious credulity might again spring up. I flatter myself that my attempts to eradicate it will not prove altogether vain."

The "Whole Prophecies" continued to be printed as a chap-book down to the beginning of the present century, when few farm-houses in Scotland were without a copy of the mystic predictions of the Rhymer and his associates.

14. Nor was the name of Thomas of Erceldoune less known and reverenced in England than in Scotland. Exclusive of the fact that all the copies we have of the old romance and prophecies have come down to us at the hands of English transcribers, the English prophetic writings of the 15th and 16th centuries abound in appeals to his authority and quotations acknowledged and unacknowledged from the predictions attributed to him. The period in English History, when these

predictions were most in vogue, was that which intervened between the decline of the fortune of the House of Lancaster, about 1430, and the full establishment of the Tudors, and completion of the rupture with Rome under Henry VIII. The numerous battles during the Wars of the Roses, especially that of Barnet, the overthrow of the Yorkist cause at Bosworth, the appearance of Yorkist pretenders under Henry VII, the defeat of the Scots at Flodden, and the daring of Henry VIII in defying the pope and suppressing the religious orders, were all the theme of *soi-disant* prophetic rhymes. One of these, claiming to be a joint production of "*Venerabilis Bede, Marlionis, Thome Arslaydoun, et aliorum*" (the last being by far the most certain of the ingredients), and which is in all probability the actual "Prophisies of Rymour, Beid, and Marlyng," with which Sir David Lyndesay regaled the childish ears of James V, I have printed in Appendix II. In its commencement it is identical with the Scotch "Prophesie of Thomas Rymer," in Appendix I, and the two have evidently been expanded from the same original nucleus. It occurs both in the Lansdowne MS. of 1529, which supplies one of the copies of our romance, and in the Rawlinson MS. C. 813 at Oxford. Both texts, as will be seen, are transcripts of older ones.

The Sloane MS. 2578 also contains many kindred productions, one of which, concerned with the battles "between Seton and the Sea," at Gladsmoor, and at Sandeford, and other mysterious episodes of Fytt III of "Thomas of Ersseldowne," and giving to these an English application, is added in Appendix III; shorter "prophecies" of the same nature appear among the illustrative notes to Fytt III of the romance.

15. In Thomas's own locality of Tweedside, as well as elsewhere in Scotland, many traditional predictions ascribed to him have long been current. Several of these were recorded by Scott in "the Minstrelsy of the Scottish Border," others have since been given in the "History of the Berwickshire Naturalists' Club" and other local publications, and by Robert Chambers in his "Popular Rhymes of Scotland." (New Edition, 1870.) Among these, "the Rhymer" is said to have prophesied of the ancient family of Haig of Bemerside,—with an early member of which, Petrus de Haga, we have already seen him connected, and whose family motto, according to Nisbet, was "Tide what may,"

> Betide, betide, whate'er betide,
> Haig shall be Haig of Bemerside.

"The grandfather of the present (1802) proprietor of Bemerside had twelve daughters, before his lady brought him a male heir. The common people trembled for the credit of their favourite soothsayer. The late Mr Haig was at length born, and their belief in the prophecy confirmed beyond a shadow of doubt."—*Minstr. Scott. Bord.*, vol. iii. p. 209. Dr R. Chambers, in a note to this "prophecy" in "Popular Rhymes of Scotland," p. 297, says, "1867—The prophecy has come to a sad end, for the Haigs of Bemerside have died out." My local correspondents inform me that the condolence is premature, as Miss Sophia Haig, the 21st in uninterrupted line from Petrus de Haga, is still alive in Italy.

Sir Walter Scott continues, "Another memorable prophecy bore that the old Kirk at Kelso (fitted up in the ruins of the Abbey) should fall when at the fullest." At a very crowded sermon, about 30 years ago (1770), a piece of lime fell from the roof of the Church. The alarm for the fulfilment of the words of the seer became universal, and happy were they who were nearest the door of the doomed edifice. The church was in consequence deserted, and has never since had a chance of tumbling upon a full congregation.

"Another prediction, ascribed to the Rhymer, seems to have been founded on that sort of insight into futurity, possessed by most men of sound and combining judgment. It runs thus:—

> At Eldon tree if you shall be,
> A brigg ower Tweed you there may see.

The spot in question commands an extensive prospect of the course of the river; and it was easy to foresee that when the country should become in the least degree improved, a bridge would be somewhere thrown over the stream. In fact, you now see no less than three bridges from that elevated situation."

Others of these traditional predictions are recorded as:

> . Vengeance! vengeance! when & where?
> On the house of Coldingknow, now & ever mair!
>
> The burn o' breid, [Bannockburn]
> Sall rin fu reid.
>
> A horse sall gang on Carolside brae
> Till the red girth gaw his sides in twae.
>
> The hare sall kittle [litter] on my hearth stane
> And there will never be a laird Learmont again.

The three latter of these are evidently distorted echoes of passages in the old prophecies. The last of them, in the form "When hares kendles o the herston," is really a line of the old Cottonian prophecy describing the desolation to which Scotland was to be reduced before the end of the English War, but locally it has been adapted to the fate of Thomas's own roof-tree, and in this acceptation says Mr Currie, "I saw it, with my own eyes, fulfilled in 1839, as it may easily have been many times before. The rumour spread in Earlstoun that one of the Rhymer's most celebrated prophecies had been fulfilled, and I well remember running with all the rest of the town, to see the hare's nest; and sure enough there it was—two young hares in a nettle bush in the fire place!"

"One of the more terrible predictions of the Rhymer is as follows:—

> At Threeburn Grange, in an after day,
> There shall be a lang and bloody fray;
> Where a three thumbed wight by the reins shall hald
> Three kings' horse, baith stout and bauld,
> And the Three Burns three days will rin
> Wi' the blude o' the slain that fa' therein.

"Threeburn Grange (properly Grains) is a place a little above the press, Berwickshire, where three small rills meet, and form the water of Ale. 'Thirty years ago, this rhyme was very popular in the east end of Berwickshire; and about the time of the French Revolution, a person of the name of Douglas being born in Coldingham parish with an excrescence on one of his hands, which bore some resemblance to a third thumb, the superstitious believed that this was to be the identical 'three-thumbed wight' of the Rhymer, and nothing was looked for but a fearful accomplishment of the prophecy."[1]

"The following," says Dr R. Chambers, "is perhaps not ancient, but it expresses that gloomy fear of coming evil which marks so many of the rhymes attributed to Thomas:

> When the white ox comes to the corse,
> Every man may tak his horse.

Similar in spirit is:

> Atween Craik-cross and Eildon-tree,
> Is a' the safety there shall be,

varied in Galloway—

> A' the safety there shall be,
> Sall be atween Criffel and the sea.

"The first space is one of about thirty miles; the second much narrower. Sir Walter Scott relates that the first of these rhymes was often repeated in the Border Counties during the early years of the French revolutionary war, when the less enlightened class of people laboured under the most agonizing apprehensions of invasion. In the south of Scotland, this prophecy then obtained universal credence; and the tract of country alluded to was well surveyed, and considered by many wealthy persons, anxious to save their goods and lives, as the place to which they would probably fly for refuge 'in case of the French coming.'"

[1] *History of Berwickshire Naturalist's Club*, vol. i. p. 147.

Within my own memory a prophecy used to be quoted of a time when "men shall ride to the horses' reins in blude,—

> And if any safety there shal be
> 'Twill be 'tween Craig House & Eildon Tree,"

often varied, however, with "'tween Hawick & Eildon Tree." Craig House is a small estate, between Leader-foot and Smailholm, about a mile from Bemerside, and thus at a very short distance from Eildon. The oldest form of this couplet is found in the "Prophecy of Bertlington" of 1515, already quoted p. xxxv:

> And the little lowne [shelter] that shall be
> Is betuixt the Lowmond and the sea.

"A verse referring to the future improvement of the country may be taken as a curious specimen of foreseeing wisdom. Thomas had the sagacity to discover that the ground would be more generally cultivated at some future period than it was in his own time; but also knowing that population and luxury would increase in proportion, he was enabled to assure the posterity of the poor that their food would not consequently increase in quantity. His words were:

> The waters shall wax, the wood shall wene,
> Hill and moss shall be torn in;
> But the bannock will ne'er be braider."

"It is certain that many rhymes professedly by our hero were promulgated in *consequence* of particular events. Of this character is:

> There shall a stone wi' Leader come,
> That'll make a rich father, but a poor son;

an allusion to the supposed limited advantage of the process of liming. The Highlanders have also found, since the recent changes of tenantry in their country, that Thomas predicted that 'The teeth of the sheep shall lay the plough on the shelf.' I have been assured that the name of Thomas the Rhymer is as well known at this day among the common people in the Highlands, nay, even in the remoter of the Western Isles, as it is in Berwickshire. His notoriety in the sixteenth century is shown in a curious allusion in a witch-trial of that age—namely, that of Andro Man, which took place at Aberdeen in 1598. In his ditty, Andro is charged with having been assured in his boyhood by the Queen of Elfin, ' that thow suld knaw all things, and suld help and cuir all sort of seikness, except stane deid, and that thow suld be weill intertenit, but *wald seik thy meit or thow deit, a. Thomas Rymour did*' [that is, beg his bread]. Also: 'Thow affermis that the Quene of Elphen hes a grip of all the craft, but Christsondy [the devil] is the guidman, and hes all power vnder God, and that thow kennis sindrie deid men in thair cumpanie, and that *the kyng that deit in Flowdoun and Thomas Rymour is their.'*—*Spalding Club Miscellany*, i. 119—121.

"The common people at Banff and its neighbourhood preserve the following specimens of the more terrible class of the Rhymer's prophecies:

> At two full times, and three half times,
> Or three score years and ten,
> The ravens shall sit on the Stones o' St Brandon,
> And drink o' the blood o' the slain!

The Stones of St Brandon were standing erect a few years ago in an extensive level field about a mile to the westward of Banff, and immediately adjacent to the Brandon How, which forms the boundary of the town in that direction. The field is supposed to have been the scene of one of the early battles between the Scots and Danes, and fragments of weapons and bones of men have been dug from it.

"An Aberdeenshire tradition represents that the gates of Fyvie Castle had stood for seven years and a day *wall-wide*, waiting for the arrival of True Tammas, as he is called in that district. At length he suddenly appeared before the fair building, accompanied by a violent storm of wind and rain, which stripped the surrounding trees of their leaves, and shut the castle gates with a loud clash. But while the tempest was raging on all sides, it was observed that, close by the spot where Thomas stood, there was not wind enough to shake a pile of grass or move a hair of his beard. He denounced his wrath in the following lines:

> Fyvie, Fyvie, thou s' never thrive,
> As lang's there's in thee stanis three:
> There's ane intill the highest tower,
> There's ane intill the ladye's bower,
> There's ane aneath the water-ȝett,
> And thir three stanes ye s' never get.

The usual prose comment states that two of these stones have been found, but that the third, beneath the gate leading to the Ythan, or water-gate, has hitherto baffled all search.

"There are other curious traditionary notices of the Rhymer in Aberdeenshire; one thus introduced in a *View of the Diocese of Aberdeen* written about 1732: 'On Aiky Brae here [in Old Deer parish] are certain stones called the *Cummin's Craig*, where 'tis said one of the Cummins, Earls of Buchan, by a fall from his horse at hunting, dashed out his brains. The prediction goes that this earl (who lived under Alexander III.) had called Thomas the Rhymer by the name of Thomas the Lyar, to show how much he slighted his predictions, whereupon that famous fortune-teller denounced his impending fate in these words, which, 'tis added, were all literally fulfilled:

> Tho' Thomas the Lyar thou call'st me,
> A sooth tale I shall tell to thee:
> By Aiky side thy horse shall ride,
> He shall stumble and thou shalt fa',
> Thy neckbane shall break in twa,
> And dogs shall thy banes gnaw,
> And, maugre all thy kin and thee,
> Thy own belt thy bier shall be.'

"It is said that Thomas visited Inverugie, which in later times was a seat of the Marischal family, and there from a highstone poured forth a vaticination to the following effect:

> Inverugie by the sea,
> Lordless shall thy landis be;
> And underneath thy hearth-stane
> The tod shall bring her birdis hame.

This is introduced in the manuscript before quoted, at which time the prophecy might be said to be realized in the banishment and forfeiture of the late Earl Marischal for his share in the insurrection of 1715. The stone in which the seer sat was removed to build the church in 1763; but the field in which it lay is still called *Tammas's Stane*.

"One of Thomas's supposed prophecies referring to this district appears as a mere deceptive jingle:

> When Dee and Don shall run in one,
> And Tweed shall run in Tay,
> The bonny water o' Urie
> Shall bear the Bass away.

The Bass is a conical mount, of remarkable appearance, and about 40 feet high, rising from the bank of the Urie, in the angle formed by it at its junction with the Don. The rhyme appears in the manuscript collections of Sir James Balfour, which establishes for it an antiquity of fully two hundred years. It is very evident that the author, whoever he was, only meant to play off a trick upon simple imaginations, by setting one (assumed) impossibility against another.

"A native of Edinburgh, who in 1825 was seventy-two years of age, stated that when he was a boy, the following prophetic rhyme, ascribed to True Thomas, was in vogue:

> York was, London is, and Edinburgh will be
> The biggest o' the three.

In his early days, Edinburgh consisted only of what is now called the Old Town; and the New Town, though projected, was not then expected ever to reach the extent and splendour which it has since attained. Consequently, it can scarcely be said that the prophecy has been put in circulation after its fulfilment had become a matter of hope or imaginable possibility. It is to be remarked, however, that there is a similar rhyme popular in England. Stukely, in his *Itinerarium Curiosum*, after expatiating upon the original size and population of Lincoln, quotes as an old adage:

LOCAL TRADITION OF THOMAS'S DISAPPEARANCE.

> Lincoln *was*, London *is*, and York *shall be*
> The fairest city of the three.

"One of the rhymes most popular at Earlstoun referred to an old thorn-tree which stood near the village, and of which Thomas had said,

> This thorn-tree, as lang as it stands,
> Earlstoun shall possess a' her lands.

The lands originally belonging to the community of Earlstoun have been, in the course of time, alienated piecemeal, till there is scarcely an acre left. The thorn-tree fell during the night in a great storm which took place in the spring of 1814.

"The Rhymer is supposed to have attested the infallibility of his predictions by a couplet to the following effect:

> When the saut gaes abune the meal
> Believe nae mair o' Tammie's tale.

In plain English, that it is just as impossible for the price of the small quantity of salt used in the preparation of porridge to exceed the value of the larger quantity of meal required for the same purpose, as for his prophecies to become untrue." *Popular Rhymes of Scotland*, by Robert Chambers, LL.D. New Edition, 1870, pp. 211—224. (See some additional particulars after the *Notes*.)

There is said also to have been a popular tradition, how far independent of the written remains, one does not know—of the intercourse between Thomas and the Fairy Queen as related in the Ballad. "The popular tale bears, that Thomas was carried off at an early age to the Fairy Land, where he acquired all the knowledge which made him afterward so famous. After seven years' residence he was permitted to return to the earth, to enlighten and astonish his countrymen by his prophetic powers; still, however, remaining bound to return to his royal mistress, when she should intimate her pleasure. Accordingly, while Thomas was making merry with his friends in the Tower of Ercildoune, a person came running in, and told, with marks of fear and astonishment, that a hart and hind had left the neighbouring forest, and were composedly and slowly parading the street of the village. The prophet instantly arose, left his habitation, and followed the wonderful animals to the forest, whence he was never seen to return. According to the popular belief, he still 'drees his weird' in Fairy Land, and is one day expected to revisit earth. In the meanwhile his memory is held in most profound respect. The Eildon Tree, from beneath the shadow of which he delivered his prophecies, now no longer exists; but the spot is marked by a large stone called Eildon Tree Stone. A neighbouring rivulet takes the name of the Bogle Burn (Goblin Brook), from the

Rhymer's supernatural visitants."[1]—*Border Minstrelsy*, Vol. III, p. 209. Scott adds that "the veneration paid to the dwelling-place of Thomas even attached itself in some degree to a person, who, within the memory of man, chose to set up his residence in the ruins of Learmont's tower. The name of this man was Murray, a kind of herbalist; who, by dint of some knowledge in simples, the possession of a musical clock, an electrical machine, and a stuffed alligator, added to a supposed communication with Thomas the Rhymer, lived for many years in very good credit as a wizard." But Dr R. Chambers, in a note (Pop. Rhymes, p. 214), pronounces this account a strange distortion and mystification of the fact that a respectable and enlightened physician, Mr Patrick Murray, who "pursued various studies of a philosophical kind not common in Scotland during the eighteenth century," and is known as the author of some medical works, lived in the tower of Thomas of Ercildoun, then a comfortable mansion; and adds, "when we find a single age, and that the latest and most enlightened, so strangely distort and mystify the character of a philosophical country surgeon, can we doubt that five hundred years have played still stranger tricks with the history and character of Thomas the Rhymer?"

16. Eildon Tree, referred to in the Romance, and connected traditionally with Thomas's prophecies, stood on the declivity of the eastern of the three Eildon Hills, looking across the Tweed to Leader Water, Bemerside, Earlstoun, and other places connected with Thomas. Its site is believed to be indicated by the *Eildon Stone*, "a rugged boulder of whinstone" standing on the edge of the road from Melrose to St Boswell's, about a mile south-east from the former town, and on the ridge of a spur of the hill.[2] "The view from this point," says a correspondent, "is unsur-

[1] My friend, Mr Andrew Currie of Darnick, has sent me the following tradition of the disappearance of Thomas, which he took down 35 years ago from the mouth of "Rob Messer, a very intelligent matter-of-fact man, well versed in all traditionary lore about Earlston, and possessing a wonderful memory for a man of 85":—"Ye want to ken if ever aw heard how Tammas the Rymer disappeared?—Weel, aw can tell ye something aboot that, as aw had it frae ma graanfaither, an' nae doot he had it frae his fore-bears, for we're als auld a family in Yerlsten, —or raither Ercildoun, as it was cas'd i' thae days—we're als auld as the Learmonts. D'ye see thae auld waa's i' the front o' yeir ain shop? weel man, aw mind o' that bein' a gay an' subtantial hoose i' maa young days, an' Tammas the Rymer was last seen gaan' oot o' that hoose eae nicht afore the derknin', an' he set off up Leader for Lauder Cas'le; but he ne'er gat there—he never was sene againe. Aw've heard 'at he geade in there to get some deed signed or wutness 't, an' that he was carryan' money wi' him to some Lord or great man up there, 'at he was inimate wi'. But ma granfaither uist to say—an' nae doot he had it handit doon—that Leader was i' great fluid at the time, an' that Tammas the Rymer had been robbit an' murdert an' his body thrawn into the water, whulk micht take it to Berwick. An' that's likker-like than the Fairy story! Sae ye hae 'd, as aw had it, frae thaim 'at was afore us."

[2] Mr Currie has a verbal tradition that the tree stood not by the stone, but a quarter of a mile higher up the base of the hill, where he says "the site of it was pointed out to me thirty years ago by the late James Williamson of Newstead, and I believe I could still plant my stick

passed; on the north you have the vale of Leader almost up to Earlston, and Cowdenknowes with its 'Black Hill' rising abruptly from the bed of the stream; while downward to Tweed the undulating expanse of woody bank is so beautiful, that in the time of the 'bonny broom,' I am often tempted to bend my steps to the spot, and 'lie and watch the sight,' from a spot once 'underneath the Eildon Tree.' In the close vicinity is the 'Bogle Burn,' a stream which rises on the slope of the Eastern Eildon, and flows down a deep glen into the Tweed a little to the north of Newtown St Boswell's. From the Eildon Stone the road descends some 500 yards in a straight line to the bed of the burn, and rises at the same angle to the opposite bank in true Roman fashion. In all probability the name of Bogle Burn is derived, as Sir Walter Scott suggested, from the Rhymer's supernatural visitants."

About half a mile to the west of the Eildon Stone, and on the slope of the same hill, we find the "Huntlee bankis" of the old romance. The spot lies a little above the North British Railway, at the point where it is crossed by the road to St Boswell's already referred to, about a quarter of a mile after leaving Melrose Station. The field next the road and railway at this point (No. 2405 on the Ordinance Map) is called *Monks' Meadow;* and higher up the hill above this are two fields (Nos. 2548 and 2408) which have preserved the name of *Huntlie Brae,* and to which in old John Bower's time tradition still pointed as the scene of Thomas's vision of the "Ladye." West of these lie the site of *Gallows Hill* and *Bower's Brae,* and a long narrow strip to the east, ascending from the road to the top of Huntlie Brae, is called the *Corse Rig,* and still burdened in its charter with an annual payment for the maintenance of the Town Cross of Melrose. From the small plantation at the head of the Corse Rig, at the east end of Huntlie Brae, a magnificent view is afforded of the surrounding locality, and in particular the eye has a full sweep along the road and hill side as far as the Eildon Stone and site of the ancient Tree.[1]

on the spot." But the general voice of tradition is, and apparently has been, that the tree stood by the stone itself. "This spot," says T. B. Gray, Esq., in a note to me on the subject, "is in fact the point of vantage whence the most extensive view in the neighbourhood is commanded. Higher up the hill, or lower down the hill, or farther back on the road, Melrose and all its beauties are lost, and Huntlee Brae itself shut out from sight; while from the stone, Bemerside, Smailholm Tower, Gladswood, Drygrange, Cowdenknowes, the Black Hill, Earlstoun (almost), Leader-foot and bridge, Galtonside, Galawater, and a long stream of silvery Tweed, start at once upon the view." Mr Gray also thinks that the spot was probably in olden times the site of a cross for the special devotion of pilgrims catching their first glimpse of St Mary's shrine from the east. There was a similar one on the west, at a point called to this day "High Cross," between Melrose and Darnick; and according to old Milne, in 1743, "a little to the southwest of Dingleton was a famous Cross, yet called the Crosshillhead, but anciently the Halesing of St Wada; for those that came from the South had first a view of the church here, and of the Tomb of St Waldhaue, and bowed and said their *Ave.*"

[1] For the satisfactory identification of "Huntley Bankes" I am indebted entirely to

Sir Walter Scott seems at first to have looked for "Huntlee bankis" in the vicinity of the Eildon Tree, but, as is well known, he afterwards affected to identify the name with a wild and picturesque ravine, then called "Dick's Cleuch," which runs by the base of the Western Eildon, two or three miles to the west of this, which he, "with his peculiar enthusiasm, purchased at probably fifty per cent. above its real value, in order to include it in his estate of Abbotsford." By skilfully planting the steep and often rugged sides, and leading a romantic pathway up the margin of the burn, which with many a cascade flows through it, he made "the Rhymer's Glen," as he christened it, a place of beauty to be visited by every tourist, albeit its real associations are with the modern "wizard of Tweedside," and not with the ancient seer of legend and tradition. The locality in fact possesses no view, and is not even in sight of the Eildon Tree, distant more than two miles on the other side of the mountain mass of the Eildons, and it may be more than suspected that the desire of bringing some of the romance of the old story to his own estate, was Sir Walter Scott's reason for naming it "the Rhymer's Glen;" although he had this "hair to mak a tether o'," that the name of "Huntley Wood" appears to have been borne by a small plantation which once stood on the hill side above Chiefswood, and so not far from his glen, and his "Huntley-burn."

17. Scott, in the "Border Minstrelsy," and Robert Jamieson, in his "popular Ballads and Songs," Edinburgh, 1806, give what professes to be a traditional ballad of "Thomas and the Queen of Elfland," considered by the former to be a genuine descendant of the old romance modified by oral tradition. "It will afford great

T. B. Gray, Esq., already mentioned, who by indefatigable perseverance has succeeded in seizing the last vestiges of an expiring tradition as to the site. Mr Gray first called my attention to the following passage in old John Bower's Account of Melrose:—"At the foot of the Eildon Hills, above Melrose, is a place called *Huntlie Brae*, where Thomas the Rhymer and the Queen of the Fairies frequently met, according to tradition. A little to the east of this is the *trysting-tree stone*." Mr Gray expressed his opinion that the place referred to must be the field or bank, adjoining what is called the Gallows Hill, but he was as yet unable to find the faintest tradition of the place having borne this name. Subsequently however he writes (8th Nov. 1875): "I am happy to say that I have identified *Huntlie-Brae* to my entire satisfaction, and in such a situation as to give a vivid tone of reality to the old Romance. Through the kindness of James Curle, Esq., of Messrs Curles & Erskines, solicitors here, I have been able to confirm old Bower's statement that there was such a place, and the senior partner of the firm assures me that he recollects quite well his father (an old man when he died) pointing out the very field my suspicions had fallen upon, as 'Huntlie-Brae.' By the Parish Ordinance Map Mr Curle was able to put his finger on the identical spot as fields 2408 and 2584. And now I am pleased to add that the locality is in entire harmony with the poetical reference; for if 'True Thomas' lay on Huntlie Brae or Bank, he would have a clear and distinct view of the 'ladye gaye' all the way along the road, or the hill side, to the Eildon Stone, a distance of fully half a mile. I had the pleasure on Friday afternoon to lead our friend Mr Currie over the spot, and he agrees with me as to the entire harmony between the site and the description in the ballad."

amusement," he says, " to those who would study the nature of traditional poetry, and the changes effected by oral tradition, to compare the ancient romance with the ballad. The same incidents are narrated, even the expression is often the same; yet the poems are as different in appearance, as if the older tale had been regularly and systematically modernized by a poet of the present day." That the "as if" in the last sentence might safely be left out, and that the "traditional ballad" never grew " by oral tradition " out of the older, is clear enough to me, even without the additional particulars that the source of the verses was that Mt Athos of antique ballads, Mrs Brown's MS. Jamieson only says his copy was "procured from Scotland." The two copies differ in extent and expressions. To complete our Thomas literature they are here added in parallel columns.[1]

THOMAS THE RHYMER.

JAMIESON.		SCOTT.
True Thomas lay o'er yonder bank, And he beheld a lady gay, A lady that was brisk and bold, Come riding o'er the fernie brae.	4	True Thomas lay on Huntlie bank; A ferlie he spied wi' his ee; And there he saw a ladye bright, Come riding down by the Eildon tree.
Her skirt was of the grass-green silk, Her mantle of the velvet fine; At ilka tate o' her horse's mane Hung fifty siller bells and nine.	8	Her shirt was o' the grass-green silk, Her mantle o' the velvet fyne; At ilka tett of her horse's mane, Hung fifty siller bells and nine.

[1] Jamieson's copy apparently came from the same source as Scott's; see the following extract from a letter of Anderson, of the "*British Poets*," to Bishop Percy, given by Nicholl: " Mr Jamieson visited Mrs Brown on his return here from Aberdeen, and obtained from her recollection five or six ballads and a fragment...... The greatest part of them is unknown to the oldest persons in this country. I accompanied Mr Jamieson to my friend [Walter] Scott's house in the country, for the sake of bringing the collectors to a good understanding. I then took on me to hint my suspicion of modern manufacture, *in which Scott had secretly anticipated me*. Mrs Brown is fond of ballad poetry, writes verses, and reads everything in the marvellous way. Yet her character places her above the suspicion of literary imposture; but it is wonderful how she should happen to be the depository of so many curious and valuable ballads." See Nicholl's *Illustrations of Literature*, p. 89.
Elsewhere in the same letter we read : " It is remarkable that Mrs Brown never saw any of the ballads she has transmitted here, either in print or manuscript, but learned them all when a child by hearing them sung by her mother and an old maid-servant who had been long in the family, and does not recollect to have heard any of them either sung or said by any one but herself since she was about ten years of age. She kept them as a little hoard of solitary entertainment, till, a few years ago, she wrote down as many as she could recollect, to oblige the late Mr W. Tytler, and again very lately wrote down nine more to oblige his son, the professor."

JAMIESON.		SCOTT.	
True Thomas he took off his hat,		True Thomas, he pull'd aff his cap,	
And bow'd him low down till his knee;		And louted low down to the knee,	
"All hail, thou mighty queen of heaven!		"All hail, thou mighty queen of heaven!	
For your like on earth I never did see!"	12	For thy peer on earth I never did see."-	
"O no, O no, True Thomas," she says,		"O no, O no, Thomas," she said,	
"That name does not belong to me;		"That name does not belang to me;	
I am but the queen of fair Elfland,		I am but the queen of fair Elfland,	
And I am come here to visit thee.	16	That am hither come to visit thee.	
		"Harp and carp, Thomas," she said;	
		"Harp and carp along wi' me;	
		And if ye dare to kiss my lips,	
		Sure of your bodie I will be."—	20
		"Betide me weal, betide me woe,	
		That weird shall never daunton me"—	
		Syne he has kissed her rosy lips,	
		All underneath the Eildon tree.	24
"But ye maun go wi' me now, Thomas,		"Now ye maun go wi' me," she said;	
True Thomas, ye maun go wi' me;		"True Thomas, ye maun go wi' me;	
For ye maun serve me seven years,	27	And ye maun serve me seven years,	
Through weal and wae, as may chance to be."		Thro' weal or woe as may chance to be."	
She turned about her milk-white steed,		She's mounted on her milk-white steed;	
And took true Thomas up behind,		She's ta'en True Thomas up behind:	
And ay whene'er her bridle rang,		And aye, whene'er her bridle rung,	
Her steed flew swifter than the wind.	32	The steed flew swifter than the wind.	
		O they rode on, and further on;	
		The steed ga'ed swifter than the wind;	
		Until they reached a desert wide,	
		And living land was left behind.	36
O they rade on, and farther on,			
Until they came to a garden green;			
"Light down, light down, ye lady free,			
Some o' that fruit let me pull to thee."	40		
"O no, O no, True Thomas," she says,			
"That fruit maun no be touch'd by thee;			
For a' the plagues that are in Hell			
Light on the fruit o' this countrie.	44		
"But I have a laef here in my lap,			
Likewise a bottle of clarry wine;			
And now, ere we go farther on,			
We'll rest a while, and ye may dine."	48		
When he had eaten and drank his fill,		"Light down, light down, now, true Thomas,	
The lady said, "ere we climb yon hill,		And lean your head upon my knee;	
Lay your head upon my knee,		Abide and rest a little space,	
And I will show you ferlies three.	52	And I will show you ferlies three.	

JAMIESON.

'O see you not yon narrow road,
  So thick beset with thorns and briers?—
That is the path of righteousness,
  Though after it there's few inquires. 56

"And see ye not yon braid, braid road,
  That lies across yon lily leven?
That is the path of wickedness,
  Though some call it the road to heaven. 60

"And see ye not that bonny road,
  That winds about the fernie brae?
That is the road to fair Elfland,
  Where you and I this night maun gae. 64

"But, Thomas, ye maun hald your tongue,
  Whatever ye may hear or see; 66
For gin a word ye should chance to speak,
  You will ne'er get back to your ain countrie."

For forty days and forty nights
  He wude through red blood to the knee;
And he saw neither sun nor moon
  But heard the roaring of the sea. 72

He's gotten a coat o' the even cloth,
  And a pair of shoes of velvet green;
And till seven years were past and gone,
  True Thomas on earth was never seen. 92

SCOTT.

"O see ye not yon narrow road,
  So thick beset with thorns and briers?
That is the path of righteousness,
  Though after it but few enquires.

"And see ye not that braid braid road,
  That lies across that lily levin?
That is the path of wickedness,
  Though some call it the road to heaven.

"And see ye not that bonny road,
  That winds about the fernie brae?
That is the road to fair Elfland,
  Where thou and I this night maun gae.

"But Thomas ye maun hold your tongue,
  Whatever ye may hear or see;
For, if you speak a word in Elflyn land,
  Ye'll ne'er get back to your ain countrie."

O they rade on, and farther on,
  And they waded through rivers aboon the knee,
And they saw neither sun nor moon,
  But they heard the roaring of the sea.

It was mirk mirk night, and there was nae stern light,
  And they waded through red blude to the knee;
For a' the blude that's shed on earth 75
  Rins through the springs o' that countrie.

Syne they came to a garden green,
  And she pu'd an apple frae a tree—
"Take this for thy wages, true Thomas:
  It will give thee the tongue that can never lee." 80

"My tongue is mine ain," true Thomas said;
  "A gudely gift ye wad gie to me!
I neither dought to buy nor sell,
  At fair or tryst where I may be. 84

"I dought neither speak to prince or peer,
  Nor ask of grace from fair ladye."—
"Now ask thy peace!" the lady said,
  "For as I say, so must it be."— 88

He has gotten a coat of the even cloth,
  And a pair of shoes of velvet green;
And till seven years were gane and past
  True Thomas on earth was never seen.

DESCRIPTION OF THE MSS.

THE three fyttes of Thomas of Erceldoune are preserved in four MSS.: the THORNTON MS. in the Library of Lincoln Cathedral; the MS. Ff. 5. 48. in the University Library, CAMBRIDGE; the COTTON MS., Vitellius E. x.; and the Lansdowne MS. 762, in the British Museum; while the prophecies alone, without the introductory Fytt I., are found in a fifth, the SLOANE MS. 2578, also in the British Museum.

The THORNTON MS. (Lincoln A. 1. 17.) is a well-known repository of romances and devotional pieces in the Northern dialect, many of which have already been printed by the Early English Text Society, written mainly by Robert Thornton of East Newton, Yorkshire, about A.D. 1430—1440. It "is written on 314 leaves of paper, in a somewhat small hand, in folio, measuring 11½ in. by 8¼; but unfortunately imperfect both at the beginning and end, and also wanting leaves in a few other places." The first piece which it contains, a "Life of Alexander the Great," appears to be in an older hand, and to have been originally a distinct MS. In it the letters "þ" and "y" are distinct; while elsewhere in the MS. they are represented by the same character, except in the Romance of *Syr Perecyuelle of Galles,* also in a different hand. "Tomas of Ersseldowne" occupies nine pages, beginning at top of leaf 149, back, and ending on the 2nd column of leaf 153, back, with 15 lines, and the remainder of the column blank. It is written in double columns of from 36 to 40 lines in a column. All these leaves are more or less injured; leaf 149 very slightly so, at the lower corner, where the beginnings of ll. 35, 36 are worn off. In leaf 150, the bottom lines in the outer columns—178 on the front, and 218 on the back—are torn through; at bottom of leaf 151, the ends of lines 336—339 and the beginnings of lines 377—379 are torn off. Leaf 152 is greatly injured, the lower part having been torn out by a tear extending diagonally across from beginning of l. 446 to end of l. 440, and from beginning of l. 478 to end of 475 on the front, and from beginning of l. 512 to end of 514, and beginning of l. 555 to end of 560 on the back. Of leaf 153 there remains only a fragment containing on the front 20 lines of the first column nearly entire, the first letters of 15 more, and the four last with the whole of col. 2 gone; on the back similarly, col. 1 is gone entirely, and col. 2 wants a large part of the beginnings of the lines. The mutilated state of this MS. is the more to be regretted, that it occurs at a part of the poem originally found in the Thornton only, and now therefore entirely lost.

This MS. presents, on the whole, a very careful and accurate text; only in a few places, as mentioned in the subsequent notes, Robert Thornton has misread his original, which can however generally be restored. It is, in date probably, in form certainly, the oldest of the existing MSS., retaining the original Northern form of the language little altered; while it is free from most of the corruptions with which the next two MSS., the Cambridge and Cotton, abound.

MS. CAMBRIDGE, Ff. 5. 48. A paper manuscript in quarto, of 140 leaves, with about 30 lines on a page, English handwriting of the middle of the 15th century. It consists of five parts, whereof the first, leaves 1—66, contains 13 different pieces, the majority being devotional poems; the second, leaves 67—78, five pieces similar in character; part third, leaves 79—94, Homilies for St Michael's day, the feast of the Annunciation, Palm Sunday, &c.; part 4, leaves 95—114, four articles, of which the first is entitled *Principium Anglie;* and part 5, leaves 115—140, four articles, of which the second (No. 26 in the MS.) is *Thomas of Erseldoun*. It begins without any title on leaf 119 a, and ends leaf 128 b, occupying nearly 10 leaves, in single columns. The writing, besides confusing o and e, c and t, which in most cases can only be distinguished by the sense, is in many places so much effaced as to present great difficulties to the reader. R. Jamieson, who printed it in his *Ballads and Songs* at the beginning of the present century, says: "The Cambridge MS. has suffered by rain-water nearly as much as the Cotton has by fire, a great part of each page having become illegible by the total disappearance of the ink. By wetting it, however, with a composition which he procured from a bookseller and stationer in Cambridge, the writing was so far restored in most places, that, with much poring and the assistance of a magnifying glass, he was able to make it out pretty clearly. The greatest difficulty he met with was from the unlucky zeal and industry of some person who long ago, and in a hand nearly resembling the original, had endeavoured to fill up the chasms, and, as appeared upon the revival of the old writing, had generally mistaken the sense, and done much more harm than good." Jamieson little thought that his own "unlucky zeal and industry" would in process of time entitle him to equal or even greater reprobation, for the "composition," which he so naïvely confesses to have applied to the MS., has dried black, and both disastrously disfigured the pages and seriously increased their illegibility. Nevertheless, with the experienced help of Mr Bradshaw, to whose kindness words fail to do justice, I have been enabled to reproduce the text with greater accuracy than either of its previous editors, leaving only a very few blanks where words are quite illegible. It presents a Southernized version of the original, with the sense not seldom, and the rhyme and phraseology often, sacrificed in transliteration (as where *myght and mayne* becomes *mode and mone*, in order to rhyme with *gone*). It has also many scribal blunders, due apparently to its transcriber not being able perfectly to read his original. In its extent it often agrees with the Thornton MS. as against later interpolations and omissions, but it has also large omissions of its own. Where its readings differ from the Thornton, it is generally unsupported by the other MSS. In some places where it presents the greatest discrepancy, it can be seen that originally it had the same reading as T., but was subsequently altered, and this not always, as Jamieson thought, by some one trying to restore indistinct passages, for the original is quite distinct, but crossed through and something substituted. In several instances it misplaces one or more stanzas as to the order of which all the other MSS. agree. My opinion ot its text is therefore different from that of Mr Halliwell, who calls it "the earliest and best," and attributes it to the early part of the 15th century, not to mention the idea of Mr Wright, who considered it of the age of Edward II. Nevertheless, it is a valuable MS., especially for those parts where the Thornton and Cotton are partially or wholly destroyed.

MS. COTTON, Vitellius E. x. "A paper volume in folio, in very bad condition, consisting of 242 leaves." This is one of the MSS. that suffered severely in the fire, and consists of charred fragments of greater or less extent of the original leaves, inlaid and rebound. It contains 26 different articles of the most varied character, in very different handwriting, but apparently all of the 15th century, a "Colloquium de rebus aulicis sub initio regni Edwardi IV.," "A sermon preached at the beginning of Parliament, anno 1483," and other similar sermons in the reigns of Edward V. or Richard III. The copy of Thomas of Erseldown which it contains is in a heavy clumsy handwriting of "about or slightly after 1450." It begins on the middle of leaf 240 *b*, with the rubric, "Incipit prophecia Thome de Arseldon," and this page contains two columns of 30 lines each. But the rest of the poem is written in double lines across the page of about 50 (i. e. 100 lines) to the page, divided in the middle by a heavy red line, or (on leaves 241 *b*, 242 *a*, and part of 242 *b*) by a red paragraph mark. Occasionally the scribe has only got one line in, which throws him out, so that his following lines consist not of the two first and two last lines of a stanza respectively, but of the 2nd and 3rd, followed by the 4th and 1st of the next. The poem is written without a break from beginning to end, except that after line 301-2, line 309-10 (the first two of Fytte II.) immediately follows, but is struck out in red, and repeated after leaving a blank space of one line. Fytt I. thus wants its last three (i. e. six) lines. The poem ends at the very bottom of leaf 243 a, with the rubric . . . . *hecia thome de Arseldoune*. From the burning of the inner side of the leaves of the MS. scarcely one line of the poem is perfect; very often half the double line is burned away, so that when printed in single lines it shows in many places only the alternate ones. See lines 221, &c. The text of this MS., so far as it goes, agrees closely with the Thornton, but it omits stanzas very often, and, like all the MSS. except the Thornton, it has not ll. 577—604. It has also some singular additions of its own, as lines 109—116, and others near the end.

MS. LANSDOWNE 792, a small 4to MS. of 99 leaves of mixed parchment and paper, of about 1524—30. It contains a memorandum of the different orders of Friars in London, and their quarters, as then existing, "the writing of Valeraunce upon the xxi conjunccion of planetes in the moneth of February, the yere of our Lord 1524;" a few lines satirizing the craving for prophecies, ending

> your tethe whet in this bone
> Amonge you euerychone
> And lett Colen' cloute alone.
> The prophecy of Skylton
> 1529

also a prediction of signs and prodigies to happen

> In the yere of our lorde I vnderstande
> xv^e & one and thirty folowand.

as well as various similar predictions for later years. The second nalf of the MS. consists almost entirely of prophetic literature, articles 45, 61—74, 79, 82, 83, being of this description. "Thomas of Arsildoun" begins without title on middle of leaf 24 a, and breaks off on leaf 31 a with the first line of a stanza, some 70 lines from the end, and leaving a blank space of several lines' extent on the page. Leaves 24—28 are paper, 29—31 parchment. The writing is very neat and distinct, in single columns of 32 lines to the page, and without a single break from beginning to end, or any larger letter at the fyttes; but it is divided (in this MS. only) into double stanzas of eight lines, by paragraph marks down the margin. The omission of two lines in the 6th stanza (ll. 71, 72) causes the paragraph marks for a short way to be displaced. In addition to its unfinished ending, this MS. omits long passages, and has three additions of its own, lines 141—156, with its counterpart 237—248, and the reference to Robert II., l. 465—468.

MS. SLOANE 2578 is a paper MS. of Prophecies, small 4to (8¼ × 6 in.) of 117 leaves, of the year 1547. It contains several (unfulfilled) predictions of prodigies for the years 1550, 1553, and 1556; and the following table, which no doubt applies to the year of its compilation (leaf 31):

The Sum of y⁰ Age of ye worlde vnto y⁰ yeare of Christ 1547 after the computacion

of
- the Ebrues — 5509
- mirandula — 5041
- Eusebius — 6737
- Augustyne — 6891
- alphonse — 8522

I copy from the Catalogue the following abstract of its contents, with additions of my own:—

1. Alphabetical index of persons, places, and subjects to the ensuing collection, ff. 1—4.
2. Prophecies relative to events in English History, written in verse and prose. Among them the following may be distinguished.

[Of him that shall wyne the holy cross, leaf 5, a]
The second canto of the prophetic rhymes of Thomas of Erceldon, ff. 6—11 b.
The prophecy of Cadar and Sibilla, ff. 12—15. Beginning:—
"Cadar and Sibell bothe of them sayes
The name of Fraunce in his writinge
Kinge to be clepid in many case
In all his lyfe and his lykinge."
Ending:
"As traytours attainte all shalbe tyde
And thus their sorrow shall wax newe."
Extract from a prophecy by Merlin, ff. 15 b—17 a. Begins:
"When the cock of the northe hathe buylde his neaste."
[See ante, p. xxxii.] Ends:
"desteny shall him not dere."
[Many leaves of short prose prophecies, including those in Appendix II., and at p. lxxx, of this volume; also the computation of the year 1547 already given.]
Prophecy of events to happen in the year 1553, ff. 61—64. Begins:
"To judge the trouthe as before us hathe bene,
So judge we maye all that shall us beseme."
Stanzas f. 64. Begins:
"An Egle shall flye
Up into the Skye
With fyer in his mowthe."
Of the York and Lancaster contests, ff. 68—79. Begins:
"The Scotts shall ryse and make ado
But the Bull shall purvey therfore,
That they shall vanishe & home againe go
And forthink ther rysinge for evermore."
A prophecy of events in English History, ff. 79 b—86. Begins:
"The lande of Albion shall come to corruption by the synne of pride, letcherye, herysye and tratorye."
A prophecy of the persecutions of the Church, ff. 86—88 b. Begins:
"In the yere of our Lorde God a M.v⁰ lxv a great tyrant ageynste the Churoh with might and mayne shall sley many of the Churche."

Another copy of the verses begins :
"When the cooke of the Northe hathe bilde his neste."—f. 100 b.

3. A key to the prophecies comprised in the foregoing collection, ff. 112 b—116.

It might be worth while for one of our publishing societies to print the whole of this MS., as illustrating one phase of English thought in the middle of the 16th century. One of the prose prophecies which specially illustrates Fytt III. of Thomas of Erceldoun is here added in Appendix II., and two other short ones will be found in the Notes.

The prophecy of Erceldoun begins at top of leaf 6 a, with the heading,

¶ Heare begynethe þe ij^d fytt I saye
of *Sir* thomas of Arseldon.

It is written in single columns of 28 lines each, uninterrupted by a single break, and ends at foot of leaf 11 b with the word "Finis." A peculiarity of the text of this MS. is the very frequent omission of the first line of a stanza, to supply the place of which another is generally interpolated at the end, or some lines farther on, so as to complete the rhyme. The conclusion is also very much abridged, the writer seemingly being impatient of everything not prophetic. In other respects the text agrees very closely with the Thornton MS. both in its extent and readings, always excepting lines 577—604, found only in that MS.

PRINTED EDITIONS.

FYTTE I. of *Thomas of Erseldoune* was printed by Scott from the fragmentary Cotton MS. as a note or Appendix to the so-called "traditional ballad" in the *Border Minstrelsy.*

The whole poem was shortly after printed by Robert Jamieson in his *Popular Ballads and Songs from Tradition, Manuscripts, and Scarce editions,* Edin. 1806, from the Cambridge MS., with collations from the Lincoln and Cotton MSS. Jamieson's edition presents many misreadings and not a few wanton alterations of the text.

It was also printed in full by David Laing, Esq., LL.D., in his *Select Remains of the Ancient Popular Poetry of Scotland,* Edin. 1822, from the Lincoln MS., with the blanks of that manuscript partially supplied from the Cambridge text.

In 1845 it was printed by J. O. Halliwell, Esq., in his "Illustrations of the

Fairy Mythology of a Midsummer Night's Dream" for the "Shakespeare Society." The Editor used the Cambridge MS. (which he calls the "earliest and best," and attributes to "the early part of the 15th century"), but printed it with much more care than had been done by Jamieson. He also first indicated the existence of copies of the poem in the Lansdowne and Sloane MSS., mentioning at the same time a later transcript to be found in MS. Rawlinson C. 258, in the Bodleian Library. But a careful examination of this MS. (now C. 813) by Mr Cox shows that it contains no copy of Thomas of Erceldoune, but that its second half consists of prophecies, embracing many of those found in Lansdowne 792 and Sloane 2578, some of which quote Thomas's authority. The Rawlinson C. MSS. have lately been catalogued, and no copy of "Thomas of Erceldoune" appears among them.

Finally, Professor F. J. Child of Harvard University, U.S., in the first volume of his *English and Scottish Ballads*, London, 1861, reprinted the first fytte of the Thornton text from Dr Laing's edition of 1822, with corrections. He endorses Dr Laing's opinion that the Thornton is the earliest text, and "in every respect preferable to that of either of the other manuscripts;" an opinion, the correctness of which will be apparent on a very slight examination of the following pages.

THE PRESENT EDITION.

THE following text exhibits all the MSS. printed in parallel columns. In Fytte I., where there are only four versions, they are printed in the following order: THORNTON, COTTON: LANSDOWNE, CAMBRIDGE. But from Fytte II., where the SLOANE MS. begins, it takes the place of the Cotton in the parallels, and the fragmentary Cotton text is printed below. Up to line 88 of this edition, the lines of the Cotton text represent those of the MS., but at that point the latter begins to be written in double lines across the page, so that the printed lines represent the half lines of the MS. indicated by a red paragraph mark in middle of the line. This will explain why, in many places, full lines alternate with defective ones or blank spaces, where the beginning or end of the MS. lines are burned. But from Fytte II., where the Cotton text occupies the foot of the page, the lines are printed as in the MS. with a dot separating the two halves, though for convenience of reference they are numbered to agree with the single lines above. I have used the thorn (þ) all through wherever the MSS. represent *th* by a single character, whether or not this is identical in form with the y of the MS. In the Lincoln MS., the *thorn* is identical with the *y*, and except at the beginning of a line is regularly used for *th* in the 2nd personal pronoun and demonstrative words, according to the ordinary MS. usage. In the Cambridge and Cotton MSS., where also the þ is in form identical with the *y*, its use for *th* is still more regular. The Lansdowne uses the thorn sparingly, but where it does occur it is usually a true þ with a tall head, and quite distinct from *y*. Its usual place is here in the 2nd personal pronoun forms, also often in *oþer, anoþer;* and occasionally it turns up in strange positions, as in *fryþ,* l. 319; *þryue* and *þe,* l. 344; *þryue* again 464; *boþe,* l. 525.[1] In the Sloane MS. the thorn is more frequent, and always like a *y*.

The punctuation and inverted commas are the Editor's, but the capital letters are as in the MSS. In the Cambridge and Lansdowne MSS., however, it is often doubtful to say whether the initial A is meant for a capital or not; both in form and size, it has a sort of medial or hybrid character which passes insensibly into either the capital or small letter. In the Thornton the single and final *i* has always a tail extending below the line. It is here printed 'j'; but of course it was not a distinct letter, only a "distinguished *i*" used when the letter stood alone, or at the end of a word to render it more prominent. The barred H and h, tagged n), and other marked letters, whose meaning—if they had any—is doubtful, are retained in the text. Letters and words accidentally omitted, illegible, obscure, or in any way doubtful, are enclosed in brackets. These will be found very frequent in the Cambridge text for reasons already given in describing that MS.; and it will be understood that all words there enclosed in brackets indicate indistinct places in the MS., as to the reading of which there exists a reasonable certainty. Where I have put dots the words are quite gone, although comparison with the other texts there also generally indicates what is to be supplied.

On account of the different extent of the poem in the various MSS., and the fact that passages which are found in one are wanting in another, the arrangement of the texts in parallel columns necessitates frequent breaks in every text, and in almost every page. *There are no breaks or paragraphs in the MSS.*, which are written *straight on uninterruptedly*, with no recognition of any omitted passages. The stanzas, if indicated, are shown only by lines connecting the ends of the rhyming lines, except in the Lansdowne, which indicates them by marginal paragraph

---

[1] Through an error in the press the thorn appears in the printed text in the following places where the MS. has *th.*full : l. 44 *the,* 108 *whethere,* 133 *clothyng,* 135 *other,* 139, 140 *the,* 171 *that,* 188 *the,* 231 *the,* 261 *The,* 284 *thre,* 292 *the,* 296 *There,* 449 *The,* 544 *the.* In every other place it is as in the MS.

marks. There are no breaks even at the beginnings of Fyttes II. and III., though some of the MSS. commence these with large initial letters as shown in the printing.

In a few places where the Cambridge MS. misplaces stanzas, so that the parallel arrangement cannot be maintained, the transposition is carefully noted by the numbering of the lines, as, for example, ll. 264, 272; 628, 640.

The poem is really in 8-syllabic four-line stanzas, the first line rhyming with the third and the second with the fourth—ordinary "Long Metre" indeed—and would have been here printed as such, but for difficulties occurring where the second line of one text answers to the first of another, as is the case several times with the Sloane MS.

In numbering the lines, every line and stanza is counted that occurs in any MS., except such as are clearly accidental interpolations, like the two lines in the Thornton, between l. 136 and 137, or those added in the Sloane MS. to make up for a line previously omitted. To this numbering, which is applicable to all the texts, all references are made. To show, however, what would be the actual numbering of the separate texts, and to what lines of each any given lines of the printed edition answer, the following Collation is added, which will also serve to show more distinctly the passages present and absent in each MS. In cases where a different order of stanzas or lines occurs in different MSS., I have followed the order of the majority, or if there are only two texts, that which the sense seemed to recommend.

COLLATION

OF THE CONTENTS OF THE FIVE MANUSCRIPTS OF THOMAS OF ERCELDOUNE,

showing the lines present and absent in the various MSS., and the actual lines in each, which answer to each other and to those numbered in the printed text.

The black line indicates the absence of the passage in that MS.

(For example, the *five* lines, 89—93 of the printed text, represent ll. 81—85 of the Thornton MS., 59—63 of the Lansdowne, 61—65 of the Cambridge, and originally answered to 61—65 of the Cotton, destroyed through the partial burning of the MS. They are altogether *wanting* in the Sloane.

The *four* lines 229—232 represent 199—202 Thornton, 169—172 Cotton, 183—186 Lansdowne, 173—176 Cambridge, in which MS. they are misplaced between ll. 224 and 225 of the general numbering.)

COLLATION OF THE CONTENTS OF THE FIVE MANUSCRIPTS. lxv

PROLOGUE.

PRINTED TEXT	THORNTON	SLOANE	COTTON	LANSDOWNE	CAMBRIDGE	LINES
1—24	1—24	—	—	—	—	24

FYTT I.

PRINTED TEXT	THORNTON	SLOANE	COTTON	LANSDOWNE	CAMBRIDGE	LINES
25—41	25—41	—	1—17	1—17	1—17	17
42—45	—	—	—	18—21	—	4
46—64	42—60	—	18—36	22—40	18—36	19
65—68	—	—	37—40	—	37—40	4
69	(61) accidentally omitted	—	41	41	41	1
70	62	—	42	42	42	1
71—72	63—64	—	43—44	—	43—44	2
73—88	65—80	—	45—60	43—58	45—60	16
89—93	81—85	—	(61—65)lost	59—63	61—65	5
94—108	86—100	—	66—80	64—78	66—80	15
109—116	—	—	81—88	—	—	8
117—136	101—120	—	89—108	79—98	81—100	20
(unnumbered)	121—122	—	—	—	—	[2]
137—140	123—126	—	109—112	99—102	101—104	4
141—156	—	—	—	103—118	—	16
157—160	127—130	—	113—116	119—122	105—108	4
161—164	131—134	—	—	—	109—112	4
165—188	135—158	—	117—140	123—146	113—136	24
189—192	159—162	—	—	147—150	137—140	4
193—196	163—166	—	141—144	151—154	141—144	4
197—200	167—170	—	—	—	145—148	4
201—208	171—178	—	145—152	155—162	149—156	8
209—212	179—182	—	—	163—166	157—160	4
213—224	183—194	—	153—164	167—178	161—172	12
[229—232]	(see below)	—	(see below)	(see below)	173—176	[4]
225—228	195—198	—	165—168	179—182	177—180	4
229—232	199—202	—	169—172	183—186	(see above)	4
233—236	203—206	—	173—176	189—190	181—184	4
237—248	—	—	—	193—202	—	12
249—260	207—218	—	177—188	203—214	185—196	12
[269—272]	(see below)	—	(see below)	(see below)	197—200	[4]

ERCILDOUN.

e

lxvi   INTRODUCTION.

PRINTED TEXT	THORNTON	SLOANE	COTTON	LANSDOWNE	CAMBRIDGE	LINES
261—268	219—226	——	189—196	215—222	201—208	8
269—272	227—230	——	197—200	223—226	(see above)	4
273—302	231—260	——	201—230	227—256	209—238	30
303—308	261—266	——	——	257—262	238—244	6

FYTT II.

309—316	267—274	1—8	237—244	261—270	245—252	8
317—320	275—278	9—12	——	269—274	253—256	4
321—324	279—282	13—16	245—248	273—278	257—260	4
325—328	283—286	17—20	249—252	——	261—264	4
329	287	(21) accidentally omitted	253	——	265	1
330—332	288—290	22—24	254—256	——	266—268	3
333—336	291—294	25—28	——	——	269—272	4
337—340	295—298	29—32	257—260	——	273—276	4
341—352	299—310	33—44	261—272	277—290	277—288	12
353—356	311—314	45—48	——	——	289—292	4
357—360	315—318	49—52	273—276	289—292	293—296	4
361—364	319—322	53—56	277—280	293—298	*297—300	4
365—372	323—330	57—64	281—288	297—306	301—308	8
373—376	——	——	——	——	309—312	4
377—384	331—338	65—72	289—296	305—314	313—320	8
[397—400]	(see below)	(see below)	297—300	(see below)	——	[4]
385—388	339—342	73—76	——	313—318	321—324	4
389—396	343—350	77—84	301—308	317—326	——	8
397—400	351—354	85—88	(see above)	325—330	——	4
401—412	355—366	89—100	309—320	329—342	——	12
413—416	367—370	101—104	——	341—346	——	4
417—418	371—372	105—106	——	345—348	325—326	2
419—420	373—374	107—108	321—322	347—350	327—328	2
421—422	375—376	——	323—324	349—352	329—330	2
423—424	377—378	——	325—326	351—354	——	2
425—426	379—380	109—110	327—328	355—356	——	2
427—428	381—382	111—112	329—330	357—358	331—332	2
(extra lines)	——	——	331—332	——	——	[2]
429—430	383—384	113—114	333—334	——	333—334	2
431—432	——	115—116	335—336	——	335—336	2

COLLATION OF THE CONTENTS OF THE FIVE MANUSCRIPTS.   lxvii

PRINTED TEXT	THORNTON	SLOANE	COTTON	LANSDOWNE	CAMBRIDGE	LINES
433—440	385—392	117—124	337—344	359—366	337—344	8
441	393	125	345	367	——	1
442	394	——	346	368	——	1
443—450	395—402	126—133	347—354	369—376	——	8
(extra line)	——	134	——	——	——	[1]
451—466	403—418	135—150	355—370	377—392	——	16
467—470	——	——	——	393—396	——	4
471—472	419—420	151—152	371—372	397—398	——	2
473—474	421—422	153—154	(see below)	399—400	——	2
475—476	423—424	155—156	373—374	401—402	——	2
[473—474]	(see above)	(see above)	375—376	(see above)	——	[2]
477—478	425—426	157—158	377—378	403—404	345—346	2
479—480	(427—428)	159—160	379—380	405—406	347—348	2
481	(429)	——	381	407	349	1
482—484	(430—432)	161—163	382—384	408—410	350—352	3
[extra]	——	164	——	——	——	[1]
485—488	(433—436)	165—168	385—388	411—414	353—356	4

FYTT III.

489—492	437—440	——	389—392	415—418	——	4
493—500	441—448	169—176	393—400	419—426	357—364	8
501—504	449—452	177—180	401—404	427—430	——	4
505—508	453—456	181—184	405—408	——	365—368	4
509—512	457—460	185—188	409—412	431—434	369—372	4
513—514	458—462	189—190	413—414	435—436	——	2
515—524	(463—472)	191—200	415—424	437—446	——	10
525—527	(473—475)	201—203	425—427	447—449	373—375	3
528	476	204	428	450	376	1
529	477	——	429	451	377	1
530—536	478—484	205—211	430—436	452—458	378—384	7
[extra]	——	212	——	——	——	[1]
537—548	485—496	213—224	437—448	459—470	——	12
549—552	497—500	225—228	——	——	385—388	4
553—560	501—508	229—236	449—456	——	389—396	8
561—564	——	——	(457—460)	——	397—400	4
565—571	(509—515)	237—243	461—467)	——	401—407	7

lxviii   INTRODUCTION.

PRINTED TEXT	THORNTON	SLOANE	COTTON	LANSDOWNE	CAMBRIDGE	LINES
572—576	516—520	244—248	468—472	——	408—412	5
577—591	525—535	——	——	——	——	15
592—604	(536—548)	——	——	——	——	13
605—606	(549—550)	249—250	473—474	——	413—414	2
607—608	(551—552)	251—252	475—476	——	415—416	2
609—614	(553—558)	253—258	477—482	471—476	417—422	6
615—616	(559—560)	——	483—484	477—478	423—424	2
617—620	(561—564)	259—262	485—488	479—482	425—428	4
[637—644]	( )	(see below)	(see below)	——	*429—436	[8]
621—628	(565—572)	263—270	489—496	483—490	437—444	8
629	(573)	*271	497	491	445	1
630—632	(574—576)	*272—274	498—500	——	446—448	3
633—636	(577—580)	275—278	501—504	——	——	4
637—640	(581—584)	*279—282	——	——	(see above)	4
641—644	(585—588)	*283—286	505—508	——	(see above)	4
645—660	(589—604)	287—302	509—524	——	449—464	16
661—664	(605—608)	——	525—528	——	465—468	4
665—677	(609—621)	303—315	529—541	——	469—481	13
678—680	622—624	316—318	542—544	——	482—484	3
681—684	——	——	545—548	——	——	4
685—686	625—626	319—320	549—550	——	——	2
687—688	627—628	——	551—552	——	——	2
689—692	——	——	553—556	——	——	4
693—695	629—631	——	557—559	——	485—487	3
696	632	321	560	——	488	1
697—700	633—636	——	561—564	——	489—492	4

NOTES TEXTUAL AND EXPLANATORY.

The PROLOGUE is found only in the Thornton MS., and is presumably no part of the Romance in its original form, although from its occurrence in the earliest MS. it must be little later than the completion of the poem itself as we now have it. It takes the form of a prelude by a minstrel or reciter to commend the poem to the attention of his audience who are twice committed as "ynglyschemen" to the safe keeping of Christ. Unless the word may have been changed for "Scottismen," the prologue is therefore the addition of a northern English author. Its dialect is pure Northern, less altered even than the text itself.

L. 1 *lystyns*; l. 2 *takis*, l. 10, 12 *hase*. In the Northern dialect since the 12th or 13th century the plural of the present indicative and imperative has ended in -*s*, when *unaccompanied* by its proper pronoun *we*, *ye*, *they*. When these are present there is no termination. See *Dialect of Southern Scotland*, pp. 211—214.

l. 2. *takis gude tente*, take good heed; *tent*, *no.*, care, attention, *vb.* to *attend*, *take heed*; "Tent me, billie—there 's a gullie!"—*Burns.*

l. 7. *pristly*, readily, quickly, actively.   l. 8. *blyne*, cease.
l. 11. *sere*, various, several.   l. 15. *tyte*, soon, quick.
l. 16. *sythene*, for the Northern *sen*, *syne*, as in l. 6, which would improve the rhyme.
l. 22. *by-leue*, remain; German *bleiben*, Dutch *b-lijven*.

FYTTE I.

l. 25—28. The Cotton differs considerably from the others, Th. and Ca. showing the original reading.

l. 25. *Endres-day* = *ender day*, this by-gone day. Icel. *endr*, of yore, formerly. Lat. *ante*.
         "As I myselfe lay this enders nyght
         All alone withowten any fere."—*MS. Rawl. C.* 813, *leaf* 54.

l. 26. *grykyng*, the graying, or gray of the morning:
         "It was na *gray* day-licht."

l. 28. *Huntle bankys*, on Eildon Hills, near Melrose. See Introduction, p. li.

l. 30. *Mawes, mavys*; L. corruptly *maner* for *maues*, the mavis or song thrush; but the *throstyll* of the preceding line is also the thrush, which L. accordingly changes into the *merle* or blackbird. *menyde*, Co. corruptly *movyde*, bemoaned herself, sung plaintively.

l. 30, 32. *songe, ronge*, doubtless originally the Northern sang, rang, as in l. 56.

l. 31. The *Wodewale*, the wood-lark. *beryde*, Ca. corruptly *farde*, vociferated, made a noise; "the rumour of rammasche foulis and of beystis that maid grete beir."—*Compl. of Scotl.*, p. 38, l. 24.

l. 32. *shawys* in L. for *wode* of others, still used as an equivalent, in the north. Isl. *skóg*, Dan. *skov*.

l. 36. *louely*, Ca. and L., is no doubt the original, corrupted by T. to *longe*, and glossed by Co. as *fayre*. In Ca. *lonely* would be as good a reading of MS., but was *lonely* = *al,onely*, then in existence?

l. 37. *zogh*, Co. for *þogh*, the þ and з frequently confounded by ignorant scribes.

l. 38. *wrabbe and wrye: wrobbe, wrabbe* = warble? sing; *wry* = *wray*, bewray, reveal. Or perhaps Sc. *wrable, warble, wurble*, to wriggle, and *wrye*, to twist; to wriggle and twist *with the tongue* in the attempt to find language to describe her.

l. 40. *askryed, skryed, discryued*, described; Fr. *escri-re, descri-re*.

l. 41—72. The description of the lady, in which T. and Ca. closely agree, varies much in Co. and L., the latter inserting l. 42—45.

l. 46—48. *none, schone, bone, stone*, in pure Northern would be *nane, schane, bane, stane;* which the original doubtless had. See ll. 81, 83; 345, 347.

l. 49. *Selle, sadyl, sege*, equivalents, the latter properly a seat (of honour). *Roelle bone*, called also *rewel bone, rowel bone, reuylle bone*, "an unknown material of which saddles especially are in the romances said to be made." See Chaucer's "Sir Topas," which presents several points of contact with the description here:—

"His jambeux were of cuirbouly,
His swerdes sheth of ivory,
His helme of latoun bright,
His sadel was of rewel-bone,
His bridel as the sonne shone,
Or as the mone light.

His spere was of fin cypress
That bodeth werre, and nothing pees,
The hed ful sharpe y-ground;
His stede was all dapple gray,
It goth an aumble in the way
Fully softely and round
In lond."

Rev. W. W. Skeat suggests that "*rowel* = Latin *rotella*, Fr. *rouelle*, i. e. bone rounded and polished, for the front or peak of the saddle."

l. 52. *Crapotee*, toad stone: smaragdus or emerald, "which often contains a flaw, in shape suggesting a toad." The *Promptorium Parvulorum* has "Crepawnde, or crapawnde, precyous stone (crepaud, P.) Samaragdus."

Note. "Crapaude, a precious stone, crapaudine." Palsgrave. Cotgrave explains crapaudine as signifying "the stone chelonitis, or the toad stone." In the Metrical Romance of Emare is described a rich vesture, thickly set with gems, rubies, topaze, "*crapowtes* and nakette;" the word is also written *crapawtes*. More detailed information will be found in Gesner, de quadrup. ovip. II. 9. See also Douce's Illustrations of Shakespeare, "As You Like It," Act 2, Sc. i.; and the word "toadstone" in Nares' Glossary.

l. 53. *Stones of Oryente*, Eastern or Oriental gems; the name may have been given definitely to some stones or varieties of stones only found in the East, as the *Turquoise*, which derives its name (*pierre turquoise*) from Turkestan, where alone it is found. "The name *Oriental Emerald* is given to a very rare beautiful and precious green variety of Sapphire." "The finest red *rubies* are generally called *Oriental Rubies*." So also in "Alliterative Poems," edited by Dr Morris, we have

"þe grauayl that on grounde can grynde
Wern precious *perlez of oryente*."

Oryons in Ca. may be *oryens*, as *o* and *e* are generally indistinguishable in this MS.

NOTES, TEXTUAL AND EXPLANATORY.   lxxi

l. 54. *hang*, Northern past tense of *hing*.

l. 55, 56 are properly wanting in L., but lines 71, 72 are brought from their own place instead; ll. 57—60 are quite altered in L. and Co.

l. 56. *a whylle, one* while; indef. article and numeral, identical in N. dialect.

l. 57. *garthes*, girths or garters?

l. 60. *perelle*, pearl; Ca. *perry, pierreries*, jewels, precious stones.

l. 61. *payetrelle*, "breast-leather of a horse"; Fr. *poitrail;* L. corruptly *parrell,* apparel.

Iral, T. *jral fyne*, Ca. *riall fyne*, Co. *yra* . . . . . L. *Alarane;* the original probably, *Iral-stane*, rhyming with *schane*. So in the "Anturs of Arthur at Tarnwathelan," the Ireland MS. has

"Betun downe berels, in bordurs so bryʒte
That with *stones iraille* were strencult and strauen,
Frettut with fyne gold that failis in the fiʒte."

And the Thornton MS. of the same:—

"*Stones of iral* they strenkel, and strewe,
Stiþe stapeles of stele þey strike don stiʒt."

I can get no light on *iral-stane;* the scribes also seem not to have understood it, and hence their alterations, *rial, alarane*, &c.

l. 62. *Orphare*, orfevrie, goldsmiths' work; Lat. *aurifaber*, Fr. *orfèvre*, a goldsmith.

l. 63. *Reler* in L. perhaps corrupt for *silver*, as *gold*, which the others have, had been already put in the rhyming line.

l. 65—68 in Co. look like a variation of the stanza before, with the lines,

"A semly syʒt it w[as to se]
In euery joynt [hang bellis thre]."

l. 65. Ca. for *iij, four* was originally written and struck out.

l. 67—70 in Ca. are clearly an awkward interpolation in the midst of an original stanza; the lines are omitted in MS., but written at side and foot with marks of insertion.

l. 68. *lire* in Ca. (A.S. *hleor*) face, cheek.

l. 69. *grewe hound*, the Grey hound or Greek hound, *Canis Graius*, still called in Scotland a *Grewe*, which was the Older Scotch for a *Greek*.

l. 70. *rache*, a hound that follows by the *scent*, as the Grewe does by *sight*.

l. 71. *halse*, neck; A.S. *heals*.

l. 72. *flone*, properly *flane*, to rhyme with *rane* above, an arrow; A.S. *flán*.

l. 74. *ane* semely tree, bespeaks a Scotch original.

l. 75. *He sayd:* so l. 87, *and sayd;* l. 157, *scho sayd;* l. 161, *And sayd*. These words, as in the old Romances generally, are *extra-metrical*, and are rather directions to the reader or reciter, like the names of speakers in a Shakspearian play, or our modern inverted commas, than part of the poem, to be said or sung. They were *read* only by a change of tone or a gesture.

l. 75, 77. *ʒone*, Th.; the other MSS. show that this demonstrative was already little used in English proper.

l. 80, 84. *Eldoune tree*. A solitary tree that formerly stood on the slope of one of the three Eildon Hills near Melrose; see Introduction, p. l. Ca. does not understand the local reference, and makes *eldryne* = eldern, like oaken, beechen.

NOTES, TEXTUAL AND EXPLANATORY.

l. 81. *radly, rathely;* A.S. *hrædlice,* quickly, readily. The Northern *rase,* when altered to *rose* in the other three MSS., ceases to rhyme with *sayes.*

l. 83. *als the storye sayes,* and again 123, *als the storye tellis full ryghte,* implies an older version of the tale than that in the poem. See Introduction, p. xxiv.

l. 87. *and sayd,* T. and Co. See l. 75, *n.*

l. 89. *mylde of thoght* in T. and L., shown by the rhyme to be the original.

l. 94. *payrelde,* apparelled.

l. 95. *fee* in the original sense of A.S. *feoh,* Germ. *Vieh,* beasts, cattle.

l. 96. *rynnys,* Northern pl. with noun subject, of which Ca. *rannen* for *rennen* is Midl., and L. *rennyng,* a scribal misconception of the latter.

l. 98. *balye* in Ca. mistake of scribe for *folye;* so l. 31, *farde* for *beird.*

l. 99. *wysse, wyce, wise,* rhymes with *price.* It is still always so pronounced in North.

l. 102. Ca. reads *let meb me be.*

l. 104. *synne* in T. probably an interpolation; gives rise to mistake in L. of *syne,* then, thereafter.

l. 106. L. read *dwelle.*   l. 107. *trowche = trowthe.*

l. 108. *by leues.* See l. 22.

l. 109—116, interpolated in Co., are not in keeping with the context, but probably the boast which the lady fears was true to the manners of the age.

l. 115. *crystenty;* Fr. *chretienté,* Christendom.

"Three blither lads that lang lone nicht
Were never found in *Christendee.*"—*Burns.*

l. 116. Co. *wryede,* accused, bewrayed; A.S. *wréȝean, wreȝod.*

l. 119. T. *chewys þe werre;* Co. *cheuyst,* achievest, succeedest, comest off, the worse; Ca. glosses *thryuist,* and L. corrupts to *chece hit,* perhaps *chesit,* chose !

l. 125. *the[e] lykes,* impersonal, *te delectat.*

"At first in heart *it liked me* ill
When the king praised his clerkly skill."—Scott, *Marmion,* vi. 15.

l. 126. *byrde,* bride, married lady; Piers Plowman has *burde, buirde, birde, berde; deel = dele,* deal, probably the original; Ca. has *dwel.*

l. 132. *are,* A.S. *ǽr,* ere, before.

l. 135. *hir a schanke blake,* her one leg black, her other grey. Ca. had originally,

"þe too shanke was blak, þe toþur gray
and alle hir body like þe leede."

which is the same as T. (þe *too,* þe *toþur =* þet *oo,* þet-oþur, the one, the other); but the second hand has altered it into the reading of the text, where *bloo, beten,* and *leed,* may be equally *blee, beton, lood.*

l. 139. *fasyd* in L., a scribal error for *fadyd.*

l. 141—156. L. The conduct attributed to Thomas is unworthy, and the whole scene out of keeping. The rhymes also break down into mere assonances.

l. 157. *scho sayd,* T. See l. 75, *n.*

l. 158. Ca. again brings in the *eldryne tre.*

l. 159. *gone* can hardly be original, as the pure Northern would be *gaa.* I suggest *wone = dwell.*

l. 160. *Medill-erthe;* A.S. *middan-eard;* Isl. *mid-gard,* the Earth, as the *middle region* of the Old Northern cosmogony.

l. 161—164. Ca. has a remarkable variation, bringing out more clearly that Thomas invokes not the lady, but the *Queene of Heuene, Mary mylde.*

l. 167. *by-teche, be-teche;* A.S. *be-tæcan,* to deliver, commit.

l. 169. *Eldone Hill,* on the Tweed, near Melrose; a mountain mass divided into three summits. See Introduction, p. xlix. Ca. again says *eldryne tre,* but the latter word is erased, and *hill* substituted.

l. 170. *derne,* secret. Ca. has *grenewode tre,* the last word obliterated, and *les* substituted.

l. 171. Ca. had originally,

"It was derk as mydnyght myrke,"

as in Th., but this is altered to,

"Wher hit was derk as any hell."

The former would seem to be the correct reading, though it rhymes with itself, instead of l. 169, and the attempt to make it rhyme with the latter has caused the three different readings in Ca., Co., and L.

l. 173. *montenans,* amount; glossed *space* in Ca., mistaken in L.

l. 176. *fowte* in Ca. looks like *fewte; fawte* is correct; Fr. *faute,* failure, want.

l. 177. *herbere,* garden of herbs or trees, enclosed garden, *later* summer-house. The original word appears to have been the O.Fr. *herbier,* a herbary, in O.E. *herber, erber;* but to have been confounded with the O.E. *herberʒe, hereberwe, herborwe, herbor, herber,* A.S. *hereberge,* Icel. *herbergi,* O.H.G. *heriberga,* harbour, shelter, hospitium. "*Wo bist du sur Herberge,*" John i. 38.—*Luther.* Then it has been misspelt in modern times *arbour* from its assumed connexion with *trees.* At Cavers, in Roxburghshire, there is a hill called the *Herber Law* or Pleasure-garden Hill (pronounced as in "to *herber* [harbour] thieves." The *Herbere* in the poem was clearly a garden of fruit trees. Note that *Orchard* (in South Sco. *Wurtshert*) now a *garden of fruit trees,* was originally also a *garden of herbs* or *vegetables, Wyrtʒeard.*

l. 180. *damasee,* the Damascene, or Damson:

"þer weore growyng so grene
þe Date wiþ the Damesene."—*Pystil of Swete Susanne.*

"The plum is a native of Caucasus and Asia Minor. Cultivated varieties, according to Pliny, were brought from Syria into Greece, and thence into Italy. Such was, for instance, the *Damson* or *Damascene* Plum, which came from *Damascus* in Syria, and was very early cultivated by the Romans."—*Treasury of Botany,* p. 932.

l. 181. *wyneberye,* the grape; A.S. *win-beriʒe. pynnene* in L. is perhaps adjective from *pine,* but *fre* is no doubt for *tre.*

l. 182. T. *nyghtgale,* A.S. *nihtegale,* night-singer, night-gladdener; the others have the inserted *n, nyghtyn-gale,* found in the South as early as Chaucer.

l. 183. *payeioys;* Ital. *papagallo,* i.e. Pope-cock; Sp. *papagay;* O.Fr. *papegay,* Russian *popagay,* a parrot or "popinjay;" Sc. *Papingo.*

l. 191. *or,* ere, before; "*or* ever they came at the bottom of the den," Dan. vi. 24. Or is still the regular Northern form of *ere, antequam.*

l. 193. *hyghte,* call, command, *past* used for *present.*

l. 199. *paye*, to pacify, please, satisfy, *and hence* pay; Lat. *pacare;* Ital. *pagare;* Fr. *payer*.

l. 201—216. The MSS. differ much in particulars, but, with exception of Co., all make *four* ways, which seem to be to heaven, purgatory, and hell, and (but coming first in the list) from purgatory to heaven, "whan synful sowlis haue duryd ther peyn."

l. 204. *rysse, ryce, rese, rise;* A.S. *hris*, twig, brushwood. Still in common use in N.

l. 209—212. Wanting in Co., and varies greatly in the others. *tene & traye*, pain and trouble; A.S. *teóna* and *tréga*. *drye*, Ca. endure; A.S. *dreógan;* Sc. *dree*.

l. 219. *it bearis the belle*, occupies the first rank, surpasses all, alluding to the leader of a flock or herd which has a bell round its neck.

l. 223. *me ware leuer*, impersonal, *mihi fuerit satius*, I had rather = I *would* rather have it.

l. 225. Here Ca. transposes two stanzas, but the order is obvious. The lady takes the most certain means of preventing Thomas from divulging secrets by binding him to answer no one but her.

l. 230. L. *thirty bolde barons and thre:* this jingling combination of numbers distinguishes the later prophecies, and modern-antique ballads, but is not found in the earlier.

l. 231. *desse, deyce*, the raised daïs (O.Fr. *deis;* Lat. *discus*) at top of the hall.

l. 235. *as white as whelys bone*, the *ivory* of the narwhal or walrus.

l. 237—252. These inquisitive demands of Thomas are only in L., but seem old.

l. 250. *hir raches couplede*, her hounds having been coupled again.

l. 261. Ca. here again transposes three stanzas.

l. 267. T. *bryttened*, cut up, broke down; A.S. *brytan*, to break; *brytnian*, to dispense; L. *tryllege*, scribal error for *bryttning*, as in Ca.; *wode*, mad.

l. 274. *parde*, per deum.

l. 276. *My lufty lady sayd to me;* so all the older MSS. L. alone changes it into 3rd person,
"To hym spake that ladyẻ fre."

l. 277. *þe buse* = (it) behoves thee; past tense, *bud, byd*, behoved; be *byd* be a fule!

l. 286. *thre ʒere;* Ca. says *seuen*, which is the traditional period.

l. 288. *skylle*, reason, cause, *as well as* the reasoning faculty.

l. 289. *to-morne*, still Northern English, "to-morn 't morn," to-morrow morning; Scotch *the morn*.

l. 290. *amange this folke will feche his fee*, refers to the common belief that the fairies "paid kane" to hell, by the sacrifice of one or more individuals to the devil every seventh year.

"Then wod I never tire, Janet,
In Elfish land to dwell;
But aye at every seven years
They pay the teind to hell;
And I'm sae fat and fair of flesh,
I fear twill be my-sell."

"I'd paid my kane seven times to hell
Ere you'd been won away."—*The Young Tamlane.*

l. 291. *hende*, gentle, *also* skilful.

l. 294. *hethyne*, hence; the scribes, with the exception of Co., misunderstand this Northern word, and write *heven*.

NOTES, TEXTUAL AND EXPLANATORY.   lxxv

l. 296. *I rede*, I counsel; A.S. *raedan;* Germ. *rathen.*
l. 200. *fowles singes ;* see l. 1.
l. 301—304. This stanza, though in all, comes in very awkwardly, nor can I explain to what it refers.
   l. 303. T. *Erlis ;* Ca. *yrons*, an *erne's* or sea eagle's.
   l. 306. *yon benttis browne.* L. distorts into *yowre brwtes broune.*
   l. 303—308. These lines are wanting in the Co. MS., which after l. 301-2 proceeds to l. 309-10, but this is first struck out, and then repeated after one blank line.

FYTTE II.

The Sloane MS. begins here. For the first 70 lines, the MSS. closely agree, though L. omits numerous passages, as all that about the Baliols, l. 324—340.
   l. 313. *carpe*, speak, or sing. Thomas has the choice of excelling in instrumental, or in vocal (rather *oral*) accomplishments; he prefers the latter, "for tonge is chefe of mynstralsie."
   l. 314. *chose,* the choice; often so spelled in Scotch.
       "in our Inglis rethorick the rose,
        As of Rubeis the Charbunckle bene *chose.*"—*Lyndesay, Papyngo*, 26.
   l. 317. *spelle,* discourse ; A.S. *spellian;* in Ca. corruptly *spill ;* L. and S. gloss, *speke*.
   l. 318. *lesynge,* lying, falsehood. *Lesynge thow sall neuer lee ;* from this characteristic Erseldown derived the name of " True Thomas," generally given to him in the later prophecies and traditional rhymes.
   l. 319. *frythe or fell,* enclosed field or open hill.
   l. 324. *ferly,* a wonder, strange thing or event. Usually derived from A.S. *fœrlic,* sudden; *fœr,* fearful; but I think more truly both in form and meaning from A.S. *feorlic, feorlen,* far away, foreign, strange. Compare *strange* from *extraneus*.
   l. 327. *wyte ;* A.S. *wit-an,* to depart, decease. Ca. has *dwyne ;* A.S. *dwin-an,* to pine, dwindle away.
   l. 329. T. *baylliolfe* for *baylliolse* or *baylliolfs ;* Co. *bali]oues ;* S. misreads *baly of ;* Ca. scribal error *folkys ;* see before, l. 101, *balye* for *foly*. The Baliols' blood, the family of John Baliol, the rival of Robert Bruce for the Scottish crown, and his son Edward, rival of David Bruce.
   l. 331—332. The *Comyns, Barclays, Russells,* and *Friseals,* or *Frasers. Semewes* in Ca. is a very simple misreading of *Comenes* in old writing, and the *Sea-mews* suggest the *teals, telys,* probably for barclys, with the *ar* contracted of the original. The *Comyns* and *Frasers* were prominent, though on different sides, during the English War in the minority of David II. David Cumyn, the dispossessed Earl of Athol, was one of Edward Baliol's leaders, when the latter invaded Scotland in 1332, was appointed viceroy of Scotland by Edward III. in 1335, and soon after slain in the forest of Kilblane, by Sir Andrew Moray, when, according to Buchanan, "fortissimus quisque Cuminianorum aut in praelio aut in fuga caesus est." This is the battle for which Barbour quotes a prophecy of the Rhymer, ante, p. xvii. Walter Cumyn was also slain in the Battle of Annan, 1332, and his brother Thomas executed after the battle. Of the Frasers, Buchanan has, "*Fraser* vel *Frisel*, cog. in varias familias tributum in quibus eminet Lovetiae, Saltonii, & Fraseriæ Reguli, cum suis quisque tribulibus."

Alexander Fraser was one of the commanders at Dupplin, 1332; James and Simon Fraser, after capturing Perth from Baliol, were slain at Halidon Hill, 1333. Of the Barclays: in 1345 David de Berklay waylaid and assassinated William Bullock, the able English ecclesiastic so intimately connected with the intrigues of the period. Sir Walter de Berklay was also concerned in the plot against Robert Bruce, and tried before the Black Parliament of 1320, and in 1322, according to Fordun's Annals, "on the 1st of October, Andrew Barclay was taken, and having been convicted of treachery, underwent capital punishment." The *Russels* I cannot trace; and the word may be a scribal error for some of the other names conspicuous in the history of the period—the *Rosseis*, for instance.

l. 333. *wyte, dwyne.* See l. 327.

l. 335. *spraye*, to spread out, sprout out, like *spray* of water, or a *spray* of blossom; Platt-Deutsch *spreden, spreën;* G. *sprühen*, to sputter, flow forth.

l. 341—348. Thomas's inquiry is as to the issue of the doubtful contest between the Bruce and Baliol families, 1332—1355.

l. 341. *whatkyns*, of what kind; used adjectively, "what kind of" *qualis*.

l. 344. *thryue* and *thee* (A.S. þeon) are synonymous; S. changes to *vnthrive*.

l. 345. *none; tane* in l. 347 shows that the original had the Northern *nane*.

l. 352. Co. *halyndon hill;* L. *helydowne hill;* T. and L. *Eldone;* Ca. *ledyn* for *Eldyn*. I think there is little doubt, though the two oldest MSS. say otherwise, that the Battle of Halidon Hill, 1333, is meant. "So great was the slaughter of the nobility, that, after the battle, it was currently said amongst the English that the Scottish wars were at last ended, since not a man was left of that nation who had either skill or power to assemble an army or direct its operations."—*Tytler*, quoting *Murimuth*, p. 81. But there may have been a legendary prophecy as to Eldone Hill, which was after the event changed to Halidown Hill, as "Spincarde Clough" was to Pinkie-cleuch.

l. 353—354. *Breton's—Bruyse blode*, the common terms in this Fytte for *English* and *Scotch*. The English claims to the superiority of Scotland were founded upon the Cymric version of the legend of the Trojan *Brutus*, from whom the name of Britain was "derived," who was said to have divided the realm, after he had conquered it from the giants, between his three sons, Locrinus, Cymber, and Albanactus, eponymi of English, Welsh, and Scotch, with the feudal supremacy to Locrinus. Thus adopting the *Brute, Breton*, or *British* legend, the English were the *Brutes* or *Bretons blode*. There was, of course, an alliterative antithesis between *Bretons* and *Bruces;* but in some of the MSS. the latter word might be either *Bruces* or *Brutes*, confounding the two opposites. I have printed *Bruces*, the word originally meant, though perhaps the scribes thought it *Brutes*.

l. 354. *spraye;* Gaelic *spreidh*, booty, prey. Gawain Douglas has *spreith, spreicht*.

l. 357. The foregoing passage refers to a cluster of events in the minority of David II., 1332—1345. They seem to have been written at that time. What follows to the end of the Fytte, and perhaps even to l. 520 in Fytte III., is a general sketch of battles and other events in Scotland from 1298 to 1400 or so, and was probably written about the latter date, when the poem took its present form. l. 357—364 refer to the battle of *Falkirk* (S. and L. do not understand the proper name); Ca. Co. and L. erroneously make the Scotch win.

l. 367—376. The lady wishes to go because her hounds are impatient. Thomas detains her, giving (in Ca. only) a reason.

NOTES, TEXTUAL AND EXPLANATORY.   lxxvii

l. 371. *god schilde*, Dieu defende! God defend! God forbid.

l. 375. Ca. *reyke*, roam, ramble.

holtely or ? *holteby* I cannot explain; it is probably a proper name. *Holt* is of course a *wood*, but it is a word not now current in the North.

l. 377—388. The battle of Bannockburn, June, 1314; here all the MSS. agree that the *Brucys-blode* shall win, though Ca. corrupts to *Brutys*, and L. to Ebruys (!).

l. 379—380 seem to be the origin of the traditional prophecy attributed to Thomas (ante, p. xliv),
" The burn of breid
Sall rin fu' reid."

a *bannock* being a cake of (home made) bread.

l. 381—385 describe the well-known device of Bruce of defending his flank by pits dug, and concealed by hurdles and turf. *snapre* L. = stumble.

l. 389, 390. The death of Robert Bruce, leaving a son of 6 years old, so that Scotland kingless stood.

l. 391—412. The tercelet, or young falcon, is Edward Baliol, who now seeing his opportunity took with him *tercelettes grete & gay*, the dispossessed lords, Henry Percy, Lord Wake, Henry Beaumont, David Cumyn and others, and landed (l. 401) at Wester Kinghorn, 1332, where Alexander Seton, with a handful of followers, threw themselves upon them, but was overpowered and cut in pieces on the sands (l. 402). They then pushed on towards Perth, surprised the Scottish army at Duplin Moor, by the River Earn, which flows over the old red-sandstone (ll. 403—408), with great slaughter, and next day took Perth, the "town of great renown near the water of Tay."

l. 400. T. *Royalle blode;* S. *baly of blud*, corruptly for *Balyolues blode*, as in Co.

l. 414. *cheuede*, achieved.   l. 415. *bowne*, ready.

l. 416. *the werre of Fraunce*. Edward III., thinking Scotland reduced under Baliol, declared war against France in 1337, and in 1339 invaded that country.

l. 417—436. The text is here in great confusion, none of the MSS. apparently being complete. The event itself is also misplaced, as the coronation of David II. really occurred before Baliol's invasion, and not now (1341) when he returned from his exile in France to reign. Ca. does not mend the matter by reading *Robert*, as the events which follow belong to David.

l. 427, 428 in L. refer to the special bull obtained from Rome for the anointing of David II.

l. 423. *More and myne*, greater and lesser.

l. 425. *skyme*, T., error for Skynne = Scone or Skune.

l. 427. *beryns* = *bernys;* A.S. *beorn*, chieftains, barons, nobles.

l. 429—448. David II.'s invasion of England in 1346, six years after his return from France, when he took Hexham (l. 431); was defeated at Beaurepair, close to Durham (l. 433, 434); and himself, after being grievously wounded (l. 440), taken prisoner (l. 444), and led to London (l. 447).

l. 430. *lygges*, lies (A.S. *licgan*); the Northern form still well-known.

l. 437. *taggud*, togged, confined, encumbered, for *tane* of T., Ca. has *teyryd*, ? for *teþryd*, *tethered*.

l. 439. *nebbe*, nose; A.S. *nyb*.

l. 441, 442. *fode*, a brood. The *fals fode*, who betray the king, points to the High

Steward, and the Earl of March, who escaped with their division from the field, and were blamed for not adequately supporting David.

l. 448. *the goshawke fynd his Make*, David II. find his *mate* or consort, Joanna, sister of Edward III.

l. 453—456 I cannot explain, unless they refer to the slaughter in Ettrick Forest of the Knight of Liddesdale, who had been gained over to the English interest by Edward.

l. 457—460 describe the great exertions made in Scotland to raise the enormous sum of the king's ransom (equal to £1,200,000 of modern money); for *fulle and fere* I suggest *felle and flese*, or *Wolle and fell, full many ane*. The money was principally raised by granting to the king all the wool and wool-fells in the kingdom at a low rate, to be exported and sold at a profit abroad.

l. 464. *bygge & browke the tre*, apparently to *build* (their nests) and *use* or enjoy the tree.

l. 467. Robert II., the first of the Stewarts, ascended the throne 26 March, 1371.

l. 469—484. The *Cheuanteyne* or *Cheftan* is the Earl of Douglas (l. 480), who invaded England 1388, burned and plundered, especially in the bishopric of Durham (l. 473-4), rode to Newcastle, and challenged Hotspur (l. 475-6), and was by him overtaken and slain at Otterbourne, in a marsh by the Reed (l. 477—480). Hotspur was taken prisoner (l. 481) and led to Scotland.

l. 479. *in fere*, together, in company (A.S. *gefera*).

l. 480. Co. *doglas*, i. e. Douglas; misunderstood, and variously corrupted in the others.

l. 486. The original seems to have been as in l. 306, *Me by-houis ower yone bentis browne*, variously corrupted in L. and S.

FYTTE III.

The first stanza, wanting in Ca. and S., differs greatly in the others.

l. 489. *gente*, handsome, elegant; *hende*, see l. 291.

l. 492. *worthe*, become, A.S. *weorðan*.

l. 494. *wandrethe*, trouble, sorrow. Isl. *vandrœdi*; *woghe*, A.S. *woh*, injustice, wrong; *wankill*, A.S. *wancol*, unstable, shaky.

l. 496. *spynkarde cloughe, slough, spynar hill;* I can find no trace of this locality, and do not know if it refers to any actual event (unless it be the skirmish between Sir John Gordon and Lilburn " in a mountain pass" on the border, in 1378); but it was quoted in the later prophecies as *Pinken* or *Pinkie cleuch*.

l. 505—512 perhaps refer to the invasion of Scotland and siege of Edinburgh by Henry IV. in 1400, although it more recalls that of Richard II. in 1385.

l. 509. T. *Sembery* is a curious error for *Edinbery*, but very simply made in the MS.

l. 513—516, a repetition of l. 409—412 in the preceding Fytte.

l. 521. From this point the prophecies are not historical; they constitute a series of legendary predictions. They are principally occupied by three battles, that between Seton and the Sea, and those of Gladsmoor and Sandyford, and the career of "the Bastard out of the west," which I take to be a distorted Arthurian legend. These four ideas fill all the later prophecies, Scottish and English alike, of the battles. Dr Robert Chambers says:—" It is broadly notable throughout the history of early prophecy in

Scotland, how strongly the notion was impressed that there was to be a great and bloody conflict near Seton, or at the adjacent Gladsmuir, both in East Lothian [about 7 miles E. of Edinburgh]. There had existed, before the battle of Pinkie (1547), a prophetic rhyme:

> Between Seton and the sea,
> Mony a man shall die that day.

And we know that the rhyme and the day were so from the following passage in Patten's *Account of the Expedition of the Duke of Somerset*, printed in 1548: 'This battell and feld [Pinkie] the Scottes and we are not yet agreed how it shall be named. We cal it Muskelborough felde, because that is the best towne (and yet bad inough) nigh to the place of our meeting. Sum of them cal it Seton felde (a town thear nigh too), by means of a blind prophecy of theirs, which is this or sum such toye : Betwene Seton and the seye, many a man shall dye that day.' The same rhyme is incorporated in the long irregular and mystical poems which were published as the prophecies of Thomas in 1615. We humbly think that our countrymen strained a point to make out the battle of Pinkie as the fulfilment of a conflict at Seton, which is four or five miles distant; not to speak of the preciseness of the prophecy in indicating *between Seton and the sea*.

"That there should be a great and bloody fight at Gladsmuir appears in the old Scotch prophecies. A traditionary one, attributed as usual to 'True Thomas,' bare reference to the fate of Foveran Castle in Aberdeenshire, long ago the seat of a family named Turing:

> 'When Turing's Tower falls to the land,
> Gladsmuir then is nigh at hand:
> When Turing's Tower falls to the sea,
> Gladsmuir the next year shall be.'

A local writer about 1720 (*View of the Diocese of Aberdeen, Spalding Club*) gives this rhyme, and adds: 'It seems that Gladsmuir is to be a very decisive battle for Scotland ; but if one fancy the place of it to be Gladsmuir on the coast of East Lothian, he will find himself mistaken ; for

> 'It shall not be Gladsmoor by the sea,
> But Gladsmoor wherever it be.'

[See before, p. xxxv ; also the English Prophecy in Appendix II. 1. 80.] That is, the number of corpses will make it a resort of birds of prey, and so a *Gled's muir*.

"When the battle of Prestonpans took place in 1745, the victorious Highlanders were for calling it 'Gladsmuir,' in reference to the old prophecy [see before, p. xli, xlii] ; but in truth, the scene of conflict was nearly as far from Gladsmuir as Pinkie was from Seton. It must be admitted to have been near to Seton, though not strictly *betwixt Seton and the Sea*."—*Popular Rhymes of Scotland*, 1870, p. 218.

The "Whole Prophecies of Scotland, &c.," 1603, already discussed (p. xxx), are full of references to these battles. But they were equally famous in England, as is shown by the prose prophecy of 1529, quoted in Appendix II. from the Sloane MS., and many other references in the same volume. At an earlier date, the Battle of Barnet, doubtless on account of the enormous carnage by which it was distinguished, as well as its decisive effect on the Wars between York and Lancaster, was called by contemporaries the Battle of Gladsmoor. In the following quotation from Holinshed, the name occurs as belonging to the site, but I suspect it was an *ex post facto* one : " Hervpon remouved they towards Barnet, a towne standing in the midwaie betwixt London and saint Albons aloft on a hill; at the end whereof towards saint Albons there is a faire plaine for two armies to meet vpon, named Gladmore heath, on the further side of which plaine towards saint Albons the earle pight his campe."—*Holinshed*, ed. 1587, vol. iii. p. 684.

Compare Drayton, *Polyolbion*, Song xxii (Chalmers's English Poets, vol. iv. p. 345) :—

"the armies forward make,
And meeting on the plain to Barnet very near,
That to this very day is called Gladmore there."

As to *Sandyford*, I can offer no conjecture, even of the place hinted at; but the battle at Sandyford is equally prominent in the other Scottish and English prophecies, as in the following, culled from the Sloane MS. already quoted :—

" Ou*er* Sandiford shalbe sorowes sene on the southe side on a mondaye, wheare gromes shall grone on a grene, besides englefield yere standethe a Castelle on a mountaine Clif the *which* shall doo y*ei*r enemyes tene, & save england yat day./ (leaf 41 *a*.)

" At Sandiford betwix ij parkes a pallace & a parishe churche, a hardy prince downe shall lyghte. troye vntrue yen shall tremble & quake yat daye for feare of a deade man when yei heare him speake. all tho*ffyceris* y*er*in shall caste him the keyes, from vxbrydge to hownslowe y*e* bushment to breake, and fare as a people that weare wudd. the ffather shall sleye y*e* sone y*e* brother y*e* brother, y*t* all London shall renn bludde." (leaf 44 *b*.)

l. 541—544. A vivid picture of the desolation to be produced ; this seems the origin of one of the traditional sayings of Thomas quoted on p. xliv :

"A horse sal gang on Carolside brae,
Till the red girth gaw his side in twae."

Carolside, properly *Crawhillside*, lies on the bank of the Leader about a mile above Earlstoun.

l. 549. T. omits *baners*. This line and the next in Ca. have been overwritten so as to make the original words irrecoverable. The words *eneglych shal rone away* have thus been inserted, probably for *nyght shal dee*.

l. 553. *trewe*, the correct singular ; of which *trewis*, *trewes*, *truce* is properly the plural. Fr. *trève*, *trèves*.

l. 555. *dere*, A.S. *derian*, to hurt, harm.

l. 557. *betwene twa sainte Marye dayes*. The same date is given to Gladsmoor in the English prose prophecy in Appendix III.

l. 560. S. *claydon moore*, above this in the MS. *dvnnes more* is written, referring perhaps to Dunse Moor, and the "Warden Raid" of 1378.

Ca. *gleydes more*, the moor of the *gleydes* or kites ; but in the next stanza in Ca. only, and evidently an afterthought, the word is played on as *glads*-moor. This stanza is quoted in the prophecy of Bertlington, ante, p. xxxvi, and in many other prophecies, Scotch and English.

l. 565—576. See as to the Crow and the Raven, Introduction, p. xxxii, &c.

l. 576. *wayloway*, A.S. *wá lá wá*, wo ! O wo !

l. 577—604. In T. only (where also l. 592—604 are lost) contain a list of the lords described by their armorial bearings, by which they might no doubt still be identified. " The publication of predictions, either printed or hieroglyphical, in which noble families were pointed out by their armorial bearings, was, in the time of Queen Elizabeth, extremely common; and the influence of such predictions on the minds of the common people was so great as to occasion a prohibition, by statute, of prophecy by reference to heraldic emblems. Lord Henry Howard also directs against this practice much of the reasoning in his learned treatise, entitled 'A Defensation against the Poyson of Pretended prophecies.'"—Scott, *Border Minstrelsy.*

l. 619. *boune*, ready, prepared.

l. 621—644. In great confusion in the MSS. Ca. seems to transpose two stanzas, putting the death of the bastard before Sandyford, while the others put it last, and make it the cause of the lady's emotion. S. agrees with Co. and L. so far as these are entire, in the order of the stanzas, but as elsewhere mixes up their lines greatly.

l. 625. *braye*, T. had probably *braa*, a brae, or steep incline. Ca. corruptly *wroo.*

l. 633. *Remnerdes*, what this word is corrupted for cannot be ascertained through the defects in the other MSS.

l. 635, *dynge*, Isl. *dænga*, Sw. *dänga*, to knock, push violently, drive.

l. 640. *bod-word*, message.

l. 644. *that mycull may*, who hast great might.

l. 651. *ladys shall wed laddys* 3*ong*; compare the Harleian prophecy, addressed to the Countess of March, "When laddes weddeth lovedies," and Waldhaue's quotation of Thomas's prophecy, ante, p. xxxix.

l. 660. S. *annes*, perhaps rather *aunes. Blak Agnes of Donbar*, the heroic daughter of Earl Thomas Randolph, and wife of Patrick Earl of March, so famed for her defence of the Castle of Dunbar, which, in absence of her husband, she held for five months (1338) against the assault of an English army, led by the earls of Salisbury and Arundel, and at last obliged them to raise the siege. Her husband's career was marked by much oscillation between Scotland and England, and his son finally took the English side, which may account for the hostility to the family here displayed. Thomas of Erceldowne lived a whole generation earlier than Black Agnes, and it is probable that traditions of his relation with an earlier Countess of March, who was "sothely lady at arsyldone" (see Introd., p. xi, xiv), were transferred to her more famous successor.

l. 661—664 differ much in Ca. and Co. The latter is doubtless the original.

l. 664. *ploos*, Ca. looks as like *plees* or *ploes.*   l. 666. *the*, thrive, flourish.

l. 672. *magrat*, O.Fr. *malgrat, maugret*, in spite of.

The conclusion, l. 673—700, differs a good deal in the four MSS. wnich possess it. Co. being fullest, T. next, and perhaps had all the original text. S. is roughly curtailed.

l. 695. *Helmesdale* in Sutherland, in the far north, whence fairies and witches were believed to come.

APPENDIXES I. AND II.

It is not very easy to define the relations between these two compositions, which have about 70 lines in common at the beginning, but are otherwise entirely different. Apparently, the original nucleus consisted of a prophecy referring to the Wars of the

Roses, and the Battle of Glad-moor, seemingly identified with Barnet. This seems to be preserved in lines 1—44, and 73—180 of the English prophecy. Afterwards this composition was extended to embrace the early fortunes of the House of Tudor, and the Battle of Flodden, and probably at this time, 1515—1525, the episode of the English and Scottish knight, l. 45—72, which comes in very awkwardly, was introduced, as well as the later part of the poem. The compiler of the Scottish prophecy then borrowed this introduction as far as line 72, and made it the commencement of a different account of the Battle of Flodden suited to Scottish needs, and alluding, l. 119, to the idea long cherished that James IV. did not die in the battle. Apparently, after the Battle of Pinkie, 1547, and perhaps about the time of the marriage of Queen Mary to the Dauphin, 1558, this was rewritten with interpolations referring to these events—lines 193 and 194 being cleverly adapted from l. 496 of the Romance of Thomas, and lines 239—244 from "the Prophecy of Bertlington:" see ante, p. xxxvi. The copy printed in 1603, and here followed, is much modernized, and bears traces in every line of the original having been pure northern. Thus in L. 65, *gone* must have been *went*; l. 69, *said* for *saw*; l. 71, *two* for *twa*; l. 79, *so* for *swa*, rhyming with *ta = take*; l. 114—121, the rhyme breaks down, and the text is in confusion; l. 139, *two* for *twa*, rhyming with *na ma*, changed into *no more* in l. 141; l. 146, *hurte and woe* for *trouble and tene*, rhyming with *shene*; l. 163 is corrupt; l. 171, *blew* for *bla*, rhyming with *sla* in 173, and in l. 178, 180, *blew*, *two*, for *bla*, *twa*; l. 182, 184, *goe*, *slay* for *ga*, *sla*; l. 224, *stone* for *stane*. Many lines and pairs of lines are also lost at various places. Perhaps one day an older and more perfect copy may be found.

APPENDIX II. I have ventured to apply to this a title recorded by Sir David Lyndesay, about 1528 (*The Dreme*, l. 43), which agrees also with the rubric at end of the MS. It is found in the Lansdowne MS. of 1529, which supplies one of the texts of the Romance of Thomas, and in the Rawlinson MS. C. 813, of a later date. The Lansdowne is evidently a copy by a southern scribe of an older northern text, the true readings of which he has often mistaken and made into nonsense. Still more frequently the rhyme has been injured in the transliteration, as in lines 229—236, where the rhyming words *blowe*, *lee*; *knowe*, *swaye*; *fall*, *hie*; *call*, *dye*, represent an original *blaw*, *le*; *knaw*, *swe*; *fa'*, *he*; *ca'*, *de*. The Rawlinson copy is still more modernized, and as a whole weaker, but it contains fewer absolute blunders, and so often enables us to restore the sense of the original. Only the more important of its variations are here given as notes to the Lansdowne text; but occasionally where the latter is very corrupt, it is relegated to the notes (there marked L.), and the Rawl. reading placed in the text. Words, &c., added from R. in the text are in brackets.

The last historical event recorded in it is the Battle of Flodden, or rather the capture of Tournay by Henry VIII. a few days later. Its date is no doubt shortly after this, and nearer to 1515 than 1525. England is of course still faithful to Rome, and the pope occupies a prominent place in the concluding events; but in the Rawlinson copy, curiously enough, the word "pope," wherever it occurs, is struck out by a line drawn across it, a witness to the feelings of a later date.

Besides the ascription at the end, the authorities for the different sections of the prophecy are cited at l. 135, as "saint Bede;" l. 291, "bredlynton;" l. 292, "bede;" l. 294, "Arseldowne;" l. 346, "Arsalldoune;" l. 380, "Merlyon;" l. 409, "Marlyon;" l. 444, "Arse[l]doun;" l. 445, "the holly man that men calles Bede." Opposite some of these the name is repeated in larger letters in the margin; thus, opposite

NOTES, TEXTUAL AND EXPLANATORY. lxxxiii

to l. 346, *Arysdon;* opp. l. 380, *Merlyon;* opp. l. 409, *Marlyon;* opp. lines 428 and 445, *Bede.*

l. 15, 16. Comp. l. 195, 196 of *Thomas.*

l. 21, &c. Comp. the description of the lady in l. 41 of *Thomas.*

l. 45—72. An interpolation dislocating the natural sequence between the l. 44 and 73. The two knights, St George and St Andrew, of course symbolize England and Scotland.

l. 60 *bis.* a superfluous line, interpolated as if the first of next stanza. Allowed for in R. by omitting l. 72; but of course the proper one to omit was l. 68.

l. 68. Note the Anglo-Saxon and Danish '*burgh* and *by.*'

l. 70. *wrong heyres.* e. g. Henry IV., Edward IV., Richard III., Henry VII.

l. 72. The fling at the Scots here and in line 183 indicates an English author.

l. 73 naturally follows 44. The Lady having consecrated the ground, now declares that it will be the site of the battle of *Gladmoor* (? Barnet), and vanishes. The writer applies to the "lytell man" to give him more distinct information about Gladmoor; the latter predicts the dissension (between the Nevilles and Woodvilles); the son fighting against the father (Clarence and Warwick); falsehood and envy (the House of York) reigning in England for 33 years. (The Duke of York took up arms in 1452, and the Battle of Bosworth was in 1485.) A king reigning without righteousness (Edward IV.); then a break when "he that hath England hent (Warwick) shall be made full lowe to light." Two princes have their deaths with treason dight; then when all expect peace, the landing of Henry VII. and Battle of Bosworth. Henry is crowned, and known as the "king of covatyce." "The fourth leaf of the tree (the house of York) dies, that lost hath bowes moo"—almost all the descendants of Edward III. are extinct; traitors taste the Tower (Warwick and ? Richard, Duke of York, nicknamed by the Tudors, Perkin Warbeck), and Henry VII. dies.

l. 77. gladismore that shall glad vs all,
        yt shalbe gladyng of oure glee;
identical with lines 561-2 of *Thomas.*

l. 79. yt shalbe gladmore wher eu*er* yt fall,
        but not gladmore by the see.

Also in the prophecy of Bertlington, p. xxxv; and see *Notes* to l. 521 of *Thomas.*

l. 181—284 describe the Battle of Flodden, naming the localities of Millfield, Branxton, and Flodden itself. The "red lion" is of course James IV.; the "white lyon," Sir Edmund Howard; and the "Admyrall," Thomas Howard, who commanded the English right. The MS. (Lansd. 762) contains, on leaf 70, a contemporary explanation of the emblems under which various persons are designated in the prophecies. They include the following :—

The mowlle the Erle of Westmerlonde.   The white Lyo*u*n Duke of Norffolk.
The wolffe the lorde Martyn*e.*   The Crepawde Rex Frauncie.
The mone the Erle of Northumberlonde. The Red Lyo*u*n Rex Scotor*u*m.
The Blew bore Erle of Oxford*e.*   The Lylye the Duke of Lancaster.
The Red drago*u*n barne of Clyfford*e.* Pye, Lorde Ryvers.

The Scots are referred to in l. 250 and 298 as "*Albenactes* blode," from the legendary Albanactus, son of Brutus, eponymus of the *Albannaich* or Scottish Celts.

l. 285. "*The prynce that is beyonde the flode*" (Henry VIII. now in France) takes two towns (Terouanne and Tournay).

l. 296. An allusion to True Thomas's absence from earth, which the later tradition extends to seven years. See *Thomas*, l. 286, Cambridge Text.

l. 297. The passage commencing here may originally have referred to the arrival in Scotland of the Duke of Albany, already mentioned more than once; but at this point the "prophecy" ceases to be historical.

l. 305. *stanis more*, this battle figures also in the prose prophecy in Appendix III.

l. 317. "*A king*" or "*duke of Denmark*," and "*the black fleet of Norway*," shew that even now, five hundred years after their invasions had come to an end, the name of the Danes and Norseman was still mentioned in terror.

l. 341. *sondysfurth*, on *the south side*, and l. 371, "*beside a well there is a stronde*," compare the prophecy of Merlyne, p. xxxiii, and the prose prophecy in Appendix III.; see also l. 624—632 of *Thomas*, and *Notes* to l. 521 of the Romance.

l. 373. *Snapeys-more* is referred to also in the prose prophecy, Appendix III.

l. 385—388. *Gladmore* and its doubtful issue; see in *Thomas*, l. 549—560.

l. 405—408. The "*okes thre*" and the "*headless cross of stone*," compare *Thomas*, l. 569—578, and l. 629, 630. See also various similar passages in "the Whole Prophecies of Scotland."

l. 543. "*In the vale of Josephate shall he dye*." So in the end of the "koke of the north" prophecy, edited by Mr Lumby; see ante, p. xxxii, and *Thomas*, l. 641, "The bastarde shall dye in the holy land."

l. 609. *he sayd*, "*a long time thow holdest me here;*" compare the lady's repeated remonstrances in *Thomas*.

l. 627. *when he thynketh tyme to talle*. Query *too tall*, i. e. *too long*; or error for *to calle*.

ADDITIONAL NOTES TO THE INTRODUCTION.

EARLSTOUN CHURCH AND RYMOUR'S STONE.—In part correction of the note to p. xiii Mrs C. Wood of Galashiels, a native of Earlstoun, writes:—"The present church was renewed in 1736, but there are many stones in the churchyard as old as 1600, and the bell, which was cast in Holland, bears the date of 1609. The older building stood a few yards further forward, more to the south. Chambers, in his 'Picture of Scotland,' says that the inscription on the stone built into the wall of Earlstoun Church was defaced by a person named Waterstone, who considered it interfered with his right of property to the burial-place. I believe that this is quite correct, and also that the characters of the former inscription were very ancient. In a plan I have of the churchyard, made in 1842, there are 16 graves belonging to 'Lermonts,' 11 of which lie in a row, and the first of these has the date 1564. But none of the Learmont graves are near the church; in fact, there is only one gravestone in the vicinity of the Rhymer's Stone, and this belongs to the Waterstones." This disposes of any inference in favour of Rymour's name having been Learmont.

HAIG OF BEMERSIDE, p. xliii.—In the account of the family of Haig, written by the Earl of Buchan, we find: "Zerubabel Haig, 17th Baron of Bemerside, who married Elizabeth Gordon, daughter of Thomas Gordon, Esq., Clerk to the Court of Justiciary, by whom he had one son and twelve daughters. . . . . This Zerubabel Haig died in 1752." This was the gentleman referred to by Sir Walter Scott.

RHYMER'S THORN, p. xlix.—Mr James Wood, Galashiels, says, "Rhymer's Thorn stood in a garden belonging to the Black Bull Inn, occupied by a man named Thin. It was a large tree, and sending out its roots in all directions, it absorbed much of the growing power of the soil. Thin set his son to cut the roots all round, and clear the garden of them. This was in the spring of 1814, and the Thorn which had defied the blasts of probably 900 years, now shorn of its roots, succumbed shortly after to a violent westerly gale. It was immediately replanted, with several cart loads of manure dug in round about it; but, notwithstanding all the efforts of the people to keep it alive, it never took root again. In 1830 the ground on which it stood came into the possession of the late John Spence, writer, Earlstoun, who built a high wall round the garden, leaving a square opening near the top to mark the site of the tree.

"The Thorn is described by John Shiel, a native of Earlstoun, 12 years old when the tree was blown down, and now 73, as 'the grandest tree ever I saw; it was a big tree, wi' a trunk as thick as a man's waist, an' its branches were a perfect circle, an' sae roun i' the tap! I' the spring it was a solid sheet o' white flourishin', scentin' the whole toon end, an' its haws—there was na the like o' them in a' Scotland! they were the biggest haws ever I saw in my life; ay, I've been up the tree scores o' times pu'ing them when I was a laddie.'

"Rhymer's Thorn must have been an object of the utmost veneration to the people of Earlstoun, as they believed their prosperity to be bound up in its existence; and on the day it was blown down, a great many people ran with bottles of Wine and Whisky, and threw their contents on it, so as, if possible, to preserve it alive. It was always said that the Rhymer prophesied that Earlstoun should prosper so long as the Thorn stood; and it was a remarkable coincidence that the year it was blown down all the merchants in Earlstoun 'broke.'"

THOMAS'S DISAPPEARANCE, p. l.—"The late Mr Whale, who was a great repository of the traditions of Earlstoun, said, that the Public House, at the door of which the Rhymer sat when the white hind went through the village, stood in the Close, behind the present Reading-Room. There is, however, another tradition known in Earlstoun connected with the sudden disappearance of Thomas. It is said, that on the night when he so mysteriously disappeared, he had attended a banquet given by the Earl of March at his Castle in Earl's Town, and on his way home to the Tower was waylaid and murdered, either by some of the neighbouring barons, or by agents of the Earl of March, to whom he was an object of fear and dislike, in consequence of his close and intimate friendship with Sir William Wallace. The road between Earl's Town and Ersildoun passed in those days to the south of the present road, and a large two-handed sword, which was dug up a good many years ago in the garden (through which the old road is said to have crossed) of the late Mr George Noble, was purchased lately by a descendant of the Earlstoun Learmonts, on account of its supposed connection with this tradition."—C. W.

"This 'sword of Thomas the Rhymer' was a huge two-handed sword, in pretty good preservation. From the form of handle, it may have possibly been of the 12th or 13th century."—A. C.

THE OLD HARLEIAN PROPHECY, p. xviii.

I DID not think of insulting the reader by a translation of this, but as I have been asked more than once "what does it mean?" here it is:—

The Countess of Dunbar asked Thomas of Erceldoune when the Scottish war should have an end, and he answered her and said:

When people have (*man has*) made a king of a capped man;
When another man's thing is dearer to one than his own;
When Loudyon [or *London*?] is Forest, and Forest is field;
When hares litter on the hearth-stone;
When Wit and Will war together;
When people make stables of churches, and set castles with styes.
When Roxburgh is no burgh, and market is at Forwylee;
When the old is gone and the new is come that is worth [or *do*] nought;
When Bannockburn is dunged with dead men;
When people lead men in ropes to buy and to sell;
When a quarter of 'indifferent' wheat is exchanged for a colt of 10 merks;
When pride rides on horseback, and peace is put in prison;
When a Scot cannot hide like a hare in form that the English shall not find him;
When right and wrong assent together;
When *lads* marry *ladies*;[1]
When Scots flee so fast, that for want of ships, they drown themselves.
When shall this be? Neither in thy time nor in mine;
But [shall] come and go within twenty winters and one.

[1] In the 14th, of course, and not the 19th century meaning of these words, when the "lads" in a shop may wed the "ladies" behind the counter, without any disparity. But *lads* have "looked up," and *ladies* gone, well-a-day! a long way down, since Thomas's time; although in old-fashioned country districts the farm-servants are still "the lads," and the daughters of the baron "the leddies."

One might suppose that Shakspere had these lines in view, where he makes the Fool in *Lear* (Act III. Scene ii.) parody these species of composition:

"Ile speake a Prophesie ere I go:
When Priests are more in word, then matter;
When Brewers marre their malt with water;
When Nobles are their Taylors Tutors
No Heretiques burn'd, but wenches Sutors;
When euery Case in Law, is right;
No Squire in debt, nor no poore Knight;
When slanders do not liue in Tongues;
Nor Cut-purses come not to throngs;

When Vsurers tell their Gold i' th' Field;
And Baudes, and whores, do churches build;
Then shal the Realme of *Albion*,
Come to great confusion;
Then comes the time, who liues to see 't
That going shalbe vs'd with feet.
This prophecie *Merlin* shall make, for I liue before his time."

Tomas Off Ersseldoune.

[*Thornton MS. leaf* 149, *back, col.* 1.]

Lystyns, lordyngs, bothe grete & smale,
   And takis gude tente what j will saye :
   I sall ȝow tello als trewe a tale,
Als euer was herde by nyghte or daye :   4
And þe maste meruelle ffor owttyne naye,
That euer was herde by-fore or syene,
And þer-fore pristly j ȝow praye,
That ȝe will of ȝoure talkyng blyne.   8
It es an harde thyng for to saye,
Of doghety dedis þat hase bene done ;
Of felle feghtyngs & batells sere ;
And how þat þir knyghtis hase wonne þair schone. 12
Bot jhesu crist þat syttis in trone,
Safe ynglysche mene bothe ferre & nere ;
And j sall telle ȝow tyte and sone,
Of Batells donne sythene many a ȝere ;   16
And of batells þat done sall bee ;
In whate place, and howe, and whare ;
And wha sall hafe þe heghere gree,
And whethir partye sall hafe þe werre ;   20
Wha sall takk þe flyghte and flee,
And wha sall dye and by-leue thare :
Bot jhesu crist, þat dyed on tre,
Saue jnglysche mene whare-so þay fare.   24

[*Thornton, continued.*]
[FYTTE THE FIRSTE.]

Als j me wente þis Endres daye,
   ffull faste in mynd makand my
   mone,
In a mery mornynge of Maye,
By huntle bankkes my selfe allone, 28
I herde þe jaye, & þe throstyll cokke,
The Mawys menyde hir of hir songe,
þe wodewale beryde als a belle,
That alle þe wode a-bowte me ronge. 32
Allonne in longynge thus als j laye,
Vndyre-nethe a semely tree,
. . . . . . j whare a lady gaye
. . . . ouer a longe lee. 36
If j solde sytt to domesdaye, [col. 2]
With my tonge, to wrobbe and wrye,
Certanely þat lady gaye,
Neuer bese scho askryede for mee. 40
Hir palfraye was a dappill graye,

Swylke one ne saghe j neuer none;
Als dose þe sonne on someres daye,
þat faire lady hir selfe scho schone. 48
Hir selle it was of roelle bone,
ffull semely was þat syghte to see!
Stefly sett with precyous stones,
And compaste all with crapotee, 52
Stones of Oryente, grete plente;
Hir hare abowte hir hede it hange;
Scho rade ouer þat lange lee; 55
A whylle scho blewe, a-noþer scho sange.

THORNTON

[*Cotton, Vitell. E .x. leaf 240, back.*]
[1]Incipit prophecia Thome Arseldon
[¹ col. 1]

IN a lande as I was lent,
   In þe grykyng of þe day,
Me a lone as I went,
In huntle bankys me for to play.
I sawe þe throstyl & þe Iay;
þe mawes movyde of hyr songe;
þe wodwale sange notes gay,
þat all þe wod a boute range.
In þat longynge as I lay,
vndir nethe a dern tre,
I was war of a lady gay,
Come rydyng ouyr a fayre le.
ȝogh I sulde sitt to domysday,
With my tonge to wrabbe & wry,
Sertenly, all hyr aray,
It beth neuer discryuyd for me.
hyr palfra was dappyll gray,

Syche on say I neuer none;
. . . als son in somers day,
All abowte þat lady schone.
hyr sadyl was of a jewel bone,
A semely syȝt it was to se;
. [w]roght with mony a precyouse stone,
And compasyd all with crapote.
Stones of [ȝ]osrt gret plente;
. . . . . a boute hyr hede it hang;
. . . . þe fair le
. . . . . shee blewe anoþer she sange.

COTTON

HER PALFREY, HARNESS, AND ATTIRE, SHINE WITH GOLD AND GEMS. 3

[*Lansdowne* 762, *leaf* 24.] [*Cambridge Univ. Lib. MS. Ff.*, *leaf* 119.]
[FOOTT THE FIRST.] [FYTTE THE FIRSTE.]

As I me went this thender day,	As I me went þis Andyrs day,
So styll makyng my Mone,	ffast on my way makyng my mone,
In a Mery Mornyng of May,	In a mery mornyng of may,
In huntly bankes My self alone, 28	Be huntley bankis my self alone,
I harde the Meryll and the Iay,	I herde þe iay, & þe throstell,
the Maner Menede of hir song,	þe mavys menyd in hir song,
the wylde wode-wale song notes gay, 31	þe wodewale farde as a bell.
that alle the shawys abowte hem Rong.	þat þe wode aboute me rong.
¶ But in a loning, as I lay,	Alle in a longyng, as I lay,
Vnder neth a semely tre,	Vndurneth a cumly tre,
I saw where a lady gay	Saw I wher a lady gay
Cam rydyng ouer a louely le. 36	Came ridand ouer a louely le.
thowh that I leue styll tyll domys day,	ȝif I shuld sitte till domusday,
with any my tonge to worble or were,	Alle with my tong to know & se,
The certayn sothe of hir Array	Sertenly, alle hur aray,
May neuer be descreued for me. 40	Shalle hit neuer be scryed for me.
¶ Hir palfray was of daply gray,	Hir palfray was of dappull gray,
[1]The farest Molde that any myght be;	
here sadell bryght as any day. [1 leaf 24, bk]	
Set with pereles to þe kne. 44	
And furthermore of hir Aray,	
Diuers clothing she had vpon;	Sike on se I neuer non;
And as the sonne in somerys day,	As dose þe sune on somers day,
Forsouthe the ladye here sylffe shone. 48	þe cumly lady hir selfe schone.
¶ here sege was of ryall bone,	hir sadill was of reuyll bone,
Syche one sau I neuer with ye!	Semely was þat sight to se!
Set with many A precious stone,	Stifly sette with precious ston,
And cumpasyde all with crapote. 52	Compaste aboute with crapote,
With stonys of oryoles, grete plenty;	Stonys of oryons, gret plente;
Dyamondes thick aboute hir honge;	hir here aboute hir hed hit hong
She bare a horne of gold semely,	She rode out ouer þat louely le
And vnder hir gyrdell a flone. · 56	A while she blew, a while she song;

LANSDOWNE CAMBRIDGE

Hir garthes of nobyll sylke þay were,
The bukyll's were of Berelle stone, 58
Hir steraps were of crystalle clere,
And all with perelle ouer-by-gone. 60
Hir payetrelle was of jrale fyne,
Hir cropoure was of Orpharë;
And als clere golde hir brydill it schone,
One aythir syde hange bellys three. 64

[. . . . . no break in the MS.]
And seuene raches by hir þay rone;
Scho bare an horne abowte hir halse,
And vndir hir belte full many a flone. 72
Thomas laye & sawe þat syghte,
Vndir-nethe ane semly tree;
He sayd, 'ȝone es marye moste of myghte,
þat bare þat childe þat dyede for mee. 76
Bot if j speke with ȝone lady bryghte,
I hope myne herte will bryste in three!
Now sall j go with all my myghte,
Hir for to mete at Eldoune tree.' 80
Thomas rathely vpe he rase, [¹ leaf 150]
¹And he rane ouer þat Mountayne hye;
Gyff it be als the storye sayes,
He hir mette at Eldone tree. 84
He knelyde downe appone his knee,
Vndir-nethe þat grenwode spraye;
And sayd, 'lufly ladye! rewe one mee,
Qwene of heuene als þou wele maye!' 88
Than spake þat lady Milde of thoghte,
'Thomas! late swylke wordes bee;
Qwene of heuene ne am j noghte,
ffor j tuke neuer so heghe degre. 92

THORNTON

. . . . er of cristall cler,
. . . . war þay sett;
Sadyll & brydil wer a . . . . . [col. 2]
with sylk & sendell fy . . . .
hyr paytrel was of y . . . . . .
And hir croper of yra . . . .
hyr brydil was of g . . . . . .
on euery syde for soth . . . .
hyr brydil reynes w . . . . . .
A semly syȝt it w . . . . . .
Croper & paytrel . . . .
In euery joynt . . . .
She led thre gre . . . .
& racches cowpled . . . . . .
She bare an horn a . . . . . .
& vndir hyr gyrdyll . . . . .
Thomas lay & sawe . . . . . .
In þe bankes of h . . . . . .
he sayd 'ȝonder is ma . . . . .
þat bar þe child þat . . . . . .
certes bot I may s . . . .
ellys my hert w . . . .
I shal me hye with . . . .
hyr to mete at ȝo . . . .
Thomas rathly up a . . . . . .
& ran ouyr mountay . . . . .
if it be sothe þe story . . . . .
he met hyr euyn a . . . . . .
Thomas knelyd down on h . . .
vndir nethe þe gr . . . .
And sayd 'louely lad . . . . . .
Qwene of heu . . . .
. . . . [leaf 241]
. . . .
. . . .
. . . .

COTTON

¶ She blewe a note, and treblyd als,
the Ryches into the shawe gan gone;
There was no man that herd þe noyes,
Saue thomas there he lay a lone.   60
here cropyng was of ryche gold,
here parrell alle of Alaran;
here brydyll was of Reler bolde;
On every side hangyd bellys then.   64

¶ She led iij greue hwndes in a leshe,
Seue richys aboute hir syde ran;   70

Thomas ley and beheld this syght,
vnder neth a sembly tre;
'yendyr ys that ladye most of myght,
That bare the chylde that blede for me.
But yf I speke with that lady bryght, 77
I trowe my harte wolde breke in thre;
¶ I wyll go wyth all my myght,
And mete with hir at Elden tre.'   80
Thomas Raythly vp a Rose,
And Ran ouer that Montayne hye;
yf it be as the story sais,
[1]He met with hir at elden tre.   84
He knelyd vpon his kne,   [¹ leaf 85]
Vndernethe a grene wode spraye;
¶ 'Louely lady! rewe on me;
Quene of heuyn, as ye wele may!'   88
Then said that lady Mylde of þought,
'Thomas, lat suche wordes be!
For quene of heuyn am I not,
I toke neuer so hye degre.   92
LANSDOWNE

[2]Hir garthis of nobull silke þei were,
hir boculs þei were of barys ston; [² leaf 119, back]
hir stiroppis thei were of cristall clere,
And alle with perry aboute be gon.
Hir paytrell was of a riall fyne,
Hir cropur was of Arafe;
Hir bridull was of golde fyne;
On every side hong bellis thre.
She led iij grehoundis in a leesshe,
viij rachis be hir fete ran;
To speke with hir wold I not seesse;
Hir lire was white as any swan.
fforsothe, lordyngis, as I yow tell,
Thus was þis lady fayre begon;
She bare a horne aboute hir halce,
And vndur hir gyrdill mony flonne.
Thomas lay and saw þat sight,
Vndurneth a semely tre;
he seid, yonde is mary of myght,
þat bare þe childe þat died for me.
But I speke with þat lady bright,
I hope my hert wille breke in thre;
But I will go with alle my myght,
Hir to mete at eldryn tre.
Thomas radly vp he rose,
And ran ouer þat mounteyn hye,
And certanly, as þe story sayes,
he hir mette at eldryne tre.
he knelid downe vpon his kne,
Vndurneth þe grenewode spray;
louely lady! þou rew on me;
qwene of heuen, as þou well may!
Than seid þat lady bright,   [leaf 120]
Thomas, let such wordis be!
ffor quen of heuon am I noght,
I toke neuer so hye degre.
CAMBRIDGE

Bote j ame of ane oþer couɳtree,
If j be payrelde moste of prysse;
I ryde aftyre this wylde fee,
My raches rynnys at my devyse.' 96
'If þou be parelde moste of prysee,
And here rydis thus in thy folye,
Of lufe, lady, als þou erte wysse,
þou gyffe me leue to lye the bye!' 100
Scho sayde, 'þou mane, þat ware folye,
I praye þe, Thomas, þou late me bee;
ffor j saye þe full sekirlye, 103
þat synne will for-doo all my beaute.'
'Now, lufly ladye, rewe one mee,
And j will euer more with the duelle;
Here my trouthe j will the plyghte,
Whethir þou will in heuene or helle.' 108

'Mane of Molde! þou will me marre,
Bot ȝitt þou sall hafe all thy will;
And trowe it wele, þou chewys þe werre,
ffor alle my beaute will þou spylle.' 120
Downe þane lyghte þat lady bryghte,
Vndir-nethe þat grenewode spraye;
And, als the storye tellis full ryghte,
Seuene sythis by hir he laye. 124
Scho sayd, 'mane, the lykes thy playe:
Whate byrde in boure maye delle with the?
Thou merrys me all þis longe daye, [col. 2]
I praye the, Thomas, late me bee!' 128

THORNTON

. . . .
. . . . most of prise
. . . .
. . . . at my devys.'
. . . .
. . . . lady in strange foly,
. . . .
þou ȝeue me leue to lige ȝe by.'
. . . . oly
⁕I pray þe, thomas, late me be!
. . . . erly
þat wolde fordo all my bewte.'
. . . . rew on me,
& euyr more I shal with þe dwell;
. . . . nowe I plyght to þe,
where þou byleues in heuyn or hell.'
'. . . . t þou myght lyg[e] me by,
vndir nethe þis grene wode spray,
. . . . . tell to morowe full hastely,
þat þou hade layne by a lady ga[y.]'.
'. . . . . I mote lygge by þe,
vndir nethe þis gren wode tre,
. . . . ll þe golde in crystyenty,
sulde þou neuyr be wryede for me.'
'. . . on molde, þou will me marre,
And þe, bot þou may hafe þi will,
. . . þou wele, thomas, þou cheuyst þe
foll al my bewte wilt þou spyl[l.]' [warre,
. . une lyghtyd þat lady bryȝht,
vndir nethe þe gren wod spray;
. . . . þe story sayth full ryȝt,
Seuyn tymes by hyr he lay.
'. . . . yd, man, þou lyste þi play,
what berde in boure myȝt dele with ȝe?
. . . . . . es me all þis longe day,
I pray þe, thomas, lat me be!'

COTTON

¶ I am of a nothere contre,
Thowgh I be perlyd moste in pryce;
And ryde here after the wylde fe,
My raches rennyng att my deuyce.'   96
'Yf þou be perled most in price,
And ryde here in thy foly,
louely lady, ware wyce,
yeue me leue to lye the bye.'   100
¶ She said, 'man, that were foly;
I pray the Thomas lett me be;
For I the say sekerelye,
Syn wolde þou for-do al my bewte.'   104
'A lowly lady! reu ofie me,
And euer I wole withe the dwell·
My trowche I plyght to the,
whe þere þou wylt to hevyne or hell.' 108

But I am a lady of anoþer cuntre,
If I be parellid moost of price;
I ride aftur þe wilde fee,
My raches rannen at my deuyse.
If þou be pareld most of price,
And ridis here in þi balye,
Lufly lady, as þou art wyse,
To gif me leve to lye þe by.
Do way, thomas, þat were foly;
I pray þe hertely let me be;
ffor I say the securly,
þat wolde for-do my bewte.
Lufly lady, þou rew on me,
And I shall euermore with þe dwell;
here my trouth I plight to þe,
Whedur þou wilt to heuon or hell.

¶ 'A Man of Molde! þou wolte me Mare,
And yete þou shalte haue all thy wyll;
But wete þou well, þou chece hit the war,
For all my bewte þou wolte spyll.'   120
A downe alyght that lady bryght,
vnder nethe that grene wode spraye;
And, as the story tellythe ryght,
Seuen sythes by hir he laye.   124
¶ 'A man, þe lykythe wele thy playe:
Whate byrde in bowre may dele with the?
Thou marrest me here this long day,
I pray the, Thomas, [lett] me be!'   128

Man of molde! þou wilt me marre,
But ȝet þou shalt haue thy wille;
But trow þou well, þou thryuist þe warre,
ffor alle my beute þou wille spille.
Down þen light þat lady bright,
Vndurneth a grenewode spray;
And, as þe story tellus ful right,   [lf 120, bk]
vij tymes be hir he lay.
She seid, thomas, þou likis þi play:
What byrde in boure may dwel with þe?
þou marris me here þis lefe long day,
I pray the, Thomas, let mé be!

THORNTON	COTTON
Thomas stode vpe in þat stede,	. . . . . . ode vp in þat stede,
And he by-helde þat lady gaye ;	& behelde þat lady gay ;
Hir hare it hange all ouer hir hede,	. . . . . hange downe a bowte hyr hede ;
Hir eghne semede owte, þat are were graye.	hyr eyn semyt oute be sorow grey. 132
And alle þe riche clothynge was a-waye,	. . . . . . thynge was all away,
þat he by-fore sawe in þat stede ; 134	þat he before had sene in þat stede ;
Hir a schanke blake, hir oþer graye,	. . . . blake, þat oþer gray,
And all hir body lyke the lede. 136	hyr body als blo as ony lede.
Thomas laye & sawe þat syghte,	
Vndir-nethe þat grenewod tree ;	
þan said Thomas, 'allas! allas! 137	. . . . de, & sayd 'allas!
In faythe þis es a dullfull syghte ;	Me thynke þis is a dulfull syght ;
How arte þou fadyde þus in þe face,	. . . . fadyd in þi face,
þat schane by-fore als þe sonne so bryght[e]!' 140	before þou shone as son so bryȝt.'

                         [& Mon[e]],

Scho sayd, 'Thomas, take leue at sonne	'. . . . . e, thomas, at son & mone,
And als at lefe þat grewes on tree ; 158	at gresse & at euery tre ;
This twelmoneth sall þou with me gone,	. . . . ethe sal þou with me gone,
And Medill-erthe sall þou none see.' 160	Medyl erth þou sall not se.'
He knelyd downe appone his knee,	

Lansdowne	Cambridge
Thomas stode vp in that stede, [leaf 25, bk]	Thomas stondand in þat sted,
And behelde that shulde be gay;	And beheld þat lady gay;
hure here honge aboute hir hede,	hir here þat hong vpon hir hed,
here yene semyd out that were gray. 132	hir een semyd out, þat were so gray.
¶ And all hir cloþyng were Awaye,	And alle hir clothis were Away,
There she stode in that stede;	þat here before saw in þat stede;
her colour blak, oþer gray,	þe too þe blak, þe toþur gray,
And all hir body as betyn lede. 136	þe body bloo as beten leed.
T[h]an said Thomas, 'Alas! alas!	Thomas seid, Alas! Alas!
This is A dewellfull sight;	In feith þis is a dolfull sight;
now is she fasyd in þe face, 139	þat þou art so fadut in þe face,
that shone be fore as þe sonne bryght!'	þat before schone as sunne bright!
¶ On euery syde he lokyde abowete,	
he sau he myght no wharo fle;	
Sche woxe so grym and so stowte,	
The Dewyll he wende she had be. 144	
In the Name of the trynite,	
he coniuryde here anon) Ryght,	
That she shulde not come hym nere,	
But wende away of his syght. 148	
¶ She said, 'Thomas, this is no nede,	
For fende of hell am I none;	
For the now am I grete desese,	
And suffre paynis many one. 152	
this xij Mones þou shalt with me gang,	
And se the maner of my lyffe;	
for thy trowche thou hast me tane,	
Ayene þat may ye make no stryfe. 156	
¶ Tak thy leue of sone and Mone,	Take þi leve, thomas, at sune & mone,
And the lefe that spryngyth on tre;	And also at levys of eldryne tre;
þis xij monthes þou most with me gone,	This twelmond shall þou with me gon,
Middylle erthe þou shalt not se.' 160	þat mydul erth þou shalt not se.
	he knelyd downe vpon his kne,

LANSDOWNE   CAMBRIDGE

Vndir-nethe þat grenewod spraye ; 162
And sayd, 'lufly lady ! rewe on mee,
Mylde qwene of heuene, als þou beste maye.
Allas !' he sayd, ' & wa es mee !
I trowe my dedis wyll wirke me care ;
My saulle, jhesu, by-teche j the, 167
Whedir-some þat euer my banes sall fare.'
Scho ledde hym jn at Eldone hill,
Vndir-nethe a derne lee ;
Whare it was dirke als mydnyght myrke,
And euer þe water till his knee. 172
The montenans of dayes three,
He herd bot swoghynge of þe flode ;
At þe laste, he sayde, ' full wa es mee !
Almaste j dye, for fawte of f[ode.]' 176
Scho lede hym in-till a faire herbere,
Whare frwte was g[ro]wan[d gret plentee ;]
¹ Pere and appill, bothe ryppe þay were,
The date, and als the damasee ; [ᴛ ʟғ 150, bk.]
þe fygge, and als so þe wyneberye ; 181
The nyghtgales byggande on þair neste ;
þe papeioyes faste abowte gane flye ;
And throstylls sange wolde hafe no reste.
He pressede to pulle frowyte with his
    hande, 185
Als mane for fude þat was nere faynt ;
Scho sayd, 'Thomas ! þou late þame stande,
Or ells þe fende the will atteynt. 188
If þou it plokk, sothely to saye,
Thi saule gose to þe fyre of helle ;
It commes neuer owte or domesdaye,
Bot þer jn payne ay for to duelle. 192
Thomas, sothely, j the hyghte,
Come lygge thyne hede downe on my knee,
And [þou] sall se þe fayreste syghte,
þat euer sawe mane of thi contree.' 196
He did in hye als scho hym badde ;

THORNTON

. . . . ll wo is me !
I trowe my dedes will werke me care :
. . . . ake to þe,
Whedir so euyr my body sal fare.'
. . . . h with all hyr my3t,
vndir nethe þat derne lee ;
. . . . . . s derke as at mydny3t,
& euyr in watyr vnto þe kne.
. . . . of dayes thre
he herde but swowynge of a flode ;
. . . . s sayde, 'ful wo is me,
Nowe I spyll for fawte of fode.'
. . . . she lede hym tyte ;
þer was fruyte gret plente ;
. . . . les þer were rype,
þe date & þe damese ;
. . . . fylbert tre ;
þe nyghtyngale bredynge in hyr neste ;
. . . . a bowte gan fle.
þe throstylkoke sange wolde hafe no . . .
. . . . . . pulle fruyt with hys hande ;

as man for fawte þat was . . . . .
. . . . 'lat all stande,
er els þe deuyl wil þe ataynte, 188

. . . . tomas, I þe hy3t,
& lay þi hede vp on my kne ;
. . . . a fayrer sy3t,
þat euyr sawe man in þu kontre.

COTTON

'Alas!' he said, 'full wo is me,
I trowe my werkes wyll wryche me care;
My soule, Ihesu, I be take the,
Where on erthe my body shall fare.' 168
¶ She lede hym downe at elden hyll,
vnder neth a derne le,   [¹ leaf 26]
In weys derke þat was full ylle,
And euer water vp to his kne.   172
The monetaynis of dayes thre
he harde but swoyng of the flode;
Att the last he said, 'full wo is me!
All most I dye for defawte of fode.' 176
· ¶ Sche browght hym tyl A fayre erbore,
where fruyt growyd grete plente;
Peres and Apples Rype they were,
Datys and the damyse;   180
the fyges and the pynnene fre;
the nyghtyngalle byldyng hire nest;
the popyngay abowte gan fle,
the throssell song hauyng no rest. 184
¶ Thomas presyd to pull the frute with
    his hand,
As man for fode hade been feynte;
Sche said, 'Thomas, let that stonde, 187
Or elles þe dewele wole the Ateynte:
Yf þou pull there of Asay,
Thowe myght be damned into hell;
Thowe commyst neuer owte agayne,
But euer in payn) þou shalt dwell. 192
¶ But Thomas southly I the heght,
Come ley thy hed on my kne,
And þou shall se the farest sight,
that euer saw man of thy contrey. 196

LANSDOWNE

To mary mylde he made his mone:
Lady! but þou rew on me,
Alle my games fro me ar gone.
Alas! he seyd, woo is me,   [leaf 121]
I trow my dedis wil wyrk me woo;
Ihesu, my soule beteche I the,
Wher so euer my bonys shall goo.
She led hym to þe eldryn hill,
Vndurneth þe grenewode lee,
Wher hit was derk as any hell,
And euer water tille þe knee.
þer þe space of dayes thre,
he herd but þe noyse of þe flode;
At þe last, he seid, wo is me!
Almost I dye, for fowte of fode.
She led hym into a fayre herbere,
þer frute groande was gret plente;
peyres and appuls, bothe ripe þei ware,
þe darte and also þe damsyn tre;
þe fygge and also þe white bery;
þe nyghtyngale biggyng hir nest,
þe popyniay fast about gan flye,
þe throstill song wolde haue no rest.
he presed to pul þe fr[ute with] his honde,

As man for fode was nyhonde feynte;
She seid, thomas, let þem stande,
Or ellis þe feend [will] þe ateynte.
If þou pulle, þe sothe to sey, [leaf 121, back]
þi soule goeth to þe fyre of hell;
hit cummes neuer out til domus day,
But þer euer in payne to dwelle.
She seid, thomas, I þe hight,
Come lay þi hed on my kne,
And þou shalle se þe feyrest sight,
þat euer saw mon of þi cuntre.
He leyd down his hed as she hym badde;

CAMBRIDGE

THORNTON	COTTON
Appone hir knee his hede he layde,	
ffor hir to paye he was fuH glade,	
And þans þat lady to hym sayde : 200	
'Seese þou nowe ȝone faire waye,	. . . . . . tomas, ȝone fayre way,
þat lygges ouer ȝone heghe mountayne ?—	þat lyggys ouyr ȝone fayr playn ?
Ȝone es þe waye to heuene for aye, 203	. . . . ay to heuyn for ay,
Whene synfuH sawles are passede per	whan synfull sawles haf ful 204
Seese þou nowe ȝone oþer waye, [payne.	. . . . is ȝone secund way,
þat lygges lawe by-nethe ȝone rysse ?	þat ligges lawe vndir þe rese ?
Ȝone es þe waye þe sothe to saye,	. . . . ay, sothly to say,
Vn-to þe joye of paradyse. 208	. . . to þe joyes of paradyse.
Seese þou ȝitt ȝone thirde waye,	
þat ligges vndir ȝone grene playne ?	
Ȝone es þe waye, with tene and traye,	
Whare synfuH saulis suffirris þaire payne.	
Bot seese þou nowe ȝone ferthe waye,	. . . . s ȝone thyrde way,
þat lygges ouer ȝone depe deHe ? 214	þat lygges ouyr ȝone . . .
Ȝone es þe waye, so waylawaye,	. . . . sothly to say,
Vn-to þe birnande fyre of heHe.	to þe brynnyng fyer of hell.
Seese þou ȝitt ȝone faire casteHe,	. . . . ȝone fayr castell,
[þat standis ouer] ȝone heghe hiH ? 218	þat standes ouyr ȝone . . .
[1] Of towne & towre, it beris þe beHe ;	. . . . [leaf 241, back]
In erthe es none lyke it vn-tiH. [1 col. 2]	. . . .
ffor sothe, Thomas, ȝone es myne awenne,	. . . . tomas . . . . . .
And þe kynges of this Countree ; 222	. . . .
Bot me ware leuer be hanged & drawene,	. . . hade leuer be han . .
Or þat he wyste þou laye me by.	. . . .
When þou commes to ȝone castelle gaye,	whan þu comyst in ȝone . .
I pray þe curtase mane to bee ; 226	. . . .
And whate so any mane to þe saye,	what so any man to þe say,
Luke þou answere none bott mee.	s . . . .
My lorde es seruede at ylk a mese,	My lorde is seruyd at eche mese,
With thritty knyghttis faire & free ; 230	with thry . . . .
I saH saye syttande at the desse,	I sall say, syttynge on þe dese,
I tuke thi speche by-ȝonde the see.'	I toke þi sp . . . .
Thomas stiH als stane he stude,	Thomas stode as still as stone,
And he by-helde þat lady gaye ; 234	& byhelde þat lady . . . .

HOW HE MUST BEHAVE, ON REACHING HER COUNTRY, AND SPEAK TO NONE BUT THE LADY.

LANSDOWNE

Seest thow yender that playn way,
That lyeth ouer youre playn so cuyne?
That is the wey, sothely to say,
To the hight blysse of hewyne. 204

¶ Seyst þou yendyr, A noþer way,
That lyeth yendyr vnder the grene Ryce?
T[h]at is the wey, sothely to say,
To the Ioye of paradyce. 208

Seyst þow yender thrid way,
¹That lyeth vnder that hye Montayne?
that is the wey, sothely to say, [¹ leaf 26, bk]
where synfull soulis sofferis payne. 212

¶ Seyst þou yendur forthere way,
that lyeth yendur full fell?
hit it the wey, sothely to saye,
To the brynyng fyer of hell. 216

Seist þou yonder, that fayre castell,
that standyth hye vpon that hyll?
of Townys and towris it berys the bell;
On erthe is lyke non oþer tyll. 220

¶ Forsothe, Thomas, that is myne owne,
And the kyngis of this countre;
Me were as goode be hengyd or brent,
As he wyst þou layst me bye. 224

when thou commyst to þe þendyr castell
I pray the curtace man þou be; [gay,
And what any man to the say,
loke þou answere no man but me. 228

. ¶ My lorde is seruyd at the Messe,
with xxxᵈ bolde barons and thre.
And I wyll say, sittyng at þe deyce,
I toke the speche at elden tre.' 232

Thomas stode styll as stone,
And behelde this lady gay;

CAMBRIDGE

His hed vpon hir kne he leide,
hir to pleese he was full gladde,
And þen þat lady to hym she seide: 200
Sees þou ʒondur fayre way
þat lyes ouer ʒondur mownteyne?
ʒondur is þe way to heuen for ay,
Whan synful sowlis haue duryd þer peyn.

Seest þou now, thomas, ʒondur way,
þat lyse low vndur ʒon rise?
ʒondur is þe way, þe sothe to say,
Into þe ioyes of paradyse.

Sees þou ʒonder thrid way,
þat lyes ouer ʒondur playne?
ʒonder is þe way, þe sothe to say,
þer sinfull soules schalle drye þer payne.

Sees þou now ʒondur fourt way, [leaf 122]
þat lyes ouer ʒondur felle?
ʒonder is þe way, þe sothe to say,
Vnto þe brennand fyre of hell.

Sees þou now ʒondur fayre castell,
þat stondis vpon ʒondur fayre hill?
Off towne & toure, it berith þe bell;
In mydul erth is non like þer-till.

In faith, thomas, ʒondur is myne owne,
And þe kyngus of þis cuntre;
but me were bettur be hengud & drawyn,
þen he wist þat þou lay be me.

My lorde is serued at ilk a messe, (229)
with xxxᵗⁱ knyʒtis fayre & fre;
And I shalle say, sittyng at þe deese,
I toke þi speche be ʒonde þe lee. (232)

Whan þou comes to ʒondur castell gay,
I pray þe curtes man to be; (226)
And what so euer any man to þe say,
Loke þou answer non but me. (228)

Thomas stondyng in þat stode,
And be helde þat lady gay;

| Scho come agayne als faire & gude, | þan was she fayr & ryche onone, |
| And also ryche one hir palfraye. 236 | & also ryal on hyr .... |

Hir grewehundis fillide with dere blode;	þe grewhondes had fylde þaim on þe dere,
Hir raches couplede by my faye;	& ratches ....
Scho blewe hir horne, with mayne & mode,	she blew hyr horne, thomas to chere,
Vn-to þe castelle scho tuke þe waye. 252	& to þe castel she to ......
In-to þe haulle sothely scho went;	þe lady in to þe hall went,
Thomas foloued at hir hande;	thomas folowyd at hyr h ....
Than ladyes come, bothe faire & gent,	þar kept hyr mony a lady gent,
With curtassye to hir knelande. 256	with curtasy & lawe kne ....
Harpe & fethill bothe þay fande,	harpe & fedyl both he fande,
Getterne, and als so þe sawtrye;	þe getern & þe sawtery;
Lutte and rybybe bothe gangande,	Lut & rybib þer gon gange,
And all manere of mynstralsye. 260	þer was all maner of mynstralsy.
þe moste meruelle þat Thomas thoghte,	þe most ferly þat thomas thoght,
Whene þat he stode appone þe flore;	whan he come o myddes ......
ffor feftty hertis jn were broghte,	fourty hertes to quarry were broȝt,
þat were bothe grete and store. 264	þat had ben before both sty ...
Raches laye lapande in þe blode,	lymors lay lapynge blode,
Cokes come with dryssynge knyfe;	& kokes standyng with dressynge ...
Thay brittened þame als þay were wode,	& dressyd dere as þai were wode,
Reuelle amanges þame was full ryfe. 268	& reuell was þer wonder r ...
[1] Knyghtis dawnesede by three and three,	knyȝtes dansyd by two & thre,
There was revelle, gamene, and playe;	all þat leue lange day;
Lufly ladyes faire and free,	ladyes þat were gret of gre,

Sche was as white as whelys bone,
And as Ryche on hir palefray.   236

¶ Thomas said, 'lady, wele is me,
that euer I baide this day;
nowe ye bene so fayre and whyte,
By fore ye war so blake and gray!   240
I pray you that ye wyll me say,
lady, yf thy wyll be,
why ye war so blake and graye?
ye said it was be cause of me.'   244

¶ 'For sothe, and I had not been so,
Sertayne sothe I shall the tell;   [leaf 27]
Me had been as good to goo,
To the brynnyng fyre of hell;   248
My lorde is so fers and fell,
that is king of this contre,
And fulle sone he wolde haue y⁰smell,
of the defaute I did with the.'   252

¶ In to the halle worldely they went,
Thomas folowde at hir honde;
Forthe came ladyes fayre and gent,
Curtesly Ayene hir kneland.   256
Harpe and fythell bothe they foynd,
the sytoll and the sawtery;
the gytorne and rybbe gan goyn,
And all maner of Menstrally.   260

¶ þe noeste ferly that thomas hade,
when he was stondyng on the flowre,
the gretest hert of alle hys londe,
that was stronge, styfe, and store;   264
Raches lay lapyng of his blode,
And kokes with dressyng knywys A hande,
Trytlege the dere, as they were wode,
there was Ryfe, reuoll Amonge.   268

¶ Knyghtys dawnsyng by iij and thre,
there was reuell, game, and play;
louely ladyes, fayre and fre,

LANSDOWNE

She was as feyre and as gode,
And as riche on hir palfray.

[1] Hir greyhoundis fillid with þe dere blode;
Hir rachis coupuld be my fay;   [1 lf 122, bk]
She blew hir horne, on hir palfray gode,
And to þe castell she toke þe way.
Into a hall sothly she went;
Thomas folud at hir hande;
Ladis came, bothe faire & gent,
fful curtesly to hir kneland.
harpe and fidul both þei fande,
þe getern, and also þe sautry;
þe lute and þe ribybe both gangand,
And alle maner of mynstralcy.   260
knyʒtis dawnsyng be thre & thre,
þer was revel, both game & play;
þer ware ladys, fayre and fre,
Dawnsyng [one ric]he aray.   (272)
þe grettist ferlye þat thomas thoʒt,
when xxx^ti hartis ley [up]on flore;
And as mony dere in were broght,
þat was largely long & store.   (264)
Rachis lay lappand on þe dere blode,
þe cokys þei stode with dressyng knyves;
Brytnand þe dere as þei were wode;

CAMBRIDGE

That satte and sange one riche araye.
Thomas duellide in that solace 273
More þane j ȝowe saye parde;
Till one a daye, so hafe I grace,
My lufly lady sayde to mee: 276
'Do buske the, Thomas, þe buse agayne;
ffor þou may here no lengare be;
Hye the faste with myghte & mayne,
I sall the brynge till Eldone tree.' 280
Thomas sayde þane with heuy chere,
'Lufly lady, nowe late me bee,
ffor certis, lady, j hafe bene here
Noghte bot þe space of dayes three!' 284
'ffor sothe, Thomas, als j þe telle,
þou hasc bene here thre ȝere & more;
Bot langere here þou may noghte duelle,
The skylle j sall þe telle whare-fore: 288
To Morne, of helle þe foulle fende.
Amange this folke will feche his fee;
And þou arte mekill mane and hende,
I trowe full wele he wolde chese the.
ffor alle þe golde þat euer may bee, 293
ffro hethyne vn-to þe worldis ende,
þou bese neuer be-trayede for mee;
þere-fore with me j rede thou wende.'
Scho broghte hym agayne to Eldoñe tree,
Vndir-nethe þat grenewode spraye; 298
In huntlee bannkes es mery to bee,
Whare fowles synges bothe nyght & daye.
'fferre owtt in ȝone Mountane graye,
Thomas, my fawkone bygges a neste;
A fawconne es an Erlis praye, 303
ffor-thi in na place may he reste. [¹ col. 2]
¹ffare wele, Thomas, j wend my waye,
ffor me by-houys ouer thir benttis browne.'
loo here a fytt more es to saye,
All of Thomas of Erselldowne. 308

THORNTON

sat & sange of ryche aray.
Thomas sawe more in þat place,
þan I kan discry pard[e];
Til on a day, allas! allas!
My louely lady sayd to . .
'buske þe, thomas, þou most agayn,
here þou may no la . . . . .
hy þe ȝerne at þou wer at hame,
I sall þe brynge to . . . .'
thomas answerd with heuy chere,
& sayd, 'louely lady, lat . . . .
for I say þe sertenly, here
hafe I be bot þe space of d . . . . .'
'Sothly, tomas, as I tell þe,
þou hath ben here thre ȝere . . . . .
& here þou may no langer be,
& I sall tell þe a skele . . . . . .
to morowe, of hell þe foule fende,
A mang ours . . . .
for þou art a large man, & an hende,
trowe þou wele . . . .
for all þe golde þat may be,
fro hens vnto þe wor . . . . . .
sal þou not be bytrayed for me;
& þer for sall þou hens . . . .
She broȝt hym euyn to eldon tre,
vndir neth þe gr . . . . . .
In huntle bankes was fayre to be,
þer breddis syng . . . . . .
Ferre ouyr ȝon montayns gray,
þer hathe my facon . . . . .

COTTON

Lansdowne	Cambridge
Satte syttyng in A ryall Araye. 272	Reuell was among þem rife. (268)
Thomas dwellyd in that place	There was reuell, game, & play, [leaf 123]
longer þan I sey, parde,	More þan I yow say parde
Tyll one day, by fyll that cace,	Tille hit fel vpon a day,
To hym spake that ladyes fre. 276	My lufly lady seid to me :
¶ 'Buske the, Thomas, thou most	Buske þe, thomas, for þou most gon,
for here þou may no lenger be; [Ayene,	ffor here no longur mayst þou be;
¹hye the fast with Mode and Mayne,	hye þe fast, with mode and mone ;
I shalte the bryng at elden tre.' [¹ lf 27, bk]	I shalle þe bryng to eldyn tre.
Thomas said, with heuy chere, 281	Thomas answerid with heuy chere,
'louely lady, lat me be !	Lufly lady, þou let me be ;
For certaynlye, I haue ben here	ffor certenly, I haue be here
But the space of dayes þre.' 284	But þe space of dayes thre.
¶ 'Forsoth, Thomas, I wolle the tell,	ffor sothe, thomas, I þe telle,
thou hast been her iij yere and More ;	þou hast bene here seuen ȝere and more ;
And here þou may no lenger dwell,	ffor here no longur may þou dwell,
I shall the tell A skele wherefore ; 288	I shal tel þe the skyl wherfore :
To morowe, a fowle fend of hell,	To morou, on of hel, a fowle fende,
A Mongis this folke shall chese his fe,	Among þese folke shal chese his fee ;
And for thou arte long man and hende,	þou art a fayre man and a hende,
I lewe wele, he wyll haue þe. 292	fful wel I wot he wil chese the.
¶ And for all the goode that euer myght be,	ffor alle þe golde þat euer myght be,
For hevene to the worldris ende,	ffro heuon vnto þe wordis ende,
Shalt þou neuer be bytrayed by me ;	þou beys neuer trayed for me ;
þere fore I rede the with me wend.' 296	ffor[th] with me I rede the wende.
She browght hym Ageyn to elden tre,	She broght hym agayn to eldyn tre,
Vnder neth A grene wode spray ;	Vndurneth þe grenewode spray ;
In huntely bankes is man) to be,	In huntley bankis þis for to be, [leaf 123, bk]
Where fowlis syngith nyght and day. 300	ther foulys syng boþe nyȝt & day,
¶ 'For ouere youre Montayne graye,	'ffor out ouer ȝon mownten gray,
Where my fawcone beldith his nest,	Thomas, a fowken makis his nest ;
the fawcone is the herons pray,	A fowkyn is an yrons pray,
therefore in no place may she Rest. 304	ffor þei in place will haue no rest.
Faire wele, Thomas, I wende my way,	ffare wel, thomas, I wende my way,
Me bous ouere yowre brwtes broume.'	ffor me most ouer ȝon bentis brown.'
Here is A foott, And tway to say,	This is a fytte ; twayn ar to sey,
Of Thomas of Asseildoun. 308	Off Thomas of Erseltown.
LANSDOWNE ERCILDOUN.	CAMBRIDGE

[Sloane 2578, leaf 6 (begins at Fytt 2).]

[FYTT THE SECONDE.]   [FYTT THE SECOND.]

¶ Heare begynethe þe ij^d fytt I saye
of Sir thomas of Arseldon.

'Fare wele, Thomas, j wend my waye,   'Farewell, thomas, I wend my waye; 309
I may no lengare stande with the!'   I may no lenger dwell with the.'
'Gyff me a tokynynge, lady gaye,   'Guyve me some token, Lady gaye,
That j may saye j spake with the.'   312   that I may saye I spake with the.'   312
'To harpe or carpe, whare-so þou gose,   'to harpe or carpe, whither thowe can,
Thomas, þou salt hafe þe chose sothely.'   thomas, þou shalt haue sothely.'
And he saide, 'harpynge kepe j none;   he said 'herpinge kepe I none;
ffor tonge es chefe of mynstralsye.'   316   for tonge is chief of mynstrelsy.'   316
'If þou will spelle, or tales telle,   '& þou wilt speake, & tales tell,
Thomas, þou salt neuer lesynge lye,   thowe shalt neuer leasynge lye ;
Whare euer þou fare, by frythe or felle,   whither þou walke by frythe or fell,
I praye the, speke none euyll of me!   I pray the, speake none ivell by me! 320
ffare wele, Thomas, with-owttyne gyle,   Fare well, thomas, withouten gile,
I may no lengare duelle with the.'   322   I may no lenger abide with the.'
'Lufly lady, habyde a while,   'Lovly lady, abide a while,
And telle þou me of some ferly!'   and some ferly tell thowe me!'   324
'Thomas, herkyne what j the saye: 'thomas, herken what I shall saye:
Whene a tree rote es dede,   326   when a tre rote is deade,
The leues fadis þane & wytis a-waye;   the leaves faden & fallen awaye,
& froyte it beris nane þane, whyte ne rede.   Fruyt it bearethe none on in elde.   328
Of þe baylliolfe blod so salt it falle :   [No break in the MS.]
It salt be lyke a rotyne tree ;   330   the baly of blud it shalbe,
The comyns, & þe Barlays alle,   their comens, & þer barons all,
The Russells, & þe ffresells free,   the Russelles, & þe fresselles fre,   332

THORNTON   SLOANE

Continuation of Cotton Manuscript.

[FYT THE SECOND.]

Fare wele thomas I wende my way · I may no lang
   [Gyfe] me a tokyn lady gay · If euyr I se ȝow w
   [To ha]rpe or carp wher þat þou gon · þou sal hafe þ   312
   thomas sayde harpyng kep I non · for tonge is che[f   316
   [Fare] wele thomas for nowe I go · I will no langer sta[y

HE ASKS TO HEAR SOME FERLY; SHE PREDICTS THE RUIN OF THE BALIOLS. 19

[FOOTT THE SECOND.]   [FYTTE THE SECOND.]

¶ 'Fare wele, Thomas, I wend my way;
I may no langer dwell with the.'
['G]yf sum tokyne, my lady gay, [leaf 28]
that euer I saw the with my ye'   312
'To harp or carp, where euer I gone,
Thomas, þou shalt chese soþele.'
'I, lady, harpyng wyll I none,
For townge is cheffe Mynstralye.'   316
¶ 'Yf þou wolte speke, or talis tell,
lesynges shalt þou neuer lye;
But where þou go by fryþ or fell,
I pray the, speke no ewylle by me!   320
Fare wele, Thomas, I wend my wey;
I may no langere dwell with the.'
'yete, louely lady! goode and gay,
A byde and tell me More ferlye.'   324

'Fare wel, Thomas, I wend may,
   I may no lengur stand with the!'
'gif me sum tokyn, lady gay,
þat I may say I spake with the.'   312
To harpe or carpe, thomas, wher so euer
Thomas, take þe chese with the. [ȝe gon,
harpyng, he seid, kepe I non,
ffor tong is chefe of mynstralse.   316
'If þou wil spill, or talys telle,
Thomas, þou shal neuer make lye;
Wher so euer þou gos, be frith or felle,
I pray þe, speke neuer no ille of me!   320
ffare wel, Thomas, and wel þou be;
I can no lengur stand þe by.'
'Lovely lady, fayre & fre,
Tel me ȝet of som farley!'   324
'Thomas, truly I þe say: [leaf 124]
Whan a tre rote is ded,
þe levys fal, and dwyne away;
ffrute hit berys, nedur white nor red.   328
So shalle þis folkys blode be fall,
þat shal be like ȝon roten tre;
þe semewes & þe telys all,
þe resull & þe frechel fre,   332

LANSDOWNE   CAMBRIDGE

COTTON

[Louely] lady wo is me so · A byde & tell me [some] fe   324
[Herken] thomas as I þe sey · whan þe trees rode is de
[The leues] fallyth & wastyth a way · it beryth no fruy   328
[.........bali]oves blode be fall · I lyken to þe ro
[.........] & þes elders all · all for soth a way   332

Thornton	Sloane
All sall þay fade, and wyte a-waye ;	all shall fade & fall awaye,
Na ferly if þat froyte than dye. 334	no farly then if þat fruyt dye'!
And mekill bale sall after spraye,	and mykell bale shall after spraye, [lf 6, bk]
Whare joye & blysse was wonte [to bee ;]	wheare that blis was wont to be. 336
ffare wele, Thomas, j wende m[y waye]	farewell, thomas, I wend my waye ;
I may no langer stand w[ith the.]' 338	I maye no lenger stande with the.'
'Now lufly lady gud [and gay]	'Lovly Lady, good & gaye,
Telle me ȝitt of some ferly !' [leaf 151, back]	tell me yet of somme farle !' 340
'Whatkyns ferlys, Thomas gude,	'what kyns farly, thomas good,
Sold j þe telle, and thi wills bee?' 342	shuld I the tell, if thi will be?'
'Telle me of this gentill blode,	'tell, of the gentle blud
Wha sall thrife, and wha sall thee :	who shall vnthrive, & who shall the; 344
Wha sall be kynge, wha sall be none,	who shalbe kynge, who shalbe none,
And wha sall welde this northe countre?	who shall weld þe northe contre?
Wha sall flee, & wha sall be tane, 347	who shall fle, who shalbe tane,
And whare thir batells donne sall bee?'	& wheare þe battellȝ done shalbe?' 348
'Thomas, of a Batelle j sall þe telle,	'of a battelle I will the telle,
þat sall be done righte sone at wille :	that shalbe done sonne at will :
Beryns sall mete bothe fers & felle, 351	birdes shall mete, both fresshe & fell,
And freschely fighte at Eldone hille.	& fyersly fight at eldon hill. 352
The Bretons blode sall vndir fete,	the brusse blud shall vnder gonge,
þe Bruyse blode sall wyne þe spraye ;	the bretens shall wynne all þe praye ;
Sex thowsande ynglysche, wele þou wete,	thre thowsand scottes, on þe grownde,
Sall there be slayne, þat jlk daye. 356	shalbe slayne that ilk daye. 356
ffare wele, Thomas, j wende my waye ;	farewell, thomas, I wend my waye ;
To stande with the, me thynk full jrke.	to stand with the me thynk it irk.
Of a batell j will the saye,	of a battell I will the saye,
þat sall be done at fawkirke : 360	that shalbe done at fowse kyrk ; 360

COTTON

[Farew]ele thomas I wende my waye · I may no langer s
[Louely lady] gentyl & gay · a bide & tele me so   340
      { [2 *lines lost at top of page*]   [leaf 242]
      { . . . .
      ll] weld þe north cun

LANSDOWNE

¶ 'What kynne, Thomas, ferly gode,
wold ye fayn) wete of me?'
'Lady, of this gentyll blode
who shall þryue, and who shall þe ; 344
who shalbe kyng, and who shall be none,
And where any battell done shall be,
who shall be slaye, who shalbe Tane,
And who shall wyne the north Contre?'

¶ 'Of A batell I shall the tell, 349
that shalbe done sone at wyll :
Barons shall mete, boith fers and fell,
And freslye fyght at helydowne hyll. 352

Fare wele, Thomas, I wende my way,
To stande here me thinke it yrke ;
But of A batell I shall the say
that shalbe don) at faw Chirch. 360

CAMBRIDGE

Alle shalle falle, & dwyn away ;
No wondur þoȝ þe rote dy.
And mekill bale shal aftur spray,
þer ioy and blisse were wont to be. 336
ffare wel, thomas, I wende my way ;
I may no lengur stand þe by.'
'lufly lady, gude and gay,
telle me ȝet of som ferly !' 340
'What kyns ferly, thomas gode,
Shuld I tel þe, if þi wil be?'
'telle me of þis gentil blode,
Who shal thrife, and who shal the ; 344
Who shal be kyng, who shall be non,
And who shal weld þe north cuntre ;
Who shall fle, & who shal be tane,
And wher þes batelis don shal be?' 348
'Off a batelle I will þe tell,
þat shall come sone at will : [¹ leaf 124, back]
¹ Barons shall mete, both fre and fell,
And fresshely feȝt at ledyn hill. 352
the brucys blode shalle vndur fall,
the bretens blode shall wyn þe spray ;
C. thowsand men þer shal be slayn, 355
Off scottysshe men þat nyght and day.
ffare wel, thomas, I wende my way ;
To stande with the, me thynk full yrke !
Off þe next bat[elle] I will þe say,
þat shall be at fawkyrke : 360

COTTON

e] wher þes batels don sal b[e] 348
þ' sal be done ful son at wyll
r]yke & fell · & freshly fyȝt at halyndon hill 352
e]nde my way · to stonde with þ° me thynk ful yrke
sall] ye say · þat sal be don at fawkyrke 360

Baners sall stande, bothe lang & lange ; Trowe this wele, with mode & mayne ; The bruysse blode sall vndir gane, 363 Seuene thowsande scottis þer sall be slayne. ffare wele, Thomas, j pray þe sease ; No lengare here þou tarye mee ; 366 My grewehundis, þay breke þaire lesse, And my raches þaire copills in three. Loo ! whare þe dere, by twa and twa, Haldis ouer зone Montane heghe.' 370 Thomas said, 'god schilde þou gaa ! Bot telle me зitt of some ferly.' 372	baner3 shall stand, longe & longe ; trowe þou well, with mode & mayne ; the brusse blod shall vnder gonge, [leaf 7] v. thowsand scottes shalbe slayne. 364 farewell, thomas, I praye the cease ; no lenger heare þou tary me ; my greyhowndes breaken the flesshe, & my ratchettes their coupulles in thre. loke howe þe deare, by ij & ij, 369 rvnn ouer yonder mountain high !' thomas said, 'god ahild thowe goo ! but tell me yet of some farly.' 372
['Of a] batelle, j sall the saye, 377 [That sall] gare ladyse morne in mode ; [. . . .]e, bothe water & claye Sall be mengyde with mannes blode : [col. 2] Stedis sall stombill with tresoune, 381 Bothe Baye & broune, grysselle and graye ; Gentill knyghtis sall stombill downe, Thorowe þe takynge of a wykkide waye. þe Bretons blode sall vndir falle ; 385 The Bryusse blode sall wyne þe spraye ; THORNTON	'of a battell I will the saye, that shall garr ladies to morne in mode : at bannokburne, bothe water & claye, it shalbe mynged with red blud. 380 steades shall stvmbull with treason, with blak & browne, grysell & graye ; & ientill knyghtes shall tvmbull downe, thurghe takinge of a wicked waye. 384 þe bretens blud shall vnder fall, the brusse shall wynne all the praye ; SLOANE

COTTON

sal stonde both large & lange · trowe þou wel .t. with mode & mayn
blode sal vndir gange · vj thowsand of ynglych þer sal be sla[yn] 364
le .t. for now I go · I may no langer stande with þe
hondes breke þair leches in two · my raches shere hyr coples in thre 368
зone dere by two & two · holdes ouyr зone lange le

¶ Baners shall stande there A longe,
Trowe þe wele, with Mode and Mayne;
the bratones blode shall vndere gange,
[1]A thowsand englysche there shalbe
   slayne.   [1 leaf 28, back]
fare wele, Thomas, I pray þou sese,   365
I May no langere dwele with the;
My greyhondes brekyng here leyse,
And my Raches here Cowples a thre. 368
¶ Lo, where the dere, by two and ij,
holdes owere yoñe Montayn) hye!'
'God forbeide!' saide Thomas, 'þou fro
   me go,
Or More of the warres þou tell me.' 372

'Of a batale I shall the say,
that shall Make ladies morne in Mode:
Bankes bourne, wattere and clay,   379
Shall be Mengyd with Mannis blode;
¶ Stedes shall snapre throwght tresoun,
Bothe bay and browñe, bresyll and gray;
Gentyll Knyghtes shall tumbell downe,
thrwgh takyn) of A wrong way.   384
Bretons blode shall vndere fall,
the Ebruys there shall wyne the pray;
              LANSDOWNE

þe bretans blode shalle vndur fall,
þe brucys blode shalle wyn þe spray;
vij thousynd Englisshe men, grete &
   smalle,
ther shalbe slayne, [þat] nyght and day.
ffare wel, [tho]mas, [I] pray þe sees; 365
No lengur here þou tary me;
lo wher my grayhoundis breke þer leesshe;
My raches breke þeir coupuls in thre. 368
lo, qwer þe dare goos be too & too,
And holdis ouer ȝonde mownten hye!'
Thomas seid, 'god [schilde thou] goo,
But tell me ȝet of sum ferly!   372
holde þi greyhoundis in þi h[onde,]
And coupill þi raches to a [tre;] [2 leaf 125]
[2]And lat þe dere reyke ouer þe londe;
ther is a herde in holtely.'   376
'Off a batell I wil þe say,
þat shalle gar ladys mourne in mode:
At barnokys barne is watur & clay, 379
þat shal be myngyd with mannys blode.
And stedys shalle stumbull for treson,
bothe bay and brown, grisell & gray;
And gentil knyȝtis shalle tombull doun,
thoro tokyn of þat wyckud way. 384
the Bretans blode shalle vndur fall,
the brutys blode shalle [wyn] þe spray;
              CAMBRIDGE

COTTON

say lady gode shelde ȝe go · abyde & tel me som ferle   372
attel I can þe say · Sal gar ladies morn in mode
kes borne both water & clay · It sal be mengyd with rede blode 380
[Stedes] sal stumbyl thrugh tresoun) · both bay & broun) gresel & gray
l knyghtes sal tumbyl doun) · for takyng of a wylsom way   384

Sex thowsand ynglysche, grete & smalee,	vj thowsand Englishe, greate & small,
Sall there be slane, þat jlk a daye. 388	shalbe slayne þat ilk daye. 388
Than sall scottland kyngles stande;	then shall scotland stande;
Trow it wele, þat j the saye!	trowe thowe well, as I the saye!
A tercelet, of the same lande,	a tarslet of the same land
To bretane sall take þe Redy waye, 392	to breten shall wynde þe redy waye; 392
And take tercelettis grete and graye,	& take tarslettes, greate & gaye,
With hym owte of his awene contree;	with him, owte of his awne contre;
Thay sall wende on an ryche arraye,	ther shall winde in riche araye, [leaf 7, back]
And come agayne by land and see. 396.	& comme againe by land & seye. 396
He sall stroye the northe contree,	he shall stroye þe northe contre,
Mare and lesse hym by-forne;	moare & les him before;
Ladyse sall saye, allas! & walowaye!	lades, welawaye I shall crye,
þat euer þat Royalle blode was borne.	þat euer þe baly of blud was borne. 400
He sall ryse vpe at kynke horne, 401	he shall ryse vp at kynkborne,
And tye þe chippis vn-to þe sande.	& slaye lordes vpon the sand;
At dipplynge more, appone þe Morne,	to foplynge moore, vpon þe morne,
Lordis will thynke full lange to stande;	lordes will think full longe to stand. 404
By-twix depplynge and the dales, 405	betwin þe depplinge & þe dasse—
The watir þat rynnes one rede claye—	þe water þer rennynge on þe red claye—
There sall be slayne, for sothe, Thomas,	þer shalbe slayne, forsothe, thomas, 407
Eleuene thowsandez scottis, þat nyghte & daye.	xi thowsand scottes, þat night & daye.
Thay sall take a towne of grete renownne,	they shall take a towne of greate renowne,
þat standis nere the water of Taye; 410	that standethe neare þe water of taye;
þe ffadir & þe sone sall be dongene downe,	the father & þe sonne shalbe donge downe,
And with strakis strange be slayne a-waye.	with strokes stronge be slaine awaye. 412
THORNTON	SLOANE

	COTTON	
	w on al þat day · both by hynde & als be fore	398*
	s]al syng welaway · þat euyr þe balyolues blod was bore	400*
	nge kyngles be · trowe þou wele thomas as I þ^e say	
	l take flyʒt & fle · to bruces lande þe redy way	392
	seletes gret & gray · with hym of hys awn contre	
	n ryche aray · bothe by lande & eke by see	396

LANSDOWNE

vij thousand ynglis, grete and smalle,
In a day there shalbe slay.   388

¶ then shall scotland kyngles be,
Trou þou well, that I the say !
A tarslet shall take his flyght, & fle
To bretons lande the Redy wey;   392
And take tarslett*es* grete and gray,
With hym, oute of his lond ;
he shall wende in A Ryche Aray,   395
And come agayu*e* by seye and londe.

¶ He shall stroye the north Contre,
More and les hym be-forne ;
Ladyes shall say 'waleway !
that eu*er* iu scotland war we borñe.' 400
He shall Ryñ vt at kyng*es* horñe,
And sley lordis on the sonde ;   [leaf 29]
At deplyng More vppoñ the Morowe,
Lordes shall thynke there long stonde. 404

¶ By twyx duplyng and the gray stoñ,
the water that Rynnes gray,
there shalbe slayne v thousand englismen,
that nyght and that day.   408

And yet they shall take A walled Towñe ;
the fader and the sone be slayñ away ;
A knyght shall wyn the warisou*n*,
w*ith* dynt of swerd for ones and ay. 412

CAMBRIDGE

viij thousand englissemen, grete & small,
ther shal be slayn, þat nyght & day.

COTTON

[397—400, *see above*]

vp at kynche horn ·   fele lordes vp on þe sande
m]ore vp on þe morn · lordes sal thynke ful lang to stand 404
ge] & a dale · þat wat*er* of Erne þat rynnes gray
w*i*]t*h* myche bale · x thowsand scottes a ny3t & a day 408
wallyd toune · standynge ful nere þe wat*er* of tay

Whens þay hafe wonne þat wallede towne,	when þei haue wonne þe walled towne,
[¹ leaf 155]	
And ylke mane hase cheuede þayre chance,	& euery man chosen his chaunce,
¹Than sall thir bretons make þame bowne,	þe bretens they shall make þem bowne,
And fare forthe to þe werre of fraunce.	& forthe to þe warres of Fraunce. 416
Than sall scotland kyng-lesse stande,	þen shall scotland without kinge stand ;
And be lefte, Thomas, als j the saye ;	beleve, thomas, as I the saye !
Than sall a kyng be chosene, so ȝynge,	thei shall chuse a kinge full yonge,
That kane no lawes lede par faye : 420	þat can no lawes leade, parfaye ; 420
Dauid, with care he sall be-gynne,	
And with care he sall wende awaye.	
Lordis & ladyse, more and Myne, 423	
Sall come appone a riche araye,	
And crowne hym at the towne of skyne,	& crowned at þe towne of scone,
Appone an certane solempe daye. 426	on a serteine solemne daye. [leaf 5]
Beryns balde, bothe ȝonge and alde,	birdes bolde, bothe olde & yonge,
Sall till hym drawe with-owttyne naye ;	shall to him drawe without naye ; 428
Euyne he sall to ynglande ryde,	into England shall thei ride,
Este and weste als lygges the waye. 430	easte, weste, as ligges the waye,
	& take a towne with greate pride,
	& let þe menn be slaine awaye. 432
Be-twixe a parke and an abbaye,	betwixt a parke & an abbaye,
A palesse and a paresche kyrke,	a pales & a parishe kirk,
Thare sall ȝour kynge faill of his praye,	there shall your kinge faile of his praye,
And of his lyfe be wondir jrke. 436	& of his lyfe be full irk. 436
He sall be tane, so wondir sare,	he shalbe taggud wunder sare,
So þat a-waye he sall noghte flee ;	so þat awaye he maye not fle ;
THORNTON	SLOANE

COTTON

yn a doun · with sore dyntes be kylled a way   412
n]ge þat is ful ȝynge · he kan no lawes lede parfay
he sal be gyn · with sorowe sal he wende a way   420
ppes both more & myn · al sal gedir to þer a ray
m]at þᵉ toun of scoyne · vp on þe trinyte Sonday   424
both ȝonge & alde · sall fal to hym with owtyn nay   428

¶ Whan they haue take that wallyd
 towne,
And euery man has chosyn his chaūs,
the bretons blode shall make hym bone
And fare to the warres of fraunce. 416
And then shall scottland be withoute kyng,
Trowe the wele that I the sey!
they shall chese a kyng full yonge,
that can not lede no laweys, perfay. 420
¶ Dauid, withoute care he shall be gyne,
And withoute care he shall wend away;
Bysshoppes and lordes, More and myne,
Shall come to hym in Ryche A Raye,
And Crowne hym at A Towne of Scone,
Forsothe vpon A Setterday. 426
Bornes blode shall wend to Rome,
To get lyve of the pope yf they may. 428

¶ By twyxte a parke and ane Abbey,
A palys and A perishe church,
there shall that kyng fayll at his pray,
And of his lyfe he shall be full yrke.
He shall be togged, the wonde sore, 437
that Away he maynot fle;

LANSDOWNE

þen shalle scotland kyngles be sen;
trow þis wel, þat I þe say!
And thei shalle chese a kyng ful ȝong,
þat can no lawes lede, parfay: 420
Robert, with care he shal be gynne,
And also he shall wynde awey. 422

lordys and ladys, bothe olde & yongg,
shalle draw to hym with outyn nay; 428
And they with pryde to Englond ryde,
Est and west þat liggys his way;
And take a toune of mycul pryde,
And sle [. . . . . . .] knyȝtes veray. 432
Betwene a parke & an abbay, [leaf 125, back]
A palys and a parissh kyrke,
ther shalle þe kyng mys of his way,
[And] of his life be full yrke. 436
He shal be teyryd(?) ful wondur sore,
So a way he may not fle;

CAMBRIDGE

COTTON

sal he holde · And bryn & sla al in hys way   extra
sal he ryde · þar sal he þat ilke day
þat wondes wyde · þat werne ful bolde in hyr aray 432
ke & an abbay · a paleys & a paryshe kyrke
s]yle of hys pray · & of hys lyfe he sal be yrke 436
ke in . . . . e ful sare · so þat a way he may not fle

THORNTON

Hys nebbe sall rynne, or he thethyne fare,
þe rede blode tryklelande vn-to his kn[ee].
He sall þan be, with a false f . . 441
Be-trayede of his awene . . . .
And wheþer it torne . . . . .
He sall byde 444
þat rau . . . .
Tho . . . .
. . . .
. . . .
[5 *lines lost at foot of page in MS.*]
. . . .

. . . .
In þe northe to do owttraye. [col. 2] 452
And whene he es mane moste of Mayne,
And hopis beste þans for to spede,
On a ley lande sall he be slayne,
Be-syde a waye for-owttyne drede. 456
Sythene sall selle scotland, par ma faye,
ffulle and fere, full many ane,
ffor to make a certane paye ; 459
Bot ende of it sall neuer come nane.
And þane sall scotland kyngles staude ;
Trowe this wele, þat j telle the !
Thre tercelettis of þe same lande 463

SLOANE

his nebbe shall or he thens fare,
of red blud, trikell to þe kne. 440
he shall, with a false fode,
[*No break in the MS.*]
whither it turne to ivell or goode ;
& he shall bide in a ravens hand. 444
the ravin shall þe Goshawke wynne,
if his fethers be neuer so black ;
& leide him strayte to London, 447
þer shall your fawcone fynde his make.
þe ravin shall his fethers shake,
& take tarslettes gaye & greate,
with him, owte of his awne contre ; [Interpol.]
& þe kinge shall him Mʳ make,
in þe northe to do owtraye. 452
when he is man of moste mayne, [Ifs, bk]
& hopes beste for to spede,
on a leye land he shalbe slayne,
beside a waye without drede. 456
then shall they sell in scotland, parfaye,
fowles & fee full many one,
for to make a sertein paye ;
but end þer of commethe neuer none. 460
þen shall scotland kingles stand ;
trowe þou well, as I the saye !
iij tarslettes, of that same land,

COTTON

1 ren with myche care · of rede blode doun) to hy[s kne] 440
a fals fode · betrayed of hys awn) lande
rn) to euyl or gode · be sesyd in to a rauyn[es hande] 444
. . goshauke wyn · be hyr fethyrs neuyr so [blake]
reght to london with hym · þer sal ȝour foule [fynd his make] 448
hyr fethyrs folde · & take þᵉ tarsletes [grete & gay]

LANSDOWNE

[1]His nose shall Rynne, or he thense go,
the blode shall trykle downe to his kne.

¶ He shall, throwght a fals fode, 441
Be betrayde of his owne lond; [1 leaf 29, bk]
Wherere it turne to ewyll or good,
He shall Abide a Rauenes honde.   444
the Rauyne shall the goshawke woym,
thowght his fedres be neuer so blake;
And lede hym to London Towne,   447
there shall the goshawke fynd his Make.

¶ þe Rawyn shall his fedres shake,
And take tasletis grete and gay;

the kyng shall hym Maister Make,
In the north for to do outray.   452
And whan he is most in his mayn,
And best wenes for to spede,
On a ley londe he shall be slayn,
By side awey without dred.   456

¶ And than most scotland, parfay,
By se & land, mony one,
For Dauid make certayn pay;   459
But end of hym commyth neuer none.
then most scotland kyngles stond;
Trowe the welo, þat I say the!
A taslet of A nother land.   463

CAMBRIDGE

his neb shall rise or he then fare,
the red blode triklond to his knee.   440

COTTON

hym maystyr bold · In þe north [sal he do owtray]   452
[? 2 *lines lost at top of page.*]   [leaf 242, back]

. en of dauy[d   459. —
sall ryde & go hyr wa[y   ?
þan sal scotlande kyngles   461. —
thre lordes of þat same londe   463. —

Saft stryfe to bygg & browke þe tree. to breten þen shall wend þer waye. 464
He saft bygg & browke the tree, he shall bigge & breake þe tre,
That hase no flyghte to fley a-waye; þat hathe no flight to fle away, 466

Thay saft with pryde to y[n]gland ryde, þai shall, with pride, to england fre,
Este & weste als lygges þe waye. 472 easte & weste as lygges þe waye. 472
Haly kyrke bese sett be-syde, holy kirk be sett beside,
Relygyous byrnede on a fyre; & religious men burne in fyre;
Sythene saft þay to a castelle gl[yde], thei shall to a castell glide,
And schewe þame þare with . . 476 & shewe þem there with mykell ire. 476
By-syde a wyft . . . . . . betwixt a well & a weare,
A wh[yt . . . . a withwell & a slyke stone,
. . . . þer shall ij cheftens mete in fere,
. . . . the on shall doughtles be slayne. 480
. . . .

. . . . the brusse blud shall with him fle,
. . . . 483 & leade him to a worthi towne;
[10 lines lost at foot of page in MS.] and close him in a castell lyght, [leaf 9]
  theare to be with greate renowme. [Interpol.]
. . . . Farewell, I wend my waye;
. . . . me behoves ouer yonder bent so browne.'
. . . . here endethe þe ij[d] fytt, I saye,
. . . . of sir thomas of Arseldon. 488
THORNTON SLOANE

COTTON
þat hath no fly3t to fle a way · In to [yng 466 . 471
& bryn & sla day by day · To a towre þan 472 . 475
And hald þer in myche ire · holychyrche is set 476 . 473
relegious þai bryn hym in a fyre 474
bytwys a wethy & a water · a well & a haly stane

Shall þryue & bygge, & browke þat tre.
¶ He shall bygge, and broke þat tre
He toke his flyght, & flye A wey;
Robert steward kyng shalbe 467
of scotland, and Regne mony A day.
[1] A cheuanteyne then shall ryse with pride,
of all scotland shall bere the floure;
he shall into Englonde Ride, [1 leaf 30]
And make men haue full sharpe schoure.
¶ holy chirche to set on syde, 473
And religyons to bren on fyre;
he shall to the new castell Ryde,
And shew hym there with grete Ire. 476

By twyx A wey of water,
A well, & A grey stone,
there cheuanteynes shall mete on fere,
And that o dowghty ther shall be slayne.
¶ that other cheuanteyne shall there
be tayne, 481
And proude blode withe hyme shall fle,
And lede hyme tyll A worthe Towne,
And close hym vp in A castell hye. 484

Fare wele, Thomas, I wend my wey;
Me bus ouer your brutes brome.'
here is a fote; anoþer to sey,
of Thomas of Assilldone. 488
LANSDOWNE

be twene A wycked way & A watur, 477
A parke and A stony way then;
ther shal a cheften mete in fere,
A ful dutey þer shal be slayn. 480
the todur cheftan shal be tane,

A pesans of blode hyme shal slee;
And lede hym a[w]ay in won,
And cloyse hym in a castell hee. 484

ffare wel, thomas, I wende my way;
ffor I must ouer ʒond . . bentis brown.'
here ar twoo.fyttis; on is to say,
Off Thomas of Erseldown. 488
CAMBRIDGE

COTTON

þer sal two chyftans met in fere · þe doglas þer sall be s[l 480
A tarslet sal in halde be tane · chyftans a way with hym
& lede hym to an hold of stane · & closo hym in a castel [h 484
Whar wele thomas I wend my way · me most ouyr ʒone be
anoþer fyt more is to say · of þe prophecy of arseldoun 488

[FYTT THE THIRD.]

[¹ leaf 152, back]

1 "Nowe, lufly lady, gente and hende,
Telle me, ȝif it thi willis bee,
Of thyes Batells, how þay schall ende,
And whate schalle worthe of this northe countre?'   492
'This worlde, Thomas, sothely to telle,
Es noghte bot wandrethe & woghe!
Of a batelle j will the telle,   495
That schall be donne at spynkarde cloughe:
The bretons blode schalle vndir falle,
The bruyse blode schalle wyne þe spraye;
Sex thowsande ynglysche, grete & smalle,
Salle thare be slayne þat nyghte & daye.
The rerewarde salt noghte weite, parfaye,
Of that jlke dulfulle dede;   502
Thay sall make a grete journaye,
Dayes tene with-owttyne drede.
And of a batelle j will þe telle,   505
That sall be donne now sone at will:
Beryns sall mete, bothe ferse & felle,
And freschely fyghte at pentland hyll.
By-twyx Sembery & pentlande,   509
þe haulle þat standis appone þe rede claye—

THORNTON

[FYTTE THE THIRD.]

'thies wordes, thomas, þat I saye,
is but wanderyng & wough;
of a battell I shall the tell,
that shalbe done at Spenkard slough: 496
the bretens blud shall vnder fall,
the brusse blud shall wynne þe praye;
vij thowsand englishe, greate & small,
shalbe slayne þat ilk daye.   500
the reareward shall not witt, parfaye,
of þat same dolfull dede;
thei shall make a greate iornaye,
dayes x without drede.   504
of a battell I will you tell,
that shalbe done sonne at will:
barons shall mete, bothe fyers & fell,
& fyersly fight at Eldon hill.   508
betwin Edynburgh & Pentland,
at þe hall þat standethe on þe redd claye,

SLOANE

COTTON
[FYT THE THIRD]

Far wel thomas I wende my way · me most ouyr ȝone bro..
sothly .t. I þe say · men sal haf rome ryȝt ny þaire dor   492
Sothly .t. as I þe say · þis world sal stond on a wondir w
of a batel tel I þe may · þat sal be don at spynkar cl   496
þᵉ gret wreth sal not persayuyd be · of þat gret vnk..

[FOTE THE THIRD.]

¶ 'Fare wele, Thomas, I wend my way;
I may no longer duell with the.'
 yet, louely lady, goode and gey,

Abyde, & tell me more ferele !'   492

'And þus, thomas, truly to tell,
hyt Is wondrand & wow;
but of a batyll I shall the tell,
that shall be don at spincar clow :   496
¶ the bretonys blode there shall vnder-
the Ebrues ther shall wyn the pray; [fall,
v thousand ynglefſ there, gret & small,
In a sunday mornyng shall be slay. 500
the fowarde shall not wit, parfey,
Certeyn of that dolfull dede ;
they shall make agayne a grete Iorney,
Dayes x withouten drede.   504

[¹ leaf 50, back]   [lond
¹¶ Bytwix Eden brought and the Pent-
the hall that stond on the Rede glay—

LANSDOWNE

[FYTTE THE THIRD.]

'Thomas, truly I þe say,
  þe worlde is wondur wankill !
Off þe next batell I wyll the say,
that shal be done at spynard [?] hill : 496
the brucis blode shall vndur fall,
the brettens blode schall wyn [the spray;]
xiij thousand per shal be slayne, [leaf 125]
Off scottisshe men þat nyght & day. 500

Off the next batell 1 wil þe telle,
þat shal be done sone at will :
Barons bothe flesshe & fell
shalle fresshely fyȝt at pentland hyll. 508
but when pentland & edynborow,
And þe hill þat standis on þe red cley,

CAMBRIDGE

COTTON

v. thowsande slayn sal be · of scottes men with outyn	500
Fare wele .t. I wend my way · I may no langer stand	
louely lady gentyl & gay · a byde & tel me more f	504
Of a batel I can þe tell · þat sal be done hastely at	
bernes sal met both fryk & fel · & freshely fyȝt at	508
by twys edynburgh & pentlande · an hyl per stand	

ERCILDOUN.   3

There schaH be slayne Eleuene thowsande
[Of scot]tis mene, þat nyghte & daye.
. . . . a townne, of grete renowne,
. . . . . . e water of Taye 514
. . . .
. . . .
. . . .

. . . .
[13 lines lost at foot of page in MS.]
. . . .
. . . .
. . . .
. . . .
. . . .
. . . .
. . . .
. . . .
The toþer oste at barboke.   [col. 2] 528
fforryours furthe saH flee,
On a Sonondaye, by-fore þe messee;
Seuene thowsandes sothely saH be slayne,
One aythir partye, more and lesse. 532
ffor þer saH be no baneres presse,
Bot ferre in sondir saH thay bee;
Carefull saH be þe after mese, 535

THORNTON

there shalbe slayne xij thowsand,
forsothe, of scottes, þat night & daye. 512
thei shall take a walled towne, [¹ leaf 2, bk]
¹ the father & þe sonne bene slayne awaye;
knightes shall wynne þer warysone,
thurghe dynt of swerd for euer & aye. 516
when þei haue wonne the wallid towne,

and euery mann chosen his chaunce,
the bretens þen shall make them bowne,
and forthe to þe warres of Fraunce. 520
thei shalbe in fraunce full
thomas, I saye, iij yeares & mare;
and dynge downe towerȝ, & castelles
to euery mann in sonder fare. [stronge,
then shall thei be bought full stronge,
betwixt Seiton & þe seye;
the bretens shalbe þe greaues amonge,
the other este at Barwik fre. 528

[No break in the MS.]

on a Sondaye before þe masse,
v thowsand sothely slayne shalbe,
of brusse blud, bothe moare & les. 532
for þat daye shuld no banerȝ presse,
but farr in sonder shall thei be;
carefull shalbe the enter messe,

SLOANE

COTTON

þer sal be slayn twelf þowsande · of Scottes [m 512
þan sal þai take a wallyd toun) · fadir & [s
knyȝtes of yngland wyn þair warysoun) · th 516
whan þai haf tak þis wallyd toun) · & ich man hath
hym to hys chance · þan sal þe bretons make
& fare in to þe werres of fraunce 520

Lansdowne	Cambridge
there shall be slayne vij m¹	vij thousande shal be slayn þere, 511
of scottes men, that nyght & day. 512	Off scottisshe men þat nyght & day.
And þet they shall take A walled Towne	
that stonde on the water of Tay ;	
knyghtes shall wyne the waryson, 515	
By dyntes of swerde for ones & Aye.	
¶ And whan they haue toke þat walled towne,	
And eche man hathe take his chaunce,	
the britons blode shall make hym boune,	
And fare agan) to werres of fraunce. 520	
then shall they be in fraunce full longe ;	
Thomas, iij yere & more ; [stronge,	
And dyng downe castellis & towres	
And then shall euery man home fare. 524	
¶ they shall mete, boþe fers & stronge,	then shalle they met, bathe stiff & strong,
By twyx Ceton and the see ;	Betwene seton and þe see ;
the englyshe shall ly in craggis amonge,	the englisshe shalle lyg þe cragys among,
That othere oste at barkle. 528	the toþur at þe est banke falleþ hye. 528
A sore semble there shall be,	the fflorence forth shall fare,
On a sonday by fore the Masse ;	Vpon a sonday before the masse ;
v thousand shalne¹ shall be, [¹ ? slayne]	v thousande þer shalbe slayne,
of bothe partes more & lesse. 532	off bothe partyes more and lesse. 532
¶ For there shall no baner presse,	ffor þat þer shall no barrons presse,
Bot fer in sundre shall they be ;	but fer asondur shalle they be ;
Carefull shall be there last Masse,	Carfull shalbe þe furst masse,

COTTON

þaj sal be in fraunce ful lang · sothly .t. thre ȝer
& bet doun) tounes & castels strange · to do owtr . . . 524
þan sal þai mete both styf & strang · by twys Seton
þᵉ Inglyshe sal lyg þe cragges amang · þᵉ frenshe 528
[freres] fast a way sal fle · On a sonday be for þe
. thowsande slayn sal be · of bernes both m 532
[þer] sal no man wyn þᵉ prise · sertenly þis I tell þ

36   A BATTLE BETWEEN SETON AND THE SEA.   [FYTTE III.

By-twixe Cetons and þe See.

Schippis sall stande appone þe Sande,
Wayffande with þe Sees fame ;   538
Thre ȝere and mare, þan sall þay stande,
Or any beryne come foche þame hame.
Stedis awaye Maysterles sall flynge,
Ouer þe Mountans too and fraa ;
Thaire sadills one þaire bakkis sall hynge,
Vn-to þe garthis be rotyne in twaa.   544
ȝitt sall þay hewe one alle þe daye,
Vn-to þe sonne be sett nere weste ;
Bot þer es no wighte þat ȝitt wiete maye,
Wheþer of thayme sall hafe þe beste.
Thay sall plante downe þaire thare,   549

Worthi mene al nyghte sall dye ;
Bot One þe Morne þer sall be care,
ffor nowþer syde sall hafe þe gree.   552
Than sall þay take a trewe, and swere,
ffor thre ȝere & more, j vndirstande,
þat nane of þame sall oþer dere,
[Nowþer] by See ne ȝitt by lande.   556
. . . . . saynte Marye dayes
. . . . . d]ayes lange
. . . . . . Baners rayse
. . . . e lande   560

THORNTON

betwin seytons & þe seye,   536
of þe brasse, bothe moare & les.   [Interpolation]
shippȝ shall stand vpon the sande,
wavand with þe seye fome,
thre yeares & moare, vnderstand,   [leaf 10]
or any barons fetche them home   540
steades maisterles shall flynge,
to the mountains to & fro ;
þer sadelȝ on þer backes hynge,
till þer girthes be rotten in to.   544
thei shall hewe on helme & sheld,
to þe sonne be sett neare weste ;
no mann shall witt, in þat fyeld,
whithether partie shall haue þe beste. 548
thei shall caste downe bannerȝ there ;

wonden many one þat night shall dye ;
vpon the morne there shalbe care,
for neither partie shall haue þe degre. 552
thei shall take a trewce, & sware,
iij yeares & moare, I vnderstand,
þat none of them shall other dare,
neither by water ne by land.   556
betwin ij Saint mary dayes,
when þe tyme waxethe longe,   558
then shall thei mete, & bannerȝ raise,
on claydon moore, bothe styf & stronge.

SLOANE

COTTON

[. . . . . .] sal þ^t ost be aftyr mes · by twys seton &   536
[Shi]ppes sal be on þe strande · wallyng with þe s
T[hr]e ȝer & more þer sal þai stande · no man . . . . . to f   540
[Sted]es maysterles a way sall flynge · to þe mountt . . . .
[Sadels on] hyr bakkes sall hynge · to þe gyrthes be   544

Bytwyx ceton & the see. 536	be twene seton & the see.	536

Shippes shall stonde ther on þe sonde,
hem selfe mene the the fome;
Seue yere & more theyr shall they stonde
And no barne shall bryng hem home. 540
[1]¶ And stedes shall maisterles fleng
To the Montayns them fro; [1 leaf 81]
the sadles shall on ther bakes hyng,
Thyll þe gerthes be rotten them fro. 544
they shall hewe on, all that day,
Tyll the sonne be sett west;
ther is no man, that wete may,
which of them shall haue the best. 548

    þen shalle þei [feʒt] with helmys & shylde
        there,   [awey;
And woundyt men al eneglych shal rone
but on þe morne þer schal be care,
ffor nedyr [side] shall haue þe gree. 552
[2]Then shalle þei take a truce & swere,
thre ʒere and more, I vndurstonde;
þer nouþer side shalle odir dere, [2 leaf 126, back]
Nouþer be se nor be londe.   556
betwene twoo seynt mary dayes,
When þe tyme waxis nere long,
then shalle thei mete, and banerse rese,
In gleydes more, þat is so long.   560

LANSDOWNE   CAMBRIDGE

COTTON

[þai sal plantt] doun hir baners þar · & wondid men s
[þis is þe] begynnyng [of þer] care · whan noþer party sa   548
[þen sal þai] take a trew & swere · thre ʒer & more   554
[þat none of] þem sal [oþer dere · noþer] by se
[. . . . .] saynt mary dayes · [when] þe da   558
[. . . . .]   560

[7 lines lost at foot of page in MS.]

. . . .
. . . .
. . . .
. . . .
. . . .

¹Bot wiete wele, Thomas, he saH fynd
  nan[e].   [¹ leaf 153]   572
He saH lyghte, whare þe crose solde bee,
And holde his nebbe vp to the skye;
And drynke of gentiH blode and free;
þane ladys, waylowaye, saH crye.   576
Ther saH a lorde come to þat werre,
þat saH be of fuH grete renown[ne];
And in his Banere saH he bere,
Triste it wele, a rede lyonc.   580
Thar saH anoþer come to þat werr[e],
þat saH fyghte fuH fayre in [   ]
And in his banere saH he ber[e]   583
A Schippe with an ankyre of golde.
ȝitt saH an oþer come to þat werre,
þat es noghte knawens by northe n[e
  southe];   586
And in his Banere saH he bere
A wolfe with a nakede childe in his
  mo[uthe].
ȝitt saH þe ferthe lorde come to þat w[erre],
þat saH grete Maystries after ma[ke];
And in his B[anere sa]H he b[er]e
The bere 592

THORNTON

iij crowned kinges, with dyntes sore,
shalbe slayne, & vnder be.
a Raven shall comme ouer þe moore;
and after him a crowe shalle flee,   568
to seke þe moore, without reste,
after a crosse is made of stone, [leaf 10, back]
ouer hill & dale, bothe easte & weste;
but trowe þou well, he shall fynde none.
he shall lyght wheare þe crosse shuld be,
& holde his nebbe into þe skye;
& drynk of ientle blud & fre,   575
of doughti knightes þat downe shall lye.

SLOANE

[Lines 577-604 not in this MS.]

. . . .

Gladysmore, þat gladis vs aH,
This is begynyng of oure gle ;
gret sorow þen shaH fall,
Wher rest and pees were wont to be. 564
Crowned kyngus þer shal be slayn,
With dyntis sore, and wondur se ;
Out of a more a rauen shaʃ cum ;
And of hym a schrew shall flye, 568
And seke þe more, with owten rest,
Aftur a crosse is made of ston ;
Hye and low, boþ est and west,
But vp he shaH [fynde] non. 572

He shalle liȝt þer the crosse shuld be,
And holde his neb vp to þe skye ;
And he shaH drynk of [ ],
Ladys shaHe cry welawey ! 576

LANSDOWNE   CAMBRIDGE

[*Lines 577-604 in no MS. but the Thornton.*]

COTTON
[*5 lines lost at top of page.*]   [leaf 243]
                    [fynd no]   572
                neb vp to þe sky   574
          [w]elaway sal cry   576
[*Lines 577-604 not in this MS.*]

40   HOW A BASTARD SHOULD COME OUT OF THE WEST   [FYTTE III.

And þa . . . .
Wh . . . .
Bot . . . .
þer 596
An . . . .
Th . . . .
þe . . . .
An 600
Be . . . .
Wh . . . .
Th . . . .
The 604
þa . . . .   frely þei shall fight þat daye,   605
V 606   to þat þe sonne be sett neare weste;
. . . .   none of them shall witt, I saye,
[4 lines entirely lost at bottom of column.] whither partie shall haue þe beste. 608
. . . .   a basted shall comme owte of a fforreste,
. . . .   in sothe england borne shalbe—
[col. 2] . . . .   he shall wynne þe gre for þe beste,
. . . .   & all þe land after bretens shalbe. 612
. . . .   then he shall into England ryde,
. . . .   easte weste, as we heare sayne.   614
. . . .
      [Col. 2 entirely torn off.]
. . . .   all false lawes he shall laye downe,
. . . .   þat ar begonne in þat contre;
. . . .   trewthe to do, he shalbe bone,
. . . .   & all þe land, after, bretens shalbe. 620
        THORNTON   SLOANE

                        COTTON
                sunn]e syt euyn weste
        w]yt may · whethir party sal hafe þe best   608
          of þe forest · In south yngland born sal be
        f]or best · And al ledes bretayns sal be   612

LANSDOWNE

¶ A basterd shall come out of the west,
And there he shall wyne the gre;
he shall bothe Est and west,
And all the lond breton shall be. 612
he shall In to Englond Ryde,
Est and west in hys tyme;
And holde A parlament of moche pryde,
that neuer no parlament byfore was seyne.

And fals lawes he shall ley doune, 617
that ar goyng in that countre;
And treu workes he shall begyn,
And bothe londes bretton shalbe. 620

CAMBRIDGE

þen shal they fiȝt with he[lme &] schilde,
Vnto þe sun be set nere west; [leaf 147]
þer is no wyȝt in þat fylde, 607
þat wottis qwylke side shall haue þe best.
A bastarde shal cum fro a forest,—
Not in ynglond borne shall he be;—
And he shalle wyn þe gre for þe best,
Alle men leder of bretan shal he be. 612
And with pride to ynglond ride,
Est and west as .... layde
And holde a parlement w[........]
Where neuer non before was sayd 616
Alle false lawes he [shalle laye doune],
þat ar begune in þat cuntre;
Truly to wyrke, he shal be boune;
And alle leder of bretans shal he be. 620

COTTON

s]al he ryde · est & west with myche tene
ment with myche pryde · þ{t} neuyr non sych be for was sene 616
es he sal dyng down) · þat wer begun in hys cuntre
o wirke he sal be bown · trewly thomas as I tell þe 620

[Leaf 153, col. 2, and 153, back, col. 1,
torn out of MS.]

thomas! trowe þat I the tell,
that it be so, eueriche worde.
of a battell I shall the spell,
that shalbe done at sandyford : 624
ney þe forde þer is a braye,
and ney þe braye þer is a well ; [leaf 11]
a stone þer is, a lytell fraye,
& so þer is, þe sothe to tell. 628
thowe may trowe this, euery wurde— 632
growand þer be okes iij ; 629
that is called the sandyford, 630
þer the laste battell done shalbe. 631
Remnerdes & Clyffordes bolde shalbe, 633
in Bruse land iij yeares & mare, 634
& dynge downe towerȝ & castellȝ high ;
to do owtraye thei shall not spare. 636
þe basted shall gett him power stronge,
all þe fyue leishe lande— 639
there shall not on him bod word brynge, 640
as I am for to vnderstand.
þe basted shall die in þe holly lande ; 641
Ihesu Criste ! þat mykell maye, 644
his sowle þou take into þi hande, 643
when he is deade & layed in claye!' [Interpolation]
& as she tolde, at the laste, 645
þe teares fell ouer hir eyen graye.

THORNTON   SLOANE

	þe bastarde shal get hym power strong,
	And alle his foes he shall doune dyng;
	Off alle þe v kyngus landis,
	þer shal non bad[word] home bryng. 640
	þe bastard shal dye in þe holy land;—
	Trow þis wel [I] þe sey;—
	Take his sowle to his hond,
	Ihesu criste, [that] mycull may! 644
And thus is that I you tell;	Thomas, [truly] I þe say,
belefe it wele euery word!	þis is [trewth] ylke a worde!
And of A baytale I wote full wele,	Off þat laste battel I þe say,
that shalbe done at Sawdyngford. 624	¹It [shall] be done at Sandeford: 624
By that forde there is a bro,	Nere sendyforth þer is a wroo, [¹ lf 127, bk]
And by that bro ther is A well:	And nere þat wro is a well;
A stone there is a lityll there fro;	A [ston] þer is þe wel euen fro;
And by the stone sothe to tell, 628	And nere þe wel, truly to tell,. 628
And at þat stone Ar cragges iij, 629	On þat grounde þer groeth okys thre,
[*The MS. here ends abruptly though there is more room on the page.*]	And is called sondyford.;
	þer þe last battel done shal be,
	Thomas, trow þou ilke a worde.' 632
	þen she seid with heuy chere;.
	þe terys ran out of hir een gray.
LANSDOWNE	CAMBRIDGE

COTTON

owe þis ful welc · þat þis is soth euery worde
[Of a bate]l I can þe telle · þat sal be done at Sandyforde   624
    [Nere þe] forde þar is a bro · & nere þe bro þer is a well
    standes þe welle euyn fro · & nere it a ston sothely to tell   628
[& nere] þat ston growith okes thre · þat men call sandyforde
    [þar þe la]st batel don sal be · thomas trowe þou wele þis euery worde 632
    e]s & clyffordes in werre sal be · In bruces lande thre ȝere & more
    n) tones & castels fre · to do owtray þai sal not spare   636
    e] þat I þe say · þe bastard sal de in þe holy lande
    þou wele may · sese hys sawle into þi hande   644
    d with mych care · þe teres ran doun of hyr eyn grey

THORNTON

[leaf 154, back, col. 1]

[Leaf 153, back, col. 1, torn out of Thornton MS.]

SLOANE

'Lady, or you wepe so faste,
take your leave & goo your waye!' 648
'I wepe not for my waye wyndinge,
but for ladyes, faire & fre,
when lordes bene deade, without leasynge,
shall wedd yomen of poore degre. 652
[1]he shall have steades in stabull fedd;
a hawke to bare vpon his hand;
a lovly lady to his bedd; [1 leaf 11, back]
his elders before him had no land! 656
farewell, thomas, well the be!
for all this daye thowe wilt me marr.
'nowe, lovly lady, tell thowe me,
of.blak annes of Dvnbarr.' 660

'of blak annes comme neuer gode,
therfor, maye she neuer the:
for all hir welthe, & worldes gode,
in london shall she slayne be. 668
the greateste merchaunte of hir blud,
in a dike shall he dye;
houndes of him shall take þer fode,
mawger all þer kynne & he.' 672

COTTON

þou wepe so sare · take þi houndes & wende þi wey 648
my way wendyng · sothly thomas as I þe say
e]s sal wed ladyes with ryng · Whan hyr lordes be slain [away 652
des in stabil fed · a fayr goshauk to hys hande
to hys bed · hys kyn be fore had neuyr lande 656
m]as & wele þe be · al þis day þou wil me mare
· of blake aunes of Dunbare 660

'lady, or þou wepe so sore,
Take þi houndis & wend þi way!' 648
'I wepe not for my way walkyng,
Thomas, truly I þe say;
But fer ladys, shall wed laddys ȝong,
When þer lordis ar ded away. 652
He shall haue a stede in stabul fed,
A hauk to beyre vpon his hond;
A bright lady to his [bed],
þat be fore had none [londe]. 656
ffare wel, thomas, I wende my way;
Alle þis day þou wil me [mar]!'.
'Lufly lady, tel þou me,
Off blake Agnes of Don[bar]; 660
¹And why she haue gyven me þe warre,
And put me in hir prison depe; [¹ leaf 128]
ffor I wolde dwel with hir,
And kepe hir ploos and hir she[pe].' 664
'Off blak Agnes cum neuer gode:
Wher for, thomas, she may not the;
ffor al hir welth and hir wordly gode,
In london cloysed shal she be. 668
þer preuisse neuer gode of hir blode;
In a dyke þen shall she dye;
Houndis of hir shall haue þer fode,
Magrat of all hir kyng of le.' 672

LANSDOWNE   CAMBRIDGE

COTTON

þe war & put me depe in hyr prisoune
with hyr · sothely lady at arsyldoun   664
e] neuyr gode · thomas sche may do not to þe
& wordely gode · In london sal she closyd be 668
xt of hyr blode · In a foule dyke sal sche dye
r sal hafe her fode · mawgre of al hyr kyn & she 673

46   THE LADY PROMISES TO MEET THOMAS AGAIN AT HUNTLEY BANKS.   [FYTTE III.

. . . .
. . . .
. . . .
. . . .
. . . .   [leaf 152, back, col. 2]
To huntlee bañkkis þou take the way[e];
[T]here sall j sekirly be bowne,   679
[And] mete the Thomas whene j maye.
[lines 681-4 found only in Cotton MS.]
[I sa]ll the kenne whare euer thou gaa,
[To ber]e þe pryce of curtaysye;   686
[For tu]nge es wele, & tunge es waa,
[And tun]ge es chefe of Mynstrallsye.'
[lines 689-692 found only in Cotton MS.]
[Scho ble]we hir horne on hir palfraye,
[And left]e Thomas vndir-nethe a tre;
[To Helmesd]ale scho tuke the waye;
[And thus] departede scho and hee!
[Of swilke] an hird mane wolde j here,
[þat couth] Me telle of swilke ferly. 698
[Ihesu], corounde with a crowne of brere,
[Bry]nge vs to his heuene So hyee!
   amene, amene.   700
      Explicit Thomas
      Of Erseledownne
   THORNTON

thomas, drere mann was he,
teares fell ouer his eyen so graye.
'nowe, lovly lady, tell þou me,
if we shall parte for euer & aye?'   676
'naye!' she saide, 'thomas, parde,
when thowe sitteste in Arseldon,
to hontley bankis þou take þe waye;
þer shall I sykerly to the recomme.   680

I shall reken, wheare euer I goo,   685
to beare the price of curtese.'   686

and thus departid she & he!   696
      Finis.

   SLOANE

COTTON

a drery man was he · þe teres ran of his eyn grey
y tel þou me · if we sal part for onys & ay   676
at arseldoun · to huntly bankes tak þi way
edy boun · to mete þe þar if þat I may   680
ende my way · I may no langer stande with þe
þe pray · tel neuyr þi frendes at home of me   684
y a lady fre · I sal þe comfort wher þat þou go

þen Thomas, a sory man was he,
þe terys ran out of his een gray ;
'lufly lady, ȝet [tell þou] me,
If we shall parte for euer and ay ?' 676
'Nay ! when þou sitt[es] at erseldown,
To hunteley [bankes] þou take thi way ;
And þer shal I be redy bowne,
To mete þe thomas, if þat I may.' 680

She blew [hir] horne, on hir palfray,
And lef[fed] thomas at eldryn tre ;
Til helmesdale she toke þe way ; [lf 122, bk]
thus departed þat lady and he ! 696
Off such a woman wold I here,
That couth telle me of such ferly !
Ihesu, crowned with thorne so clere,
Bryng vs to thi hall on hye ! 700
Explicit

LANSDOWNE   CAMBRIDGE

COTTON

profe of curtasy · tong is weke & tong is wo   688
e of mynstralsy · tong is water & tong is wyne
[Tong is che]fe of melody · & tong is thyng þat fast wil bynd   692
[þen went] forth þat lady gay · vpon hyr wayes for to w[ende]
[She blewe hi]r horn on hyr palfray · & lefte thomas vndir a [tre]   696
man wold I here · þat couth tel more of þis ferly
kyng so clere · bryng vs to þi halle [on hye]   700
[Explicit prop]hecia thome de Arseldoune

APPENDIX I.

From "The Whole prophesie of Scotland," &c. Edinburgh, Robert Waldegrave, 1603. Collated with Andro Hart's Edition, 1615.

☞ The Prophecie of Thomas Rymour. [B j, back]

Still on my waies as I went,
Out throgh a land, beside a ¹lie,
I met a ²beirne vpon the ³way.
Me thought him seemlie for to see,
I asked him ⁴holly his intent, 5
Good Sir, if your ⁵wil be,
Sen that ye byde vpon the bent
Some vncouth tydinges tell you me,
When shal al these warres be gone,
That leile men may ⁶leue in lee, 10
Or when shall falshood goe from home
and laughtie blow his horne on hie.
I looked from me not a mile,
And saw two Knights vpon a ⁷lie,
they were armed seemely new, 15
two Croces on ⁸there brestes they bare,
and they were ⁹cled in diuers hew,
Of sindrie countries as they were,
the one was red as any blood,
Set in his Shield a ¹⁰Dragone keene, 20
He ¹¹steird his Steed as he were ¹²mad,
With crabbid words sharpe and keene
Right to the other beirne him by.
His Horse was al of siluer sheene
His Shield was shaped right seemlie, 25
In it a Ramping Lyon keene.
Seemly into golde was set,
His bordour was of Asure sheene,

With silke and Sabil well was plet, [B ij]
I looked from me ouer a greene, 30
And saw a Ladie on a lie,
That such a one had I neuer seene.
the light of her shined so hie,
Attour the moore where ¹³at she fure,
The fields me thought faire and greene 35
She rode vpon a Steid ful sture,
That such a one had I seldome seene :
Her Steid was white as any milke,
His top his taile ¹⁴war both full blae
A side ¹⁵saydle sewed with silke, 40
As al were golde it glittered so,
His harnessing was of silke of ynde,
Set with precious stones free,
He ambled on a noble kinde :
Vpon her head stoode Crownes three : 45
Her garment was of Gowles gay,
But other colour saw I none,
A flying fowle then I saw,
Light beside her on a stone
A stoope into her hand she baere, 50
and holy water she had readie,
She sprinkled the field both here & there
Said heere shal many dead corpes lie.
At yon bridge vpon yon burne,
Where the water runnes bright and sheene, 55
There shal many steides spurne,

¹ Ley ² bairne ³ bent ⁴ wholly ⁵ wils ⁶ liue ⁷ Ley ⁸ their
⁹ clad ¹⁰ Dragon sheene ¹¹ stirde ¹² wood ¹³ as ¹⁴ wer ¹⁵ saddle

And Knightes die throw battles keene
¹ To the two Knightes did she say,
Let be your strife my Knightes free,
Ye take your Horse and ride your way   60
As God hath ordained so must it be, [B ij, back]
Saint Andrew thou hast the ²hight,
Saint George thou art my owne Knight,
they ³wrongous aires shall worke thee woe,
Now are they one there ⁴waies gone,   65
The Ladie and the Knightes two,
to that beirne then can I ment,
and asked ⁵tythings be my fey,
What kinde of sight was that I said?
⁶Thou shewed to me upon yone lie,   70
Or wherefrom came those Knights two
They seemed of a farre countrie,
That Ladie that I let thee see,
that is the Queene of heauen so bright
the fowle that flew by her knee,   75
that is Saint Michael much of might
the knightes two the field to ta
Where manie men in field shall fight.
know you well it shal be so,
that die shal manie a gentle knight.   80
With death shall manie doughtie daile,
the Lordes shal be then away,
there is no Harret that can tell,
who shal win the field that day,
A crowned King in armes three   85
Vnder the Baner shal be set,
two false and feyned shal be,
the third shal light and make great let
Baners fiue againe shal striue,
and come in on the other side,   90
the white Lyon shall beate them downe,
and worke them woe with woundes wide,
The ⁷Bares heade with the ⁸read Lyon, [B iij]
So seemely into ⁹read golde set,
That day shal slay the King with Crowne,   95
Though many Lordes make great let,
there shal attour the water of Forth

Set in golde the read Lyon.
And many Lords out of the North
to that battell shal make them boun,   100
there shal Crescentes come ful keene,
that weares the Croce as read as blood.
On euerie side shal be sorrow seene,
Defouled is many doughtie foode,
Beside a Lough, vpon a lie,   105
they shal assemble vpon a day,
And many doughtie men shal die
Few in quiet shal be found away,
Our Scottish King shal come full keene,
The read Lyon beareth he,   110
A feddered arrow sharpe I weene
Shal make him winke and warre to see,
Out of the ¹⁰filde he shal be led
When he is bloodie and woe for blood,
Yet to his men shall he say   115
For Gods loue ¹¹you turne againe
and giue ¹²those Sutherne folke a ¹³fray,
Why should I lose, the right is mine.
My date is not to die this day.
Yonder is ¹⁴falshoode fled away,   120
and ¹⁵laughtie blowes his horne on hie,
Our bloodie King that weares the Crowne,
Ful boldlie shal ¹⁶he battell byde,
His Baner shal be beaten downe,   124
And hath no hole his head to hide, [B iij, back]
the Sternes three that day she l die,
That beares the ¹⁷Harte in siluer sheene :
there is no riches golde nor fee,
May lengthen his life ¹⁸an howre I weene,   129
Thus through the field ¹⁹that Knight shal ride
And twise reskew the King with Crowne,
He will make many a Banner yeeld,
the Knight that beares the toddes three,
He wil by force the field to ta,
But when he sees the Lyon ²⁰die,   135
Thinke ye wel he wil be wae,
Beside him lightes beirnes three,
Two is white the third is blae,

¹ Knights then did they sey   ² right   ³ wrangous heires   ⁴ wayes   ⁵ tydings by
⁶ Then   ⁷ Beares   ⁸ red   ⁹ red gold   ¹⁰ field   ¹¹ turne you   ¹² these
¹³ frey   ¹⁴ falset   ¹⁵ loudlie   ¹⁶ the battell bide   ¹⁷ heart   ¹⁸ one houre
¹⁹ the   ²⁰ dee

ERCILDOUN.   4

the toddes three, shall slay the two,
The third of them shall make him die, 140
Out of the field shall goe no more,
But one Knight and knaues three.
 There comes a Banner red as ¹blud,
In a Ship of siluer sheene,
With him comes many ²ferlie fude, 145
to worke the Scottes much hurte and woe,
There comes a Ghost out of the west,
Is of another language then he,
to the battle bownes him best,
As soone as he the Senyour can see, 150
the Ratches workes them great wanrest,
Where they are rayed on a lie,
I cannot tell who hath the best
Each of them makes other die
A white Swane set into blae, 155
Shal semble from the South sey,
To worke the ³Northen folk great wae, [B 4.]
For knowe you well thus shal it be,
the staikes ⁴aucht with siluer set,
Shal semble from the other side, 160
till he and the Swan be met,
They shal worke woe with woundes wide,
throw woundes wide, there weeds hath wet
So boldlie will ⁵there beirnes byde,
It is no ⁶rek who gets the best, 165
they shal both die in that same tide.
 There comes a Lord out of the North,
Riding vpon a Horse of tree,
that broad landes hath beyond Forth,
The white Hinde beareth he, 170
And two Ratches that are blew,
Set ⁷into golde that is so free,
that day the ⁸Egill shal him slay,
and then put up his Banner hie:
The Lord that beares ⁹the Losanes three, 175
Set into gold with Gowles two,
Before him shal a battel be,
He weares a banner that is blew,

Set with Peeok tailes three :
and lustie Ladies heads two, 180
¹⁰Vnfane of one, each other shal be,
all through griefe to gether they goe
I cannot tel who wins the gree,
Each of them shal other slay,
the ¹¹Egill gray set into greene, 185
that weares the ¹²hartes headen three,
Out of the South he shal be seene,
to light and ray him on a lie,
With ¹³55. Knights that are keene, [B 4, back]
And Earles either two or three, 190
From ¹⁴Carlel shal come ¹⁵bedene,
Againe shal they it neuer see,
at Pinkin Cleuch ¹⁶their shal be spilt,
Much gentle blood that day,
¹⁷Their shal the ¹⁸Baire lose the ¹⁹gylt, 195
And the Eagle beare it away,
Before the water ²⁰man calles Tyne,
And there ouer ²¹lyes a brig of stone,
the ²²Baires three, looses the gree,
there shall the Eagle win his name. 200
 There comes a beast out of the west
With him shal come a faire manie,
His Baner ²³hes beene seldome seene,
A bastard trowe I best he be,
Gotten ²⁴with a Ladie sheene, 205
²⁵With a Knight in priuitie
His armes are full eath to knowe,
the ²⁶read Lyon ²⁷bears he,
that Lyon shall forsaken be,
and ²⁸he right glad to ²⁹flee away 210
Into an Orchyard on a lie,
With hearbs greene and allayes gray,
there will he inlaiked be,
His men sayes harmesay,
the Eagle puts his Baner on hie 215
and sayes the field he woone that day.
their shal the Lyon lye full still,
Into a vallie faire and bright,

¹ blood   ² ferly food   ³ Northerne   ⁴ eight   ⁵ their bairnes bide   ⁶ reck
⁷ in golde   ⁸ Egle   ⁹ *omits* the   ¹⁰ Unfaine   ¹¹ Egle   ¹² hearts heads
¹³ fiftie fiue   ¹⁴ Carlill   ¹⁵ bedeene   ¹⁶ There shall   ¹⁷ There   ¹⁸ Beare
¹⁹ guilt   ²⁰ men cals   ²¹ lies   ²² Beares   ²³ hath bene   ²⁴ betweene   ²⁵ And
²⁶ red   ²⁷ beareth   ²⁸ be   ²⁹ be

A Ladie shoutes with words shrile,
and sayes woe worth ¹the coward knight 220
Thy men are slaine vpon yon hil,   [B 5]
To dead are many ²dougtie dight,
Theareat the Lyon likes ill,
And raises his baner hie on hight
Vpon the moore that is so gray,   225
Beside a headles Croce of stone,
There shal the Eagle die that day,
And the read Lyon win the name
The Eagles three shal lose the gree,
that they haue had this manie day,   230
the read Lyon shal win renowne,
Win all the field and beare away,
One ³Crowe shal come, another shal goe,

and drink the gentle blood so free.
When all these ferlies was away   235
then sawe I non, but I and he
then to the ⁴birne couth I say
Where dwels thou or in what countrie :
Or who shal rule the Ile of Bretaine
From the North to the South sey :   240
a French ⁵wife shal beare the Son,
Shall rule all Bretaine to the sey,
that of the Bruces blood shall come,
As neere as the nint degree
I franed fast what was his name,   245
Where that he came from what countrie ?
In Erslingtoun, I dwell at hame
Thomas Rymour men calles me.   248

¹ thee   ² doughtie   ³ Crowne   ⁴ Bairne could   ⁵ Queene   ⁶ which

[My idea at first was to print the above in 4-line stanzas, thus :

Still on my waies as I went,
Out throgh a land, beside a lie,
I met a beirne vpon the way ;
Me thought him seemlie for to see.

But, though this is clearly the original structure, it breaks down in twelve places, in the copy as we have it (a clear proof of its imperfections), and in others is so uncertain, that I finally resolved to let it alone, and give it in the form in which I found it. An examination will show :—

Three regular stanzas	1—12	:	*two* lines (half stanza)	12—14 ;
two „ „	15—22	:	*three* uncertain lines	23—25 ;
nine „ „	26—61	:	*three* lines of a stanza	62—64 ;
twelve „ „	65—112	:	*nine* uncertain lines	113—121 ;
two „ „	122—129	:	*three* odd lines	130—132 ;
one „ „	133—136	:	*two* lines (half stanza)	137—138 ;
ten „ „	139—178	:	*two* lines (half stanza)	179—180 ;
four „ „	181—196	:	*six* uncertain lines	197—202 ;
one „ „	203—206	:	*two* lines (half stanza)	207—208 ;
six „ „	209—232	:	*two* lines (half stanza)	233—234 ;
one „ „	235—238	:	*two* lines	239—240 ;
one doubtful „	241—244	:		
one regular „	245—248.]			

APPENDIX II.

"THE PROPHISIES OF RYMOUR, BEID, AND MARLYNG:"
AN ENGLISH PROPHECY.

[*Lansdowne MS.* 762, *leaf* 75, *collated with Rawl. MS. C.* 813, *leaf* 72, *back.*]

WELL on my way as I forth wente
   ouer a londe beside a lee,
I met with[1] a baron[2] vpon a bente,
   Me thought hym semely for to see. 4
I prayed hym with good entente
   To abide awhile and speke with me:
Som vncowth tidynges [in] verament
   [3]That he wolde tell me ij or iij.[3] 8

'Whan shall all these warres be gone[4]
   Or trewe men lyve in love &[5] lee?
Or whan shall falshed fange[6] from home,
   Or Trewth shall blow his horne on hye?'

He said, 'man, set thy fote on myne,
   And ouer my Shulder loke thyn lie[7]
The fairest sight I shall shewe the [syne][8]
   That euer saw[9] man in[10] thy countre.'

Ouer a lande forth I blynte,[11]
   A semely sight me thought I se—
A crowned quene in verament,
   With a company of Angelles fre. 20

Her stede was grete & dappyll gray,
   her aparell was of silke of Inde;
with peryll and parrye[12] set full gay,
   her stede was of a ferly kynde. 24
[13]So Ryally[14] in her Arraye,
   I stode and mwsyd in my mynde;
all the clerkes a live to day
   So fayre a lady colde[15] none ffynde. 28

An Angyll kneled on his kne,
   and other many apon that land
went to that faire of ffelycite,
   and gave her a holy water sprynckell
   in hand. 32
her crowne was Graven in graynis iij,
   she halowyd the grownd with her
   owen[16] hand,
both ffrythe & ffelde and fforest ffree;
   and I behelde[17] and styll did stand. 36

She halowed yt both [18]farre & nere;[18]
   the Angelles after her did hie;
She said, 'Iesu, that bowght vs dere,[19]
   what here shalle many a dede corse
   lye! 40
'here most barnies[20] be brought on
   bere,
and welle away[21] shall ladyes crye,
Iesu, that bowght mankynde so dere,
   vpon the[r] soulles haue mercye! 44

then I lokyd ouer a lovely lande—
   that was a selcowth thinge[22] in
   sight—
I se come ouer a bent rydaunde
   [23]A goodly man as armyde knyght.[24] 48
he shoke his spere ferselye[25] in hand,
   Right cruell[ye] and kene;
Styfly & stowre as he wolde stonde,
   he bare a shylde of Syluer shene. 52

---

[1] R. *omits.*   [2] buron   [3—3] to tell me what hereafter shulde be.   [4] done   [5] L. or
   [6] be founde   [7] thow nye   [8] R. ffyne, L. *nil.*   [9] see   [10] of
   [11] Ouer a louely lande as I was lente   [12] L. perle = perre   [13] leaf 75, back.
[14] Soo Ryall she was   [15] can   [16] om.   [17] L. behinde yt and   [18—18] L. fere & nye
[19] L. man kynde   [20] burons   [21] L. wyll away   [22] L. *inserts* 'to se'   [23] leaf 76.
   [24] He semed In felde as he wolde ffight   [25] L. furyously

A crosse of gowles therin ¹did be;¹
  he carpyd words cruell & kene,
And shoke a shafte of a suer tree;
²I blent wele forder apon a² grene:
A nother armyd knyght I see,
  In his crest he bare, I wene,
A Rede lyon that did rawmpyng be;
  he spake words cruell & kene   60
to that other³ that was hym by.

This crowned quene rode them betwene,
  Right as fast as she colde⁴ hie,
She saith, 'men what do you meane?
  stente your Stryff & your follye, 64
Remember that ye⁵ be sayntes in heven;
  and fro my dere son comen am I
to take this ffelde you [twoo] betwene.
  whereuer yt shall⁶ fall in ⁷burghe
    or bye.'⁷   68

⁸She said 'Seint G[e]orge thow art my
    knyght
  oft wronge heyres haue done the tene;
Seint Andrew yet ⁹art thow in the⁹
    right,
  of thy men if it be syldom sene.¹⁰ 72
here [dye] shall many a doughty knyght,
And gromes shall grone apon yat
    grene,
here lordly leedes loo shall lyght,   75
And many a douty knyght bydene.¹¹

here shalbe gladismore that shall glad
    vs all,
yt shalbe gladyng of oure glee;
yt¹² shalbe gladmore wher euer yt fall,
  but not gladmore by the see.   80
¹³ouer cache more¹³ a coke shall crowe,
  of[ter] tymes¹⁴ then tymes thre,
In the thirde yere a ferly shall fall, 83
  At yermes¹⁵ broke a kynge shall dye.'

This crowned quene vanyshed awaye
  with her companey of Angilles bright,
so dide both these knyghtes that day;
  no more I ¹⁶sawe them¹⁶ in my sight.
to a¹⁷ lytell man I toke my waye,   89
I¹⁸ prayed hym with mayn & myght,
¹⁹more of this matier he wold me saye;
  he answered me with reason²⁰ Right:

'I ²¹wyll the tylle²¹ with trew Intent,
  but I haue no space to bide with the,
To tell the [the] trouth in varament
  what shall fall &²² gladismore be. 96
dissencion amonges your²³ lordes shalbe
    lent,
of them that are of blode full nye,
where many a man shall their be shent,
And doughtyly in batell dye.   100

Charyty shalbe layed awaye,
  That ryffe in londe hath been;
Come shall tene and tray,
  This man can melle & mene.   104
those²⁴ that love[s] well to-day
  belyve ²⁵shall tray & tene,²⁵
In batell ²⁶shall barons²⁶ them araye
  Right doughtely²⁷ by dene.   108

gret batell[es] in Englond men shall see,
  be yt wronge or Right;
The sone ageinst the father shalbe,
  Right frussely²⁸ to ffyght.   112
²⁹then shall truth be banysshed ouer
    the see,
And falle [bothe] mayn and myght;
then shall falcede³⁰ and envy

blowe³¹ their hornes on high[t].   116
This shall Reigne vnto the space
  of xxx^ti yeres and thre;
In Englond shalbe la[k]ke of grace,
  So much treson shall be.   120

---

¹⁻¹ I dyd see   ²⁻² & past fforwarde vppon the   ³ other buron   ⁴ might
⁵ ther   ⁶ om.   ⁷⁻⁷ L. bought or by   ⁸ leaf 76, back.   ⁹⁻⁹ thou art In
¹⁰ This line omitted in R.   ¹¹ These four lines omitted in R.   ¹² þer
¹³⁻¹³ on Cachemore   ¹⁴ ofter   ¹⁵ yernes   ¹⁶⁻¹⁶ see them   ¹⁷ that   ¹⁸ and
¹⁹ leaf 77.   ²⁰ reason and   ²¹⁻²¹ wolde tell the   ²² or   ²³ om.   ²⁴ these
²⁵⁻²⁵ shalbe traied by teene   ²⁶⁻²⁶ buryns shall   ²⁷ dulfully   ²⁸ fercelye ffor
²⁹ leaf 77, back.   ³⁰ falshede   ³¹ L. browe

A kynge shall reigne without Right-
   wysnes,
And put downe blod full hye;
Another shalbe lost for fawlte of grace,
To here shalbe [grett] petye.   124

yet shall deth haue a dynt
   In ¹tor[na]ment and fyght;¹
he that hath ynglond hent
   ²shalbe made lowe in leght.²   128
³Then wenis men³ that ware shall stynt,
   but yt Ryseth new on hight;
Then shall ij prynces harnes hent,
   with treason ther dedys be dyght. 132

wrongwise werkes lokes after wrake
   with ⁴clerkes on-wissely⁴ wrought;
Seint Bede in booke did make
   ⁵When the proffycies was sought, 136
that god he will vengyance take,
   when all Englond is on lofte;
A duke shall suffer for their sake,
   which he to dede hath brought.   140

when euery [man] wenys that ware is
   goone,
And Rest and pese shall be,
Then shall entre at Mylford haven
   vpon a horse of tree   144
A banyshed barone⁶ that is borne
   of brutes blode shalbe;
through helpe of a[n] Egyll an-one
   he shall broke all⁷ bretayne to the see.

be side bosworth a felde shalbe pight,⁸
   ther mete shall bores two,
of dyuerse colors shalbe dight;⁹
   the one shall the other sloo.   152
A hartes hed with tenes¹⁰ bright
   shall werke his armes¹¹ woo;
The white bore [to dethe] shalbe dight:
   The profficies saith soo.   156

¹²After Lordes shall to London Ride
   That mykyll is of prise;¹³
A parliament shalbe sett that tyde,
   and chose a kynge at ther devisse. 160
euery man of englond large & wyde
   ¹⁴wene[s] they ar sett of pryce,¹⁴
yet he shalbe called in that tyde
   the kynge of covetyse.¹⁵   164

when sonday goth by B and C,
   And pryme by one¹⁶ and two,
the[n] selcouthe[s] men shall see,
   that seme not to be soo.   168
Barnes¹⁷ in batell shall brednet¹⁸ be,
   And barors¹⁹ of blod full bloo;
the iiij⁺ʰ lefe of the tree shall dye,
   that lost hath bowes moo.   172

A ffedder from heth shall falle in hast,
   his name shall torne to a²⁰ tree:
²¹dulfull dede shall women wast,²¹
   ²²And make folke to felde flee.²²   176
Traytors shall towers tast,
   And doughtlesse be done to dye;
All London shall trymble in hast,   179
   ²³A dede kynge when they shall²⁴ see.

A prynce shall bowne [hym] ouer a
   flode,
Ouer ²⁵a streme straye:²⁵
those that were neuer of Consciens good
   shall broke truse on a daye.   184
Mekyll ²⁶care barnes brues;²⁶
   when they cast there truthes awaye;
then in englonde men shall here newes,
   And A kynge slaine on a day.   188

betwene a traytise of trust,²⁷
   with a ffalse assent,
A castell sone shall lost be
   Apon a Ryver [in] varament.   192

¹—¹ turnament off ffight   ²—² shall make hym lowe to light
—³ R. then men weneth; L. then wyns men   ⁴—⁴ ? werkes, R. dedes vnwisely   ⁵ leaf 78.
⁶ buron   ⁷ om.   ⁸ L. piched   ⁹ L. Right   ¹⁰ tynes   ¹¹ enemyes
¹² leaf 78, back.   ¹³ L. pryde   ¹⁴ R. thinke they be sett att prise; L. pryde
¹⁵ L. covitous   ¹⁶ iij   ¹⁷ burons   ¹⁸ beyton   ¹⁹ barons   ²⁰ om.
²¹—²¹ dulfull dedes shall warnes waste   ²²—²² make ffolkes to ffelles to fflye   ²³ leaf 28.
²⁴ om.   ²⁵—²⁵ the stremes staye   ²⁶—²⁶ bale burons bruen   ²⁷ truse

[betwen) Seyton) & the see
then) shalbe warre In verement,]
And many a towne brent shalbe
  [1]when ware is with assent.[1]   196
[2]then shall wacone woo & wrothe[3]
and barnys to batell shalbe bowne :[4]
their shall com ouer the water of[5] forth
wele arrayed in golde, a rede lyon; 200
with many a lorde out of the North,
for to bete their enymys downe.
mikell[6] blode with hym [7]& broth[7]
shalbe spyllyd vpon [bentis browne].[8]

[9]out of the south shall entre Right
a whyt lyon [vpp]on) a daye,
ageinst the Rede lyon for to fyght ; 207
but their shall begyne a dulfull fraye.
their shall dye many a doughty knyght,
And ladys [shalle] crye welle awaye !
Men of the chirch shall[10] fiersly fyght,
with shaft and shelde them to[11] asaye :

Est and west, north and south,
shall [12]some Ryall[12] in their araye :
At mylnefylde they shall splaye banars
  couth
Ageinst the Rede lyon that day. 216
they shall begyne at yerneʒmowth,
many a Ryall[13] knyght in fay ;
[14]Many a doughty[14] that day be put to
  deth ;
A[tt] flodden felde begynnys the
  afraye :   220

[15]Att Branstone[15] hill shall semble a
  herd,
and bright baners shall dysplaye ;
And many frekes shalbe a-ferde,[16]
and fewe to bere the[17] lyff away. 224

those that is brede of vncouthe erde
shall doubtlesse lese they[r] lytles yat
  day :
[18]The Rede Lyon was neuer a ferde, 227
he shall[19] doubtlesse dy[20] that day.

A beme full [21]burle shall ther[21] blowe
vnder a montayne apon a lee ;
A splayd egle that men do know
shall make a C standertes [swe].[22] 232
ther shall frekes full frely fall,
and of them he shall wyne the mon-
  tane hie ;
doutye knyghtes shall clype[23] & call, 235
and many a man that day shall dye.

A bull & a bastarde together [shalle]
  mete,
shall fyght in fylde full manfully ;
the Rede blode shall rone as rayne in
  strete,
and many a doughty that day shall
  dye.   240
the Rede lyon made shalbe full meke,
and come downe from a mountayne
  hye ;
belyve be [ffallen downe][24] vnderfete
and in yerneʒ broke slayne shall he[25]
  be.   244

A white lyon shall kepe a stale,
An admyrall shall come from the see,
And make[26] his enymys [27]for to fall,[27]
And dryve them to the mountayn hye :
their shal be-gyn a dulfull swale, 249
when the Albenackes[28] blod begyn-
  nyth to fle ;
[29]they shall be dreven) downe into a
  dale,[30]
ther fayrest flower [ther] lost shalbe.

[1-1] and warre shall waken In violent
[2] R. *inserts as first line of stanza :* That many a wiffe shall wydoo ben   [3] orthe   [4] L. bounde
[5] L. at   [6] L. Muche   [7-7] ys broghte   [8] L. a bent of brome (*this line is omitted in R.*)
[9] leaf 79, back.   [10] om.   [11] selffe   [12-12] semble rially   [13] doughtye
[14-14] and many   [15-15] L. on bramstone   [16] L. a-frayde   [17] ther   [18] leaf 80.
[19] shalbe   [20] dede   [21-21] borle ther shall   [22] L. to shake & swaye   [23] clepe
[24] L. falled, ? fouled   [25] om.   [26] doo   [27-27] mekell bale   [28] almanakes[!]
[29] leaf 80, back.   [30] *This line is omitted in R.*

the mowle¹ and the ²mayre mayden
  shall be layed awaye,²
and shalbe doñe dulfully to dye;
The golde anker shalbe slayne that day,
  So shall the besand³ with the beres
    thre;⁴   256
A white lyon in ⁵armyn graye⁶
  shall fyght that day full manfully,
to helpe the Egell [in] all he maye, 259
And make his enymys fayne to fle.⁶

the day shall fayle⁷ both leme & light,
  the nyght shall entre vpon them tho,
their enymys ther [shalbe] put to flyght
  with blody woundes & hartes woo. 264
then shall they cry & call on hight,
  vnfaithfull⁸ frendes that ⁹are goo;⁹
their shall mysse manye a Ryall knyght
  that gladly to that ffelde dyd goo. 268

on morow the day shalbe full bright,
  the people shall asemble fare in fere,
som with hevy hartes & som with ligh[t];
  who fyndes his frynde[s] shall make
    good chere.   272
¹⁰But the Rede lyon ¹¹to dede shalbe¹¹
    dight,
  and by the adwise of a woman clere
ther shall they fynde hym sone¹² full
    Right,
  or elles ¹³they wiste nott¹³ which he
    were.   276

then leyve¹⁴ every lorde shall take,
  and bowne¹⁵ them home to their
    contry,
som with weale, & som with wrake, 279
  who that haue lost their frendes fre.
but the rede lyon, welc I wot,
  to London towne browght shalbe;
the whit lyon shall grath his gate 283
  and to London [shalle] cary that fre.

then ther shall happen such a chauns;
  the prynce that is beyonde the flode
two townes shall take that longe¹⁶ to
    Fraunce,   287
  with lytyll shedyng of Crysten) blod;
boldely his people he shall avaunce,
  and nother spare for golde ne good.
bredlynton)¹⁷ this profficy grauntes, 291
  and so did bede that well vndirstoud.

when every man said yt shulde be were,¹⁸
  Arsaldowne¹⁹ then proficied he,
And said in englond ²⁰y not dere²⁰ 295
  ²¹tyll vij yere com) and goan) shulde be.
In bast ther shall²² a messynger
  In Albanack²³ from ouer the see,
that many a man shall suffer dere
  th[r]ought his falsed and sotylty. 300

A childe with a chaplet shall raye hym
    right,
  with many a hardy man of hande,
with many a helme that clyderith²⁴ bright
  And he shall com ouer soelway sand;
on ²⁵stanys more begyn to²⁵ fyght, 305
  wher lordes shall light vpon that londe,
And ²⁶aske Nothing²⁶ but his Right,
  yet shall his enymys hym with stand.

holly chirch shall harnys hent,
  and iij yeres stonde on stere,
mete & fyght vpon a bent,
  Even as the[y] seculers were.   312
the Ruff shall Ruffully be Rent,
  And stond in grete daunger,
vnto the synne of Simony be shent
  that they haue vsed here.   316

A kinge²⁷ of Denmarke shall hym dyght
  ²⁸Into Englond vpon á day,
[þat] shall make many a lorde low²⁹ to
    lyght,
  And ladyes³⁰ to say wele away!   320

---

¹ mule ²—² mairemedon shalbe awaye ³ bason ⁴ L. ther; R. om. beres thre ⁵—⁵ harnes gaye
⁶ fflye ⁷ ffade ⁸ on feithffull ⁹—⁹ is agoo ¹⁰ leaf 81. ¹¹—¹¹ vnto dede is
¹² om. ¹³ L. not wyt ¹⁴ L. lyvye ¹⁵ L. Bounde ¹⁶ L. belongeth ¹⁷ Bridlynton to
¹⁸ warre ¹⁹ L. Arsedowne ²⁰—²⁰ itt shulde not deire ²¹ leaf 81, back. ²² is
²³ Almanake ²⁴ gliderethe ²⁵—²⁵ Stanesmore begynnethe the ²⁶—²⁶ askethe noo thyng
²⁷ Duke out. L. had also originally duike ²⁸ leaf 82. ²⁹ full lowe ³⁰ many a ladye

then frekys in felde shall frely fyght;
A kynge shall com out of Norway;
The blake flet wi*th* mayn and myght
their enymys full¹ boldly shall²
asay.   324

In bretayn londe shalbe a knyght,
on them shall make a felon fray,
A bytter bere wi*th* mayn and myght 327
shall brynge a Ryall Rowt that day.
. ther ³shall dy³ many a [stalworthe]
knyght,
And dryve them to [the] flod*es* graye;
they shall losse both sayle & syght,⁴
And a crowned kynge be slayne that
day.   332

then shall the North Ryse ageinst y*e*
south,
And the est ageinste the west:
care in contry shalbe couthe,⁵
vntyll couytyce downe be caste. 336
out of a dene shall drawe a wolf
Right Radly in that rest,
And he⁶ shall come in at the south,
And bett downe of the best.   340

⁷on sondysforth shall this⁷ sorow be
sene,
⁸ ⁹on the south syde vpon a monday;⁹
The[r] gromes shall grone vpon a grene,
besyde the greues¹⁰ graye.   344
their standith a castell on a montayn
clene—
thus Arsalldoune¹¹ did saye—
which shall do there enymys tene,
and save englond that day.   348

to gethers ther shall mete wi*th* banars
bright
crowned kyng*es* tnre,
And hew on other wi*th* mayne and myght,
tyll one of them slayne shalbe. 352

the blake flet of Norway shall take y*e[r]*
flyght,
And be full fayne to flee;
they shalbe dreven ou*er* ¹²Rock*es* &
clyff*es*,¹²
And many one drowned shalbe.   356

they shall flee in the salt strond,¹³
fer forthe in¹⁴ the fome:
xx*ti* thowsand wi*th*out dynt of hand,
shall losse their lyves ylke one. 360
A darf¹⁵ dragon, I vnderstonde,
shall come yet ou*er* the fome,
And wi*th* hym bryng a Ryall
baunde,¹⁶
ther lyves shall yet be lorne.   364

this darf¹⁵ dragon, I vnderstond,
that comyth ou*er* the flode[s] browne,
¹⁷when his tayle is in Irelond,
his hede shalbe in stafford towne; 368
he shall so boldly bryng his bonde,¹⁸
thynkyng to wyn Renowne;
beside a welle ther is a stronde¹⁹
ther he shall be beten downe.   372

on Snapys more they shal be-gyne,
these doughty men & dere,
with sterne sted*es* together thring,²⁰
and hew on helm*es* clere.   376
an Egyll shall mount wi*th*out lettyng
and freshely fyght in²¹ fere,
and in a ford [shalle] kyll a kynge;
thus ma*r*lyon²² said in fere.²³ 380

knyght*es* shall rydd²⁴ in ryche araye,
and hew on ²⁵helm*es* bright:²⁵
a gerfacon shall mounte that day, 383
and iij ²⁶merlyon[s] fers of flyght.²⁶
on gladmore, I dare well say,
dye shall many a knyght;
who shall bere the gree²⁷ away
no sege can rekyne²⁸ right.   388

¹ *om*.   ² ffor to   ³—³ dye shall   ⁴ flight   ⁵ L. wroght   ⁶ *om*.
⁷—⁷ on the Southe side Sondiforde shall   ⁸ leaf 82, back.
⁹—⁹ vppon a munday In the morni*n*ge gaye   ¹⁰ grayves   ¹¹ L. arsedoune
¹²—¹² Rocke & Cliffe   ¹³ strounde   ¹⁴ on   ¹⁵ derffe   ¹⁶ L. bownde   ¹⁷ leaf 83.
¹⁸ bande   ¹⁹ fforde   ²⁰ L. therin   ²¹ on   ²² merlyn   ²³ prophesye   ²⁴ counter
²⁵—²⁵ helmett*es* clere   ²⁶—²⁶ marleons In ffere   ²⁷ L. gere   ²⁸ L. reke a

the egyll shall so wery be
  for fyghtynge, as I wene,
he wyll take ¹an Ilande¹ in the see,
  wher ²herbes is ffaire & alsoo grene;²
³then shall mete hym a faire Lady, 393
  she shall speke with voice so clene:
'helpe thy menne Right hardely⁴
loke where they dye in batelles kene!'

then shall this egyll buske with pride,
  th[r]ought counsell of this faire lady,
entre ⁵in [on] euery side,⁵   399
make xxᵗⁱ standertes ⁶for to swey.⁶
A rampyng lyon, mekyll of pride,
  In syluer sett with Armyn)⁷ free,
shall helpe the egyll in that tyde,
where shall many a doughty dye. 404

In a forest stondith⁸ Ookes thre,
  In a fryth all by ther one;
beside a hedlesse crosse of tree
  A well shall Ronne of blode alone. 408
Marlyon) said in his profecy
  that in ⁹their stondith⁹ a stone:
A crowned kynge shall heddid be
And¹⁰ to losse his lyffe alone.   412

The egyll shall fyersly fyght that day—
  to hym shall draw hys frendes nere;¹¹
a Reunaunde¹² hounde, withoute delaye,
shall ¹³brynge the chace¹³ both fere &
  nere.   416
barnes¹⁴ shall on helmettes laye
  ¹⁵doubtfull dyntes on sides sere;
twis for sworne, I dare well say,
ther song shalbe on) sorow ther.¹⁶ 420

the derf dragon shall dye in fight,
  the bere shall holde his hede on) high;
A wyld wolf low shall light;
  the brydelyd stede shall manfully 424

In felde ageinst his enymes fight,
  the dowble flowre maynteyn shall he;
a swane shall Swymne with mayn and
  myght;
this bede saith in his profecy.   428

The bull of westmerlande shall bell &
  bere,
  the boldest best in varament;
he shall afterward without were   431
  be made Iustice from tyne¹⁷ to trent.
a bastard shall do dedys dere,
  the fox he shall in handes hent,
the ffullemarte¹⁸ shalbe disfigured in
  fere,
what side soeuer he be [on] lent. 436

then shall the egyll calle on hight,¹⁹
  and say this fylde is our²⁰ to day;
then shall aliens take their flyght,
  their songe shalbe wele awaye!   440
the duble Rose shall laughe²¹ full Right,
  And bere the gre for euer & aye,
when false men) shall take ther flyght,
  as arse[l]doun²² hymself did say. 444

then spake the²³ holly man that men
  called²⁴ Bede—
  In profecy saith [he] in fere:
A childe with a chaplet shall do a dede
  ²⁵That is doughtye & deere;²⁵   448
In handes he shalbe take[n] at nede,
  and brought to his blode full nere.
he shalbe saved that day from drede
  with a prynce that hath no pere; 452

And ²⁶of that barne he shall haue grete²⁶
  pety
[that] tyll hym is leve²⁷ & dere;
And afterward, in proffecy
  as clerkes sayne²⁸ in fere,   456

---

¹⁻¹ L. in Irelonde   ²⁻² L. herkes ar faire & ale is   ³ leaf 83, back.   ⁴ egerlye
⁵⁻⁵ shall In on the Southe side   ⁶⁻⁶ to fflee   ⁷ hermens   ⁸ standes
⁸⁻⁸ the fforde ther standes   ¹⁰ & ther   ¹¹ neare   ¹² ravande   ¹³⁻¹³ ring the shawes
¹⁴ burons   ¹⁵ leaf 84.   ¹⁶ here   ¹⁷ L. tyme   ¹⁸ L. fyluer or syluer
¹⁹ R. heght; L. high   ²⁰ owres   ²¹ L. lought   ²² Arsaldoune   ²³ that   ²⁴ calles
²⁵⁻²⁵ L. that doughty dere & fere   ²⁶ om.   ²⁷ leefe   ²⁸ saye

hè shall Rayne in[1] Ryaltye
v & fyfty yere.
then [2]of them lordes shall a[2] counsell be
that doughty are[3] & dere.   460

when all this is comprehended to[4] ende,
than men may bide & blyne;
to London then[5] lordes shall wende
with that Ryall[6] kynge.   464
[7]then all wares is brought to ende
[that] hath been englonde within;
[8]Suche a[8] grace god shall send,
[that] exyled shalbe all synne.   468

then A parliament he shall make,
that kynge of high degre:
[9]truse In[9] englond shalbe take
with his blod full nye.   472
then [10]goo shall ware[10] & wyked wrake
that longe in englonde hath be,
then shall all sorow in englond slake
this saith the profecye.   476

then[11] the blake Jett of Norway is
commyn[12] & gone,
And drenchid in the [13]flode truly;[13]
Mekelle[14] ware hath bene beforne,
but after shall none be;   480
then shall truth blow his horne
truly lowde and hye;[15]
he shall Reigne both even & morne, 483
And ffalshed [16]shalle banisshed be.[16]

then shall this kyng a protector make—
his cosyn of his kynne;
then the farre[17] flode he shall take,
vncouthe londes to wyne,   488
for to fyght for Iesus[18] sake,
[19]that dyed for all our synne,
And he shall worke them woo and wrake,
or euer he byde or blyne.   492

at bareflet[20] he shall do battelles thre—
this prince of mekyl[21] myght,
And to parys wend shall he
with many a doughty knyght.   496
ther shall they yelde hym vp the kayes[22]
of all the Citie wyght,
[And] vnto Rome wend shall he
with many A doughty knyght.   500

The pope of rome with prossession
shall mete hym the[23] same day,
And all the cardynalles shalbe bowne[24]
In their best araye.   504
Ther shall knele iij kinges with crowne,
and homage make that day,
And many of the spirituall of Rome
shall brynge hym on the waye.   508

to the woodes[25] then shall he Ryde—
this comly kynge with crowne,
And wyn his enymys on euery side,
And boldely bete them downe.   512
Ther shall advaile[26] no erthly pride
in castell, towre, ne towne,
but geve they warkyng wondes wyde,
[27]who[28] ageinst hym in batell is
bowne.[28]   516

then to Iherusalem this prince[29] shall fare
as conqueror of myght
vij mortalle[30] batelles shall he wynne
there
And the turkes to dede shall dight.   520
[then to the sepulcre shalle he ffare
To see that gratious sight,
where cryst ffor vs suffred sare[31]
when he to dethe was dight.]   .   524

All the Citie of Iherusalem
shall a-Raye them with Ryalte,
And for to fyght shalbe [fulle] fayne
vpon the heithen meynye.   528

---

[1] In welthe &   [2] shall lordes off   [3] is   [4] to an   [5] these   [6] noble   [7] leaf 85.
[8—8] And suche   [9—9] L. the ruffin   [10—10] shall goo woo   [11] when   [12] L. compis
[13—13] ffome so ffree   [14] L. much   [15] L. hight   [16—16] L. shalbe vanyshed awaye
[17] faire   [18] Iesu   [19] leaf 85, back.   [20] harefleete   [21] L. mylke   [22] L. kynge
[23] that   [24] L. bound   [25] Rodes   [26] L. avale them   [27] leaf 86.   [28] L. bownd
[29] L. parrys   [30] L. Mortye   [31] MS. sore

To Synay that pr*i*nce shall bowne anone,
wher seint Kateryn doth beryed be;
vij hethe*n* kyng*es* ther shalbe slayne,
that sight or euer he [se]¹ 532

xxxij² batell*es* that crowned kynge
shall wyn, I vnderstonde,
[and] then the holly crosse he shall wyne,
And bryng yt into criston lande. 536
In hast their ³shall serue³ to hym,
that dare not him w*ith*stonde;
xxxij² hethen kyng*es*
he shall cr*is*ten w*ith* his hand. 540

he shall send this rich Relycke to Rome,
to that worthy wones:
All the belle*s*, I tell you sone,
they shall rynge [alle] at ons; 544
the pope⁴ shall mete yt w*ith* prossession,
⁵And ⁶ all the cardynall*es* for the nones,
And all the senators of Rome
shall knele on knes at ons. 548

then towar*des*⁷ Iherusalem this kynge shall hie
w*ith* many a crysten wight,
In the vale of Iosephate y*er*⁸ shall he dye
with*out* batell or fyght. 552
xxiiij⁹ kyng*es* that do crystened be
shall take that¹⁰ worthy wight,
[and] brynge hym to Rome Right hastely
before the pop*es*¹¹ sight. 556

all the bell*es* of Rome at one[s],
ye¹² shall wele vnderstond,
they shall rynge w*ith*yn those¹³ wones
w*ith*out helpe of mann*es* hand. 560

the pope shall bowne [hym] to bery his bones
in seint peter[s] mynster wher yt doth stonde,
¹⁴All that clerk*es* [of Rome] that ons¹⁴
Shall not styre that bere¹⁵ w*ith* hand.

then the pope, w*ith* many a kynge
and cardenall*es* grete plenty,
to the citie of Colyñe they shall hym brynge,
where ther ly*es* kyng*es* three, 568
that offred to Ie*s*u a ryche thinge¹⁶
that nyght he borne did be,
¹⁷bethelem that burghe¹⁷ w*ith*y*n*),
¹⁸of a Mayden free. 572

Than balthaser shall speke on heght¹⁹
and say to ²⁰Melchore in fere :²⁰
'Make a rome, curteys knyght,
²¹our fourt felow²¹ is here.' 576
A grete²² of golde hath Rased²³ in sight,
vpon a good maner,
And ther they shall bery this worthi wight
betwene thes kyng*es* dere. 580

the pope²⁴ shall ²⁵grave hym²⁵ w*ith* his hond
trewly, this holly kynge,
And all the lord*es* of faire englond
he shall geve them his blessinge. 584
They shall bowne²⁶ ouer [the] stalworth strond
Fayre englond w*ith*yn;
Many shall wayle & wryng ther hand*e*²⁷
when they here that tydynge.²⁸ 588

[then] he that was protector englond w*ith*yn
hath wrought so wordely,²⁹
In London they [shall*e*] crowne hym kynge
w*ith* gret solempnytie. 592

---

¹ MS. be   ² Two and thritte   ³⁻³ shall be sworne   ⁴ pope offe Rome [pope *crossed through*]
⁵ leaf 86, back.   ⁶ with   ⁷ to   ⁸ om.   ⁹ ffoure & thrittye   ¹⁰ th*is*
¹¹ *Crossed through in* R.   ¹² yow   ¹³ th*is*   ¹⁴⁻¹⁴ butt all the clerk*es* of Rome th*is* ones
¹⁵ beere   ¹⁶ relike   ¹⁷⁻¹⁷ In Betheleme that riall borough   ¹⁸ leaf 87.
¹⁹ L. high   ²⁰⁻²⁰ Melcheser in ffeere   ²¹⁻²¹ our ffourthe brother   ²² grate   ²³ resyd
²⁴ *Crossed through in* R.   ²⁵⁻²⁵ laye In gr*a*ve   ²⁶ bowne them   ²⁷ L. hand*es*
²⁸ R. tithing; L. tydyng*es*   ²⁹ w*o*rthelye

And so noble shalbe ¹his reigne,¹
  In tyme when yt² shalbe,
³lv yere³ Englond wit*h* yn,
  so long his Rayne shalbe.   596
than shall falshede be vanyshed away⁴
  ⁵and trouth shalbe redy
trew men both by nyght & day
  shall lyve in charytie   600
dayly, me⁶ thynke, we ought to pray
  to god in trynytie,
for⁷ to exele all vickednes away⁸
  pray we [vn]to o*ur* lady   604
I pray[ed] this littell man in fere
  that he wolde truly [vnto] me say,
when shall ⁹ this ende wit*h*out[en] were,
  or when shall come that day ?   608
he said, 'a long tyme thow holdest me
  but yet I wyll the say,   [here,
of yt¹⁰ I shall not fayle a¹¹ yere,
And thow ¹²wylt take hede¹² what I
  say :—   612

In the yere of o*ur* lorde, I vnderstonde,
  ¹³xvc yere,¹³
& one and thirty folowand,
  all this shall apere ;   616
¹⁴the crosse in¹⁴ *cris*ten men*n*es hand*e*,¹⁵
  that is worthi and dere,
yt shalbe brought I vnderstond
  to Rome ¹⁶wythouten were.¹⁶   620

betwene the walcoen & the wall
  this lytyll man mett wit*h* me,
¹⁷tolde me this proffecy all,
  And what tyme it shulde be.   624
god that dranke esell & gall
  and for vs dyed on a tree,
when he thynketh tyme to tall,
  to heven bryng you & me ! Amen.

    Explicis proficia Venerabilis
bede, Marlionis, Thome Asalaydon)
et Ali*orum*

¹⁻¹ thys realme   ² thys   ³⁻³ ffyve & ffyftye yeres   ⁴ ffor aye   ⁵ leaf 87, back.
⁶ L. my   ⁷ om.   ⁸ ffor aye   ⁹ L. *inserts* all   ¹⁰ that   ¹¹ on
¹²⁻¹² take good hede   ¹³⁻¹³ ffyffetene hundreth In ffere   ¹⁴⁻¹⁴ The hollye crosse In-to
¹⁵ L. hand*es*   ¹⁶⁻¹⁶ L. wit*h*out ware; B *adds*, ¶ finis, *and ends here*.   ¹⁷ leaf 88.

    The Lansdowne MS. 762 also contains, among a collection of short prophetical notes, the following of

THOMAS OF ERCELDOUNE.

leaf 49, back.

    Thomas of Ashledoñ sayth the fader*is* of the moder*is* church / shall cause the Roses bothe to dye in his Avne fonte ther / he was cristened.

leaf 50.

    Thomas of Asheldoñ sayeth the egle of the / trewe brute shall see all inglond in peas & rest / both spirituall and temp*or*all ; and eu*er*y estate of / in thaire degre and the maydens of englond*e* / bylde your howses of lyme and stone.

APPENDIX III.

AN ENGLISH PROPHECY
OF
GLADSMOOR, SANDISFORD, AND SEYTON AND THE SEYE,
PREDICTED OF 1553.

[*Sloane* 2578, *leaves* 38 b—41.]

The begynninge of warres & myschef in england as Bede saiethe is anno domini 1553. The first battell shalbe fowght betwin englishe men & the scottes with y* frenchmen on yer company at Somerhill beside Newecastell (the battell shalbe sore[1]) the scottes & frenchemen shall ouercom, scape who that maye, vntill a newe yeare. ¶ The next yeare after this battell, shall Philip of Spayne com in with a greate hoste betwon Seyton & the seye, beside Westcheschester,[2] and at a Skyrmyshe there shalbe slaine 5000 on bothe parties. Then shall thei mete with yer greate battelles at Gladismore we & they, & there shall our nobles fyght so greate a battell with them that it shalbe hard to saye who shall haue the better. on the morowe thei shall mete agayne at Snapes moore[3] therby wheare he shalbe slaine & all his men, and thende shalbe at [4]Sandisford downe, wheare yer shippes shall lye till y* crowes buylde yer neastes in them. ¶ Then shall com owte of Denmark a Duke and he shall come into England with 16 Lordes, with whose concent he shalbe crowned kinge in a towne of Northumberland, and shall raign 3 monethes & odd dayes. he shall fight a battell at Snapes more,[3] wheare he shalbe slaine, & xx^m of his men drowned in the seye. ¶ Then comethe Pole owte of rome and his power shalbe so groate yat he shall not cease vntill he win to London and then shall he fight so soare a battell yat none shall knowe who shall haue y* better and so on the morowe bi the mone light thei shall come to London, and thei shall fight an other battell betwin Peter, John, Jamys Gylys, & charynge crosse, then at that battell shall thei wynne London & contynue there a while doinge yer will. Then shall a Cardynall yat neuer was worthy of that estate, come to the tower of London, and take one by the hand, & saye come forthe ientle brother & though the poles haue bene so longe drye in england yat men myght wade ouer them in pynsons, which nowe ouerflowe all England. ⁵ ¶ Then shall come the frenche kinge at

---

[1] The words between ( ) are inserted in another hand.   [2] Sic.
[3] "Sandes more" written over in another hand.   [4] fol. 39.   [5] fol. 39, back.

waburne holte (or hoke)¹ 15 myles from norwiche, there shall he be lett in bi a false
mayre and that shall he kepe for his lodging a while, then at his returne he shalbe
mett at a place callid the redd bank, y* place is 30 miles from Westchester wheare
at y* first assaye shalbe slaine ix^m welchmen, and y* dowble nombre of enemyes,
then on y* morowe shall y* stranger desire a peace for 3 yeares moare, but y* pease
shall endure no lenger then ij maye² dayes when y* dayes waxe somwhat longe,
then shall mete botho parties at Sandisforde, and yer shalbe so mortall a battell
that xx^m enemyes shalbe dryven into the seye without dent of swerd ¶ then shall
our noble kinge toward London ryde, & at Stanesmore yer shall he mete & fight
with y* pole & y* spiritualtie a greate battel, so yat yer shalbe slaine xxx^m prestes
& prestes servauntes which shall haue shaven crownes as yer maisters, & made to
belevo yat thei shall dye goddes servauntes then shall the kinge ryde to London &
23 Aldermen shall lease yer heddes & a besom ³of equitie shall swepe all thinges cleane,
holly churche shall tremble & quake, therfor lett them to yer prayour3 take.
¶ A prophet of portyngale saythe, Awake englishemen & guive hede, for a tyme
shall come when a kinge with a myter shall raigne ouer you & he shalbe a wulf of
y* seye, he shall holde in him y* strengthe of ij bisshopp3, & the shadowe of a pope
shall lye in him by y* sufferaunce of a Lion, & he shall take his iourney north-
ward, & shall come againe into his contrey, & in the hemme of his mantell
shalbe lapped iij thinges hunger, pestilence, & sorowe. ¶ An heremyt of Fraunce
saithe Woo be to you englishmen, drawe neare, for it shalbe said emonge you, wuld
god I weare for 3 monethes a Foxe in a hole lyenge, a bird in the Aire Flyenge, or a
fishe in y* seye swymynge. ¶ Bedo saythe, vnto a councell in winter englishmen
make haste, and from a Feaste in Somer Fle, fle, fle. ¶ An Abbott of the laud said,
guyve you hede englishmen when a privie hatred shal be in merlyn castell⁴ betwin
a larke, or a ⁵rcaremouse, and a Raven, which shalbegynne in one daye, but shall
not be endid in 3 yeares. but within yat yeare shalbe a councell in winter and in
somer folowinge shall y* greate men of england be bidden to a feaste, amonge whom
thei shall saye, woo, woo, woo, what shall we doo, whither shall we goo, but to y*
messenger of deathe. ¶ M. shall Raise vpon you greate tribulacion & sorowe, the
kinge of y* romans & grekes shall com vpon you with a greate fury, and E. shall
rise owte of his slepe like a lyve man, whom all men thought to be deade. ¶ The
trone of constance, & thomas with his tales all said, yat y* saxons shuld chuse
them a Corde yat shuld brynge them all vnder. A deade man shuld make betwin
them a corde, & yat shuld be right myche wonder, that he yat deade is & buryed in
sight, shuld rise againe & live in lande, thurgh y* comfort of a yonge knight, yat
fortune hathe chosen to hir husband, y* wheale shall turne to hym right, yat
fortune hathe chosen to be hire ⁶feere. ¶ When Father blithe the begger can
saye ij credes, & hathe libertye to walke with his wallet, and mother symkyn of
the sowthe takethe againe hir beades, then thowe preste take hede of thi pallett.

Finis.

---

¹ Added by another hand.   ² "Midsomer" is written over "maye."   ³ fol. 40.
⁴ "Salisbury castell" written over these words.   ⁵ fol. 40, back.   ⁶ fol. 41.

ADDITIONS FOR *MEDITATIONS*.

NO. 60, ORIGINAL SERIES.

VARIOUS READINGS OF A MS. IN TRIN. COLL. CAMB. B. 14. 19.

BY THE REV. J. R. LUMBY, B.D.[1]

Line 16. ... þei may lere.
„ 18. But þat þat is proved of cristis fay.
„ 38. þat in þis cene crist haþ wrouȝt,
„ 40. þe secounde his disciplis waischyng.
„ 46. To make redi his pask aȝenus he come.
„ 49. ... as þou herd seie.
„ 54. ... þei saten him bi.
„ 58. So trist so trewe as was Joon.
„ 73. ... men han seen.
„ 74. ... of Laterain
„ 75. An oþer mancre þou understonde.
„ 80. To slepen on his brest Ioon þau liste.
„ 86. For as a seruaunt ...
„ 92. Crist seide þese wordis wiþ sad chcre.
„ 95. Forsoþe forsoþe I wole ȝou seie.
„ 101. *For ye this MS always spells* iȝe.
„ 105. Priueli Ioon to crist gan seie.
„ 127. Biholde and þenke þis in þi mynde.
„ 133. To an inner hous gunnen þanne tee.
 So seyn þat þe houshold hanne see.
 He dide hem sitten adoun in þat stide.
„ 166. Whanne he waischide ...
„ 175. In stidfast praier ...
„ 178. Into his blis þei wolen þee ledo.
„ 180. Hou dereworþili aforn his ende
„ 181. *om.* with.
„ 183. *alþer* in one word. It is genitive plural of *all*, and probably is only written *divisim* here by accident.
„ 185. ... he gan sowne.
„ 195. In memoraunce ...
„ 203. ... more cleer.

[1] Mr Lumby also notes that there is a prose version of the *Meditations* in the Bodleian MS. 789 (new number: 2643 in the ordinary catalogue), leaves 1-51, bk; and that the tract "To kunne deie" in the same volume is of worth for its dialect.

48 ADDITIONS FOR MEDITATIONS, NO. 60, ORIGINAL SERIES.

Line	207.	From hevene he list ...
,,	214.	To ʒyvc þee peyne ...
,,	216.	... quyk not deed.
,,	245.	þe þridde he tauʒte hem bi monesting To kepyng his comaunding
,,	264.	þat schulen ...
,,	267.	þese wordis and oþere þat he hem tolde kitten her hertis and waxen coolde.
,,	271.	... wiþ manye siʒyng.
,,	277.	þis sermoun at his brest he soukc.
,,	283.	Forþ þei wente ...
,,	286.	As chikenes crepten to þe dammes wyng
,,	291.	Faste þei wenten þei camen anoon.
,,	295.	om. yn.
,,	299.	Schame ...
,,	300.	For he schamed not to die for þee
,,	305.	He biddiþ ...
,,	328.	... have ʒolden a stounde.
,,	336.	þei han me prisid my woo to make.
,,	347.	... delven ...
,,	356.	He foond hem slepyng and summe he woke Her iʒen weren slepyng ...
,,	362.	... and dide more
,,	372.	... praie þi god abone.
,,	406.	To my fadir in his sete.
,,	414.	Al bisprongen ...
,,	427.	Summe bynden summe blenden him sum on him spit Summe buffetiden him and summe seyn telle who þe smyt Summe scornen him sum syngen on hym a song.
,,	436.	þerfor þou schalt have deþ as riʒt
,,	438.	Help þi silf if þou be boun.
,,	441.	Summe drugge him summe drawe him fro see to see.
,,	450.	þei wepen þei weilen her wristis þei wryngen.
,,	464.	Be brouʒt
,,	473.	Thenke man and rewe of her sekyng
,,	477.	Boþe lorels and ech gadlynge.
,,	490.	Aswoun sche fel doun in þe feeld. þanne crist was torment in moost care.
,,	502.	þo was maad frenschip þere firste was bate.
,,	505.	þei crieden on him as foule on owle.
,,	516.	þei beten him and renten hym wounde to wounde.
,,	520.	Biholdiþ he ...
,,	522.	Til þei ben weeri þei moun no more.
,,	538.	þe doyng of þe þridde our now wole I ryme.
,,	541.	... a reehed þei took.
,,	543.	þei setten hym openli in her clepyng

Line	546.	þou modi man þi sauyour biholde
,,	548.	And for oo word þou woldist men grame
		Eft soone to pilat þei camen accusyng
		And seiden saif sir Cesar we han no kyng.
,,	567.	þei punchid him forþ þorou ilke a slowȝ
,,	573.	þei hiȝen hym he goiþ wiþouten striif
,,	583.	... foloweþ a fer.
,,	585.	A schort weie sche is goon to chese.
,,	599.	For evere it semeþ aȝenus his wille.
,,	627.	To þe cross forth þei drowen him defiyng.
,,	632.	A schortere laddere biforn was set,
		þere as þe feet schortere weren.
,,	637.	Wiþout aȝen seiyng ...
,,	642.	... crucifieris hem bereiȝt.
,,	648.	... be merciful ...
,,	654.	þat oon Jew ...
,,	655.	þe oþere him drowen til veynes to brest.
,,	663.	Eueri ioynt þanne brast atwynne.
,,	702.	I praie þee somdeel hise peynes lisse.
,,	715.	... was nome.
,,	728.	... me takist.
,,	733.	He taastiþ sumdeel his þreste to liþen.
,,	737.	ȝit treuli man þirstide on rode.
,,	746.	... calle me to þee.
,,	760.	... I take.
,,	763.	... centurio gan torne.
,,	812.	Whiche I bar wemles of mij bodi.
,,	817.	... grete sone ...
,,	823.	To sle hem and caste her cors awei
		þat noon schulde se hem on sabat dai
,,	835.	... scharpli sche ran.
,,	856.	... þorow merci ...
,,	859.	þorou out his herte he preent him wiþ mood.
,,	888.	If we goon hennes þis bodi worþ stole
,,	896.	Joseph of Armathie ...
,,	934.	... for feyntise ...
,,	944.	A grettir pris myȝte nevere be brouȝte.
,,	949.	... seide marie ...
,,	960.	Prikid, brisid ...
,,	990.	And greiþide hem faste þennis to goon.
,,	1007.	But I hadde trist to his seying
		Myn herte schulde aborst at his diing.
,,	1015.	I must do nedis as þou me biddest.
,,	1023.	... now departid.
,,	1027.	If þou risist up as þou me behiȝtist
		Myn herte schal rise wiþ þe liȝtest
,,	1030.	I am stoon deed for oones and ay

50   ADDITIONS FOR *MEDITATIONS*, NO. 60, ORIGINAL SERIES.

Line 1032.   And kiþe þat þou art goddis sone.
  " 1034.   Sche romyde ...
  " 1047.   Sche sai þe cros : Abide, sche seide
  " 1087.   ... maistras.
  " 1118.   ... ho soukide it ...
  " 1123.   Fro fendis bounde to make þee free.

ADDITIONAL NOTES BY THE REV. W. W. SKEAT, M.A.

Line 328.   Read 'a stounde,' two words. At any rate, it means 'at any time.'
  " 414.   Read 'be-sprunge,' with a hyphen.
  " 513.   Read 'vndyr-neme,' with a hyphen.
  " 570.   Read 'a-sterte,' with a hyphen.
  " 577.   Dele comma after 'owne.'
Lines 632, 633.   The full stop should be at the end of l. 633, and the comma at the end of l. 632.
Line 918.   Observe that here only *one* nail is used for fastening the feet. So in Piers the Plowman—'nailede hym with *thre* nayles,' C. xxi. 51.

In the Glossary, note the following corrections :—

Angred means afflicted, not made sorry, and refers to the infliction of pain. The use of *anger* in the sense of affliction, pain, is curious, yet common. See *anger* in Stratmann.
Astounde, at any time (for *a stounde*), 328.
Besprunge, besprinkled, 414. Wrongly entered as *Sprunge*.
Cleuyn, cleave, 616. *Cleuyn on* = cleave to, cling to.
Fode, a child, 939. *Omitted.*
Iuwyse, instrument of punishment, 577. It commonly means punishment only, as in Chaucer's Knightes Tale.
Knowlechyng, recognition, 424. To *knowleche* is to recognize, to acknowledge; not 'to *know*.'
Kyþe, make manifest, shew, 1032. Not 'to *know*.'
Myþe, meek, mild, 156. See *Methe* in Halliwell. (Certainly not *mighty*.)
Owne, own; not 'only.'
Real, royal, 640. So also in ll. 33, 34. (The usual meaning.)
Ryue, rife (in great numbers, or else quickly), 839.
Seche, to seek, 621. It simply means to seek, examine.
Soke, sucked, 1118. *Omitted.*
Too, 654. The too = thet oo, the one. (Very common.)
Vndyrneme, reprove, 513. See *Vnderneme* in Prompt. Parv.; and cf. P. Pl. B. v. 115.

www.ingramcontent.com/pod-product-compliance
Lightning Source LLC
Chambersburg PA
CBHW031833230426
43669CB00009B/1329